SCHUBERT'S MUSIC FOR PIANO FOUR-HANDS

A Comprehensive Guide to
Performing and Listening to the
Dances ¤ Fantasies ¤ Marches
Polonaises ¤ Sonatas ¤ Variations
Waltzes and Other Duets

by

DALLAS A. WEEKLEY

and

NANCY ARGANBRIGHT

PRO/AM MUSIC RESOURCES, INC.
White Plains, New York

KAHN & AVERILL
London

D1474500

Pro/Am *P♪A* General Music Series GMS-6

Front cover reproduction: This rare portrait of Schubert by Josef Teltscher was published in a small magazine *Die Musik* (Berlin) Vol. IX, No. 23 in September, 1912 (not to be confused with the well known periodical *Die Musik* edited by Schünemann). At the time of its publication the drawing was in the possession of Anton Gegenbauer in Czechoslovakia, who no doubt received it from his relative Karl Gegenbauer, a fellow pupil and life-long friend of Schubert, who inscribed it "Think as often as possible on your Franz Schubert". (The Pierpont Morgan Library, New York.)

FIRST EDITION

Published in the United States of America 1990 by
PRO/AM MUSIC RESOURCES, INC.
63 Prospect Street, White Plains, New York 10606
ISBN 0-912483-55-5

Published in Great Britain 1990 by
KAHN & AVERILL
9 Harrington Road, London SW7 3ES
ISBN 1-871082-23-4

To

WALTER ROBERT

scholar, musician,

mentor and friend

CONTENTS

Preface / Acknowledgements / A Note from the Publisher . . . . *vii*

Introduction . . . . *ix*

Chapter I
   THE EARLY YEARS (1797–1813) 1

Chapter II
   A CAREER IS BEGUN (1814–1817) 10

Chapter III
   THE FIRST IMPORTANT PIANO DUET YEAR (1818) 17

Chapter IV
   MUSIC FOR THE THEATER (1819–1823) 31

Chapter V
   THE RETURN TO ZSELIZ (1824) 41

Chapter VI
   A REPUTATION IS ESTABLISHED (1825–1827) 55

Chapter VII
   THE FINAL YEAR (1828) 69

Chapter VIII
   GENERAL PERFORMANCE CONSIDERATIONS 83

Appendix
   A CRITICAL MOSAIC 93

Bibliograpy
   Selected Books and Articles 130

   Manuscripts 131

   First Editions 132

   Available Editions 133

   Supplementary Collections 137

   Recordings 137

Index of Titles 145

This painting, "Hunter's Row" (now called Praterstrasse) by Franz Scheyerer, is a typical street scene in Schubert's Vienna. (Historic Museum of the City of Vienna)

PREFACE

This book is the result of many years of devotion to Franz Schubert and his piano duets; it is written for music lovers who are particularly interested in the performance and history of these duets. As pianists who have made a career performing compositions originally written for one piano, four hands, we have a great love for, and indebtedness to Franz Schubert because of his enormous contribution to the literature.

We have traced the development of the one-piano, four-hand compositions of Schubert, presented biographical and historical events related to their composition, and analyzed them from the standpoint of performance problems. In doing so, we considered the following factors: the influences of preceding composers upon Schubert's writing, his innovative compositional techniques, and his stylistic evolution.

Historical background of a general nature has been given so that one can understand the circumstances under which the duets were composed. We have noted specifically, whenever relevant, the place and time of the compositions, dedication and publication data, and information concerning Schubert's friends with whom he performed the duets. We also searched for information on the present location of the manuscripts, made comparisons among manuscripts, first editions, and present editions, and noted discrepancies. Our own suggestions for effective performance have also been given.

We have grouped Schubert's piano duets into seven periods: (1) his youth from 1810 to 1813, (2) 1817, (3) 1818, which includes his first Zseliz visit, (4) 1819 through 1823, composed in Vienna, (5) his second Zseliz visit in 1824, (6) his mature years from 1825 to 1827, and (7) his final year, 1828. The study concludes with a chapter concerning general performance considerations.

ACKNOWLEDGEMENTS

In 1964 the authors lived in Vienna in order to experience in a personal way Schubert's beautiful city. We were most fortunate in becoming acquainted with the leading Schubertian authority, Otto Erich Deutsch (1883-1967), to whom we owe a deep debt of gratitude for his contributions and encouragement. Dr. Deutsch collected almost all existing documents pertaining to the composer, publishing them in *Schubert: A Documentary Biography* (London 1946)[1] and *Schubert: Memoirs by His Friends* (London 1958). We have relied heavily on his works for historical information.

Walter Robert, noted pianist, scholar, and Professor Emeritus of the Indiana University School of Music, has been our beloved teacher for many years. He has, in a sense, looked benevolently over our shoulders as this book has developed, and his suggestions have been invaluable.

We wish to thank Father Reinhard van Hoorickx (scholar, author and eminent authority on Franz Schubert), who has given generously of his time, knowledge, and documents toward the development of this book. The time spent with him on the island of Corsica discussing Schubert's work will always be a cherished memory.

Eva Szabo, who combined great skill as a translator with profound historical and musical understanding, was a priceless resource.

We appreciate the patience of our son, Lance, who grew from childhood to manhood during the course of this project.

---

1 *Schubert: A Documentary Biography*, 1946, is the English version of *Franz Schubert: Die Dokumente seines Lebens* ; in 1947 it was published as *The Schubert Reader: A Life of Franz Schubert in Letters and Documents*.

We wish to thank Thomas P. Lewis of Pro/Am Music Resources, who in the course of working with us has also become a friend.

Last, but far from least, we are grateful to David Thomack for his assistance, both technical and editorial, and for his constant inspiration.

A NOTE FROM THE PUBLISHER

At first, the prospect of "another" book on Schubert might give one pause — but among the many qualities which, in the publisher's view, the present volume has to recommend it, there are two of a special attractiveness.

On the one hand the book brings into clear focus a body of great music which appears to deserve much more attention than that which it customarily receives today — not only for public performance, but equally for less formal playing and/or for student attention — for learning and growth as a performer, surely, but also just for pleasure. The authors present this repertory in detail, both historically and critically.

At the same time, since Dallas Weekley and Nancy Arganbright are professional musicians who have gained a thorough familiarity with the music they describe, their readers are treated to an "insider's view" as knowing as it is caring. They communicate something of the spirit in which Schubert himself may have written these pieces — which combine, somewhat uniquely, a regard for the highest *artistic* standards with a delight in, simply, *making music*... in partnership at a single keyboard, and, among friends, within hospitable surroundings.

INTRODUCTION

Franz Schubert was the greatest and most prolific composer of piano duets (one piano, four hands) the world has ever known. One might prefer certain individual compositions of other duet composers, but the overall high quality of the more than seventy duets which Schubert composed surely places him in the forefront of all who have written for the duet medium. No major composer before or since Schubert has produced one-piano, four-hand music in such profusion.

There are at least four purposes for which Schubert wrote for this medium, and these same purposes may also give us insight as to why the duets encompass such a wide range of difficulty: they were composed (1) for professional concert performance, (2) for social gatherings, (3) for instructional purposes, and (4) for commercial reasons, for profit through publications.

If challenged to prove that Schubert composed piano duets with concert performance in mind, one might have difficulty, for it is true that only one duet, the *Overture in C, D 597* (performed March 12, 1818), was heard publicly during his lifetime; however, this fact does not prove that he did not conceive of his duets for public performance. By the same token, his symphonies were not publicly performed during his lifetime, yet they were obviously intended for the concert hall. During the early nineteenth century there were very few public concerts as we know them today; concerts were generally held in private homes. Such major and mature compositions as the *Grand Duo,* D 812, the *Divertissement à la hongroise,* D 818, and the *Fantasy in F minor,* D 940 are certainly more than mere salon pieces.

We know that Schubert felt that his piano duets were among his best compositions, because it was his *Variations on a French Song,* D 624, that he chose to dedicate to Beethoven, whom he revered above all others. Also, he chose a duet to play in his first public performance as a pianist in Vienna. Duets were enormously popular during Schubert's time, due to the new interest in the piano. The instrument featured many improvements including a wider keyboard, which made it more comfortable for two people to sit side by side. After the Napoleonic Wars, which had traumatized Vienna, piano duets took precedence over the previously popular house-orchestra as a vehicle for music-making.

In reading the diaries and memoirs written by Schubert's friends, one relives the many musical evenings usually referred to as "Schubertiads." These evenings were spent largely in performing his lieder and his piano duets, since both are so well suited to social music-making of an intimate, informal nature.

It is obvious that Schubert also composed duets for instructional purposes when we see the vast amount of duet music which was written in Zseliz (at that time in Hungary, but now in Czechoslovakia) where he was employed by Count Johann Karl Esterházy to teach his two daughters, Marie and Karoline. Through duet playing he kept the two young countesses occupied musically, giving them a feeling for melodic line and steady rhythm.

With regard to Schubert's livelihood, it seems that duets were easier to sell to the publishers than solo compositions. At least two publishers, Probst and Artaria, asked Schubert to compose piano duets to meet popular demand. Such demand was not always in the best interest of Schubert's music: in at least one instance, a publisher divided a three-movement piano duet into three separate compositions! (The *Divertissement sur des motifs originaux français* became *Marche brillante, Andantino varié,* and *Rondeau brillant.*) Of all of the opus numbers published during Schubert's life, piano duets were second only to songs in number.

CHAPTER I

The Early Years (1797–1813)

Franz Peter Schubert was born on January 31, 1797 in a very small room in his parents' crowded apartment located in the Viennese suburb of the Himmelpfortgrund. The name Schubert means shoemaker; the family tree can be traced back to the early 17th century. Schubert's father, Franz Theodor (1763-1830) came to Vienna from his native Moravia at the age of 20 to work as an assistant schoolmaster for his brother Karl. In 1785 he married Elisabeth Vietz (c. 1756-1812), a domestic servant who was born in Silesia but who was at that time working in Liechtental, a suburb next to the Himmelpfortgrund. From the marriage register for January 17, 1785 of the parish church "The Fourteen Helpers-in-Need," Elisabeth's age was given as 28 and Franz Theodor's as 25. Apparently Franz Theodor had falsified his age on the marriage register. Elisabeth was then seven months pregnant with their first child.

To this union were born fourteen children; only five survived childhood. They were Ignaz (1785-1844), Ferdinand (1794-1859), Karl (1795-1855), Franz Peter (1797-1828), and Maria Theresia (1801-1878).

Soon after their marriage, Franz Theodor became director of a school in the Himmelpfortgrund district in a house that was originally No. 72 High Street, called "*Zum roten Krebsen*" ("The Red Crab") but later renamed and renumbered as No. 54 Nussdorferstrasse. Today it is "The Schubert Museum," Schubert's birthplace.

This house contained sixteen apartments, each comprised of one medium-sized room and a small kitchen. Schubert's parents rented two of these apartments, for a total of four rooms. In 1801 the family left their overcrowded quarters and moved around the corner to a somewhat larger house on the Säulengasse which still stands, but is now a service station presently known as the Schubert Garage.

Even though the times were turbulent because of the Napoleonic Wars raging throughout Europe, young Franz's home life seemed pleasant and happy.

His father's school gradually expanded and profited, ultimately employing six assistant teachers for 300 students. Franz began to attend school at age six and received the best possible training, not only in basic studies but also in music. Ferdinand, his brother, described Schubert's early education: "In Franz, our father . . . perceived great talent for music from his early childhood. Dear, good Franz then received lessons in pianoforte playing from his brother Ignaz. Later he was taught violin and pianoforte playing, as well as singing, by the choirmaster Michael Holzer, who several times asserted, with tears in his eyes, that he had never yet had such a pupil: 'For,' said he, 'whenever I wished to impart something new to him, he always knew it already. I often looked at him in silent wonder.'"[1]

Young Franz's rapid progress in music astonished his father, who was determined to provide him with the best available education by entering him at the Imperial and Royal Seminary. Thus began his first important training in 1808. The *Wiener Zeitung* (May 28, 1808) announced that there were vacancies for two choristers for the Imperial and Royal Court Chapel, (Hofkapelle), which was an affiliate of the City Seminary, known as the Stadtkonvikt. (The word "*konvikt*" meant "communal house".) Applicants for the appointment were to present themselves on September 30 at 3 p.m. "and to undergo an examination, as regards both the progress made by them in their studies and such knowledge as they may have already gained in music, and to bring their school certificate with them."[2] It was also necessary that the boys be past their tenth birthday, be able to enter Latin class, and show evidence that they were out of the danger of smallpox. (Schubert had not had smallpox nor did he ever get the disease.)

The Imperial Court Chapel required an excellent singing voice and a knowledge of music theory and composition. Fr. Franz Innocenz Lang, head of the Stadtkonvikt, and Antonio Salieri, the court Music

---

1   O. E. Deutsch, *The Schubert Reader* (New York, 1947), 912.
2   *Ibid.*, 6.

Director (and Mozart's antagonist), were among the committee members who administered the entrance examination to Schubert.

Founded in 1803, the Stadtkonvikt was the principal boarding school for commoners in Vienna, as well as being a choir school. Schubert's secondary subjects included Latin, mathematics, natural history, general history, geography, physics and religion.

Anton Holzapfel, a fellow student and friend, was asked in 1858 to describe Schubert: "When I got to know him better, he was in the fourth grammar class, a short, stocky boy, with a friendly, round face and strongly marked features. He was not a particular favorite with the clerical teachers, but he did not cause them any particular trouble through excessive liveliness. He proved to possess one of those quiet, deep natures which, judged by the standards of superficial book-learning, may appear to have little talent. Even then, he was mentally far in advance of his years, as was proved by a long poem of his, written at that time, which I kept, but have since lost. It was in the style of Klopstock's odes, hardly understood by us pupils, but whose theme was the omnipotence of God in all creation."[3]

During this time at the seminary, Schubert's beloved mother died on May 28, 1812 of typhoid fever, a disease which would later kill Schubert himself. No contemporary documents tell us of his feelings; however, Schubert wrote a highly romantic, allegorical soliloquy ten years later, entitled *My Dream:*

> I was the brother of many brothers and sisters. Our father and mother were good people. I was deeply and lovingly devoted to them all. Once my father took us to a feast. There my brothers became very merry. I, however, was sad. Then my father approached me and bade me enjoy the delicious dishes. But I could not, whereupon my father, becoming angry, banished me from his sight. I turned my footsteps and, my heart full of infinite love for those who disdained it, I wandered into far-off regions. For long years I felt torn between the greatest grief and the greatest love. And so the news of my mother's death reached me. I hastened to see her, and my father, mellowed by sorrow, did not

> hinder my entrance. Then I saw her corpse. Tears flowed from my eyes. I saw her lie there as in the old happy past, in which according to the deceased's desire we were to live as she had done herself.

> And we followed her body in sorrow, and the coffin sank to earth. From that time on I again remained at home....[4]

This allegory fostered the groundless rumor that Schubert was banished from his father's house. Although we know that Schubert's father was a pious and stern man, there is no evidence that any such quarrel took place.

Napoleon occupied Vienna in both 1805 and 1809. He levied such a high tax on Austria that the country went bankrupt in 1811. Austrian currency was drastically devalued and new paper money was issued, called "*Wiener Währung*", worth only one-fifth of the older money. Spartan living conditions at the seminary were one result of this financial crisis. The first of the seventy-four surviving letters written by Schubert complains of his lack of money. On November 24, 1812 he wrote melodramatically to one of his brothers (probably Ferdinand):

> Straight out with what troubles me, and so I shall come to my point without beating around the bush. For a long time I've been thinking of my situation here, and have decided that, although on the whole it's reasonably good, there is still room for improvement here and there. You know from experience that we all like to eat a roll or a few apples sometimes, and especially if, after a modest-sized lunch, all you have to look forward to is a miserable supper eight and a half hours later. This persistent longing is becoming more and more frequent, and I must do something about it, willy-nilly. The few groschens that Father allows me are all gone in the first few days, so what am I to do for the rest of the time? 'Whosoever believeth on Him shall not be put to shame.' (Matthew, Ch. 3, verse 4.) I thought so too. How would it be if you were to let me have a few Kreutzer each month? You wouldn't notice it, and I, in my cell here, would be content. As I said, I rely upon the words of the apostle Matthew,

---

3   O. E. Deutsch, *Schubert: Memoirs by His Friends* (London, 1958), 57.
4   O. E. Deutsch, *The Schubert Reader*, 226-227.

where he says 'He that hath two coats, let him give one to the poor.' In the meantime, I hope that you will give an ear to the voice that calls unceasingly to you to remember

Your loving,

poor,

hopeful and again,

poor brother
Franz[5]

Franz's letter is one of several documents demonstrating the young boy's sense of humor. (The first bible quote is not from Matthew, but from Romans 10:11 and the second is a paraphrase, not from Matthew but from Luke 3:11.) Another example of his wit was found at the Stadtkonvikt on a fragment of an octet for wind instruments. The postscript states: "Finished wi' th' *Quartet*, which has been compos-ed by Franz Schubert, Chapel Master to the Imp. Chinese Court Chapppelll at Nanking, the world-famous residence of His Chinese Majesty. Written in Vienna, on a date I can't tell, in a year which has a 3 at the end, and a one-er at the beginning, and then an eight, and another one-er: that is to say — 1813."[6]

Franz's voice began to change in July 1812, for he wrote on the alto part of Peter Winter's *First Mass* in C major: "Schubert, Franz, crowed for the last time, July 26, 1812."[7] Even though Schubert was reported to call the seminary a "prison" he was generally happy with his days there. He studied composition with Antonio Salieri, who had been Beethoven's teacher, and piano and organ with Wenzel Ruzicka. He heard and sometimes participated in performances of music by Handel, Haydn, Mozart and Beethoven. Although he had numerous friends to give him encouragement and support, by 1813 he began to lose interest in remaining at the Stadtkonvikt. Emperor Franz I, himself, issued an "Imperial Resolution" that Schubert could stay at the seminary only if he improved his academic grades: "...since singing and music are but a subsidiary matter, while good morals and diligence in study are of prime importance and an indispensable duty for all those who wish to enjoy the advantages of an Endowment." (October 21, 1813).[8] A month later Schubert resigned from the seminary; he

could not accept the Emperor's dictum that music was a "subsidiary matter." He moved back home with his family, but the domestic situation had changed because of his father's re-marriage. Franz Theodor was forty-nine and his bride, Anna, was twenty years younger. From this union came five children, four of whom survived, giving Schubert's father a total of nineteen children (nine surviving). Although the apartment was crowded, Anna made a good home for Franz and his brothers and sisters.

THE DUETS OF THE EARLY YEARS, 1810-1813.

The duets of the early years are very revealing because they introduce several of the most distinctive Schubertian compositional techniques.

FANTASY IN G, D 1 ¤ ¤ ¤ ¤ ¤ ¤ ¤ ¤ ¤

Composed: April 8–May 1, 1810
Manuscript: Sketch only, pp. 1-8 scattered; pp. 9-24 Pierpont Morgan Library, New York
First publication: Gesamtausgabe [Complete works], 1888

It is significant to note that Schubert's first large composition was for piano duet. This work, the *Fantasy in G*, D 1, was composed while Schubert was a student at the Stadtkonvikt. Enrolled in this boarding school as a chorister, the young Schubert received excellent general education and musical training. Documents concerning this period shed little light on the early compositions. Joseph von Spaun (1788-1865), a devoted friend of Schubert, wrote in his memoirs of 1829 concerning this fantasy: "Already at the age of ten or eleven Schubert was trying his hand at small songs, quartets and little pianoforte pieces. His first larger work was a Fantasy for pianoforte duet which he wrote at the beginning of 1810."[9]

Since the book *Schubert: Thematic Catalog of All His Works in Chronological Order* by Otto Erich Deutsch was published in 1951, more than fifty pages of works and fragments have been found which predate this

---

5   *Ibid.,* p. 28.
6   *Ibid.,* 32.
7   *Ibid.,* 26.
8   *Ibid.,* 37.
9   O. E. Deutsch, *Schubert: Memoirs by His Friends*, 18-19.

Fantasy in G. Several of these seem to be copies of other composers' work. However, there are two fragments (one in G and one in F) which are preliminary studies for the *Fantasy in G,* D 1. These fragments, found in Vienna at the Männergesangverein, were studied by the late Christa Landon. In one work which she calls *Sonata Fragment in F Major* and attributes to early 1810, there are several themes which Schubert used later in the *Fantasy in G.* Another fragment in G major (without title) shows similarities with the adagio and allegro sections at the beginning of the *Fantasy in G.*

This first *Fantasy in G* was left to Ferdinand Schubert, the brother of the composer. An article written by Ferdinand which appeared in Schumann's Leipzig magazine *Neue Zeitschrift für Musik* (1839), entitled "From Franz Schubert's Life," describes the fantasy thus: "Schubert's very first pianoforte composition (1810) was a Fantasy for four hands in which more than twelve different movements occur, and each with a character of its own. It consists of thirty-two very closely written pages. This was followed by two further, smaller ones [fantasies]."[10] This *Fantasy in G* ends, as did most of the early compositions of Schubert, in a different key from which it began; in fact, nearly every "movement" is modulatory. Ferdinand refers to its subtitle as being *"Leichen-phantasie"* ("Death Fantasy"). He probably confused this subtitle with a Schubert lied entitled *"Eine Leichenfantasie"*, composed around 1811. Schubert's contemporaries Spaun, Fuchs and Schindler referred to it simply as "Fantasy for Pianoforte Duet."

After Schubert's death the manuscript (now at the Pierpont Morgan Library) was owned by Schubert's half-brother Andreas (1823-1893). The first eight pages of the manuscript were divided into several pieces by Andreas and given as gifts to family and friends. The remainder of the manuscript (pp. 9-24), including a cancelled page of the finale, was later owned by the late Dr. Alvin Cranz of Vienna. This latter section, which begins with m. 336 of the primo part and is joined at m. 416 by the secondo, is complete to the finale. The cancelled finale contains 65 bars of the secondo part of a fugue in C major which was not finished nor included in the first publication. Dr. Cranz owned a completed version of the finale, but it has since been lost. Dr. Deutsch believed that there were originally two different manuscripts of this Fantasy, the one which is now at the Pierpont Morgan Library, and one which he believed to have been at the *Gesellschaft der Musikfreunde* in Vienna but is now lost. He believed that the one which was supposedly at the *Gesellschaft der Musikfreunde* was the manuscript used for the first publication. We, on the other hand, after examining the manuscript at the Pierpont Morgan Library, believe this to be the one used for the first publication, because there are numerous editorial marks in the manuscript other than Schubert's. The first edition and the Henle edition are identical and these are the only ones published.

Already in the *Fantasy in G* we find Schubertian traits destined to become trade marks of his mature compositions: the "grand pause," tremolo effects, and examples of evaded cadences modulating to third-related keys. Notably absent is the near equality of both partners, which he later developed to such a high degree. In this early composition, the secondo is mere accompaniment, with one timid, brief exception in an imitative Vivace section.

The form can only be described as a series of loosely connected, unrelated episodes or movements. Schubert had not yet hit upon the idea of a unifying motive. It is interesting to speculate whether this composition might have been programmatically conceived, perhaps for the entertainment of his friends at the Stadtkonvikt. Such writing was greatly in vogue at that time, and the trumpet calls, tremolos, and very fre-

FANTASY IN G, D 1

Adagio

Presto

FINALE
Allegro maestoso

---

10   *Ibid.,* 36.

Ex. 1. Schubert, *Fantasy*, D 9, m. 20-23
(Allegro)

Mozart, *Requiem, "Kyrie"*, m. 25-26
(Allegro)

quent tempo changes bring the possibility to mind.

Schubert's study with the famed Salieri did not begin until June 18, 1812, a fact which partially explains the immaturity of the *Fantasy in G*. One can compare this work with the soprano arias accompanied by a small orchestra which Mozart composed in Milan in 1770 when he was nearly the same age as Schubert in 1810. While his precocity is in no way comparable to Mozart's, Schubert's early musical talent was remarkable. It must be admitted, however, that the *Fantasy in G* is poorly constructed and far too long. Its historical interest is greater than its performance value, although it does contain numerous lovely melodies characteristic of the highly gifted young boy.

missing portion.) The manuscript, the Gesamtausgabe edition, and the Henle edition are alike except that in measures 202 to 206 the Henle differs from the Gesamtausgabe. The Henle used for these measures a fragment from the Vienna City Library, found on the manuscript of D 62 *"Thronend auf erhabnem Sitz"*.

The *Fantasy in G minor* seems to have been inspired by the *"Kyrie"* from Mozart's *Requiem*. The contrapuntally treated primo theme (beginning with measure 20) is closely related to the second subject of Mozart's double fugue. (See Ex. 1, above.)

The "Largo" introduction and the ending are based upon the piano introduction of Schubert's song *"Hagars Klage"* (D 5) and the introduction of the *Overture for Strings* in C minor (D 8). (See Ex. 2, page 6.)

FANTASY IN G MINOR, D 9 ¤ ¤ ¤ ¤ ¤ ¤

Composed: Sept. 20, 1811
Manuscript: Deutsche Staatsbibliothek [German State Library], East Berlin
First publication: Gesamtausgabe, 1888

Among historical documents, the *Fantasy in G minor*, D 9 is mentioned only in Ferdinand Schubert's list of his brother's works, as published in the issue of the *Neue Zeitschrift für Musik* mentioned earlier. The original manuscript is complete except for the final sixteen measures of the primo part. (The editors of the Gesamtausgabe completed the

FANTASY IN G MINOR, D 9

Ex. 2. Schubert, *Hagars Klage*, D 5, m. 1-5

The form, far more meaningful than that of the previous fantasy, is: Introduction A B A C (March) B Coda. The Introduction and Coda are based upon the same theme.

There are two notably bold modulations in the work. The first, which begins at measure 108, consists of descending diminished seventh chords so mighty and serious as to be almost comical in approaching a gay, unassuming Tempo di Marcia. The second interesting modulation (measures 118-135), which leads from C minor to A major, is accomplished by means of descending open fifths over an A pedal point.

From the standpoint of performance, the most important concern is to emphasize the contrast between the Tempo di Marcia, which is a light, refreshing section in major, and the heavier materials which surround it. In this Largo introduction, as well as in any slow passage, perfect ensemble is both essential and difficult to achieve. The writers advocate an arrangement whereby the primo player is the leader, giving visual cues with the wrist, much like the technique for a conductor's baton.

There are some technically awkward areas, especially in such early pieces, which can be made much more playable by switching certain notes to the other hand (sometimes even to the other player). Examples of this type of redistribution can be found in secondo measures 52, 54, and 56, in which the second four eighth-notes could well be taken with the right hand; in the primo part beginning with measure 83, the right hand could take the eighth-note passage. At measure 112 the secondo may play an unmeasured tremolo, since a literal reading would very likely sound too heavy.

ALLEGRO MODERATO IN C and *ANDANTE IN A MINOR*, D 968 ¤ ¤

Composed: ca. 1812-1818
Note: The Allegro Moderato in C major and the Andante in A minor were originally published as one piece called *Sonatine.*
Manuscript: Stadtbibliothek, Vienna
First publication: Gesamtausgabe, 1888

O. E. Deutsch was not sure of the dates of composition of the *Allegro Moderato in C Major* and the *Andante in A minor*, and listed them among the undated compositions, hence the high Deutsch number. Later, however, certain discoveries concerning these works were made by Maurice J. E. Brown and were published in the July, 1961 *Musical Quarterly*. Mr. Brown had strong reasons for dating these duets approximately 1812.[11] The manuscripts themselves are neither signed nor dated by the composer, but they consist of large white sheets of music paper such as were not often used by Schubert. Since similar paper was found in the manuscript of the operetta *Der Spiegelritter* which was composed in 1812, it is possible that these works are of the same period.

---

11 M. J. E. Brown, "Schubert: Discoveries of the Last Decade", *The Musical Quarterly*, xlvii (July 1961), 300-303.

Ex. 3. Schubert, Franz. *Allegro Moderato*, D 968, m. 1-6.

Schubert, Ferdinand. *Pastoral Mass, "Credo"*, m.1-5.

Cre - do, Cre - do in u - num De - um, pa -trem om-ni - po -

On the other hand, Fr. Reinhard van Hoorickx, a Schubert scholar, believes that it was written in the spring of 1818 as an exercise for the daughters of Count Esterházy. Dr. Ernst Hilmar (Music Division, Vienna City Library) believes the paper is from 1817, and not from 1812 as suggested by Mr. Brown.

Penciled in the manuscript of the *Allegro Moderato* are the words from the Mass: "*Credo in unum Deum*", and in the Andante there are words from "*Et incarnatus est*". Dr. Deutsch believed that the writing is not Schubert's, but Mr. Brown pointed out that opinions differ on this matter.

Fr. Reinhard van Hoorickx has found that the *Allegro Moderato* and the *Andante* are remarkably akin to the "*Credo*" and the "*Et incarnatus est*" found in Schubert's brother Ferdinand's *Pastoral Mass* in B flat major. This Mass, according to Ferdinand's manuscript, was composed by himself in 1833, and performed in 1846. However, Ferdinand borrowed his brother Franz's "*Kyrie*", composed in March, 1813, for the opening of this Mass; Fr. Reinhard points out that Ferdinand also borrowed for his Mass portions of his brother's song "*Leichenfantasie*" (D 7), a chorus from the operetta *Die Zwillingsbrüder* (D 647), several minuets from D 41, as well as the *Allegro Moderato* and *Andante!* (See Ex. 3, above.)

In the piano duet there are two themes which alternate as follows in the *Allegro Moderato* : A B Development (of B theme) A B. This is followed by the *Andante*, which is only forty-five measures long and has basically only one theme, which is carried throughout by the primo in octave doubling. The secondo is mere accompaniment. It is among the very easiest duets. The manuscript contains fingerings, so it was probably used as a teaching piece. The piece presents some problems in balance, especially for the younger or less experienced duettists. Some examples would be at measure 9, secondo, where the right hand should be subdued (even though "f") to avoid an overly thick texture, and at measure 31 and beyond, where the broken chords in the secondo right hand should likewise be subdued.

FANTASY IN C MINOR, D 48 (*Grosse Sonata*) ¤ ¤ ¤ ¤ ¤ ¤ ¤ ¤ ¤ ¤ ¤

First published version

Composed or copied: 1814
Manuscript: (without fugue) Gertrude Clark Witall Collection, Library of Congress, Washington,D.C.
First publication: J. P. Gotthard, 1871 as "*Grosse Sonata*"

Second published version

Composed: April–June 1813
Manuscript: (complete with fugue) Stadtbibliothek, Vienna
First publication: Gesamtausgabe 1888

The *Fantasy in C minor* exists in two versions, the first without a fugue and the second with a fugue. The first was owned by Albert Stadler, a boyhood friend of Schubert at the Stadtkonvikt, who dated it 1814. The work in this form—without fugue—is obtainable in the Peters edition and the Universal edition, in each case as *Grosse Sonata in C minor*. The authenticity of this version was questioned by Dr. Deutsch, who believed that it may be a copy by Stadler, who chose to omit the fugue. Father Reinhard has made a scholarly, detailed comparison between the Washington (first version) and Viennese (second version) manuscripts. Having studied other manuscripts copied by Stadler he concludes that the Washington version is definitely in Stadler's hand, but probably copied from a now lost version (not the Viennese). Because of its many corrections and cancellations, we assume that the Viennese version is only a first draft. The Henle edition is taken from the second version — the Viennese manuscript, which is definitely in Schubert's hand and dated by him "April 1813." In examining the version called "*Grosse Sonata*" one finds no sonata-allegro form, therefore the title "Fantasy" is more suitable than the "Sonata" title of the Peters and Universal editions.

This third fantasy from the first period of duet composition does not show the economy of means displayed in the *Fantasy in G minor*, D 9. Like the first *Fantasy*, D 1, its length is not justified by the materials contained, nor is its form as cohesive as that of the second fantasy. It does, however, contain one of the best early examples of Schubert's melodic gifts, an *Andante Amoroso*. At that time Schubert was studying

with the renowned Italian composer Salieri, who emphasized the importance of a beautiful melodic line. We also find in this section a real integration of the elements in the primo and secondo. The form is as follows:

Allegro	Andante	Allegro	Adagio	Fugue
ABABA	C D C	E F	G	H

As in the previous fantasy, the sections in major provide a very welcome contrast to what surrounds them, but in this case Schubert ran into modulatory difficulties, namely from measures 69 to 71, and the result is weak. The manuscript shows that there was much agonizing over this spot. Measures 462 to 469 were written by the *Gesamtausgabe* editor, based upon Schubert's own materials of thirteen measures' length, i.e., thirteen measures were shortened to seven.

As Beethoven's "Electoral" sonatas, which he composed when he was eleven years old, foreshadowed his later works, this *Fantasy in C minor* is related to the mature *Wanderer Fantasy* (for piano solo) and the superb *Fantasy in F minor* of 1828. The three early fantasies give us insight into the character of Schubert as a young man. Spaun tells us that he was quiet and shy as a small boy, and even in his maturity he was outgoing only when with his small group of friends. This does not imply that Schubert was as misanthropic as Beethoven, for he had many acquaintances; yet, he was more at ease with close friends. Duets were, therefore, an ideal medium of expression and performance for one with his personality. Schubert never wrote a two-piano composition or a piano concerto, perhaps because by the very nature of the concerto principle, rivalry is implied. This "harmonious opposition" was foreign to Schubert's nature and interest. Conversely, the intimacy of two persons at one keyboard — each being necessary to complement the other — retained its appeal throughout his life.

It has frequently been said that the style of Schubert's composition

FANTASY IN C MINOR, D 48

shows little development and that many of his early works are as mature as any of the late ones. This is not a correct observation when the compositions of 1810 to 1814 are taken into consideration. We see here the strong influence of the Viennese classics, especially Mozart and Haydn, whose music was quite familiar to Schubert through the Stadtkonvikt orchestra. The compositions of this first period are generally more dependent on Schubert's predecessors than original, as would be expected of such early efforts, although attention has been called to various Schubertian clichés.

In concluding our consideration of the earliest duets, two ideas, which originated with writers of romantic fiction, should be re-examined. The first is that Schubert always suffered from a shortage of music paper. Even though there are documents describing Schubert's meager existence at the Stadtkonvikt, Eusebius Mandyczewski in his introduction to the revised Gesamtausgabe points out that young Schubert was extravagant with paper (hence the shortage?) but became more economical in later life, even to the point of writing smaller. The manuscripts bear this out. Another wrong notion is that Schubert was unable to write contrapuntally. There is evidence that Schubert felt himself inadequate in this respect. However, anyone studying the *Fantasy*, D 9 or the *Fantasy*, D 48 must agree that Schubert demonstrated an early gift for polyphonic writing. He sensed the value of giving equal importance to the primo and secondo parts and, at least until 1818, achieved this best in the contrapuntal sections.

Franz Theodor Schubert (1763-1830),
the composer's father, a schoolmaster.
(Historic Museum of the City of Vienna.)

Schubert's birthplace at 54 Nussdorferstrasse,
now the Schubert Museum.
(Historic Museum of the City of Vienna.)

CHAPTER II

A Career Is Begun (1814–1817)

In November 1813, two months before Schubert's seventeenth birthday, he left the Stadtkonvikt in good standing. He continued to study composition with the great Salieri for the next three years, sometimes seeing the master teacher twice a week. Music was beginning to flow from the young genius at a prodigious rate. In addition to his favored lieder, he tried his hand at compositions for piano, string quartet, symphony orchestra and an opera.

Schubert's father, a very stern, practical man, was adamant that musical genius alone was not sufficient to make one's way in life. It was decided that Schubert should remain at home with the family and study at the St. Anna Teachers' Training College. Schubert attended the school until August, 1814 when he completed his study in "theoretical and practical knowledge".[12]

The recurring suggestion that Schubert became a teacher to avoid the draft is groundless, since teachers were not exempt from conscription. During the Napoleonic Wars, Austrian conscription was for seven to fourteen years and generally dreaded, but Schubert would not have had to serve in the military anyway, because he was too short — only five feet one inch. The minimum for the military was five feet two inches.

In the fall of 1814 Schubert joined his brother Ferdinand as a teaching assistant at their father's school. Despite the long teaching hours and the strain of teaching six-year-olds, Schubert managed to compose a considerable amount — some 300 works between 1814 and 1816. His diaries show him to be depressed and unhappy, but he felt he must sacrifice his own freedom and feelings to please his father and gain security and middle-class respectability.

At about the time Schubert began to teach, Napoleon was defeated and forced into exile. Vienna was to host a congress whose purpose was to settle the affairs of Europe and prevent further wars. Between September 1814 and June 1815 the Congress of Vienna met in a carnival-like atmosphere. Representatives of all European nations were invited to Vienna regardless of their alignment in the recent war. Their idealistic goal, to avoid all future wars, was not achieved but the new map of Europe drawn up by this Congress survived until 1914. The principal leaders who attended were Prince Clemens Metternich of Austria, Charles de Talleyrand of France, Prince Carl August Hardenberg of Prussia, Viscount Robert Castlereagh of England and Czar Alexander I of Russia. Aside from these key leaders, there were two emperors, two empresses, four kings, one queen, two hereditary princes, three princes of royal blood, three grand duchesses, and all their staff and entourage. In addition there were other members of the reigning houses numbering nearly 250. These people were accompanied by military leaders and experts in various fields, such as bankers, cartographers, writers, industrial advisers and diplomats. Families brought their own maids, cooks, valets, coachmen and interpreters. In all, over 10,000 people were brought to Vienna.

Aside from the great amount of work which was accomplished, endless balls, banquets and receptions filled the evenings, causing one observer to say "The congress dances, but does not move." The Viennese waltz had already supplanted the more stately minuet, and the dignitaries and middle class alike danced it endlessly. The most popular dancing establishment was the Apollosaal, which had opened in January 1808 for the wedding of Emperor Franz. On that opening night more than 4,000 people crowded into this establishment with its five enormous ballrooms and four drawing rooms. Greenery and flowers were everywhere, as well as waterfalls, grottos and a small lake with a live swan. The Apollosaal probably rivaled the luxury of any ancient Roman hall.

Music, art and dance flourished. New fashions in clothing and hair styling were seen by this international group. Exotic foods were introduced. The revelry continued until March 1, 1815 when

12 O. E. Deutsch, *The Schubert Reader*, 43.

Napoleon escaped from Elba. He entered Paris on March 20 and the period of the "hundred days" began. Austria, Britain, Prussia and Russia went to war once more—a war which lasted until the Battle of Waterloo on June 18, 1815, in which Napoleon was defeated by the Duke of Wellington. Here ended the last hope of Napoleon. He was banished to St. Helena. The Congress of Vienna was dissolved.[13]

Schubert continued to teach in his father's school (fall 1814 to summer 1816). He still loathed the frustrations of working with elementary students and the long working hours which took him away from composing, on a salary which was only a pittance. He looked elsewhere for a position. The *Wiener Zeitung* (February 17, 1816) announced a "Music Master's Post" opening at the German Normal School in Laibach (now Ljubljana, Yugoslavia). He wanted the position very much, since it would allow him to work as a musician with a salary six times greater than he was receiving from his father. For some unknown reason, however, Schubert's application was sent

three weeks late. Was he waiting for the letter of recommendation from Salieri which he enclosed with his application? The application itself was short and hastily written. Schubert only mentioned that he had "knowledge and skill in all branches of composition."[14] No details were given. He received the disappointing news in August that the position had gone to a local teacher in Laibach.

Two months earlier, Schubert had entered in his diary (June 17, 1816): "Today I composed for money for the first time. Namely, a cantata for the name-day of Professor Wattrot [Watteroth], words by Dräxler. The fee is 100 florins, V. C. [Vienna currency]."[15] Encouraged that his music could bring in money and by the fact that his close friend Franz von Schober (1796-1882) had received a sizable inheritance, Schubert decided to leave his family and his teaching position. By December of 1816 he had moved to the Schobers' lodging in the Landskrongasse where he remained as a house guest of the Schober family for the next year.

Franz von Schober (1796-1882), one of Schubert's dearest friends. Unfortunately, he never wrote an account of his recollections of the composer. (Historic Museum of the City of Vienna.)

Josef von Spaun (1788-1865). A government official who was among the first to organize the Schubertiads, many of which were held in his home. (Historic Museum of the City of Vienna.)

Johann Mayrhofer (1787-1836). A poet who made his living as an official in the Censorship Office. Melancholy and misanthropic, he committed suicide. Schubert used many of Mayrhofer's poems for his lieder. (Historic Museum of the City of Vienna.)

13 For a more comprehensive description of the Congress of Vienna see R. Waissenberger, *Vienna in the Biedermaier Era* (New York, 1986), 9-28.

14 O. E. Deutsch, *The Schubert Reader*, 54.

15 *Ibid.*, p. 65.

Schubert and Schober had been friends for two years, having established a rapport at their first meeting. Schober was born in Sweden of a German father and an Austrian mother. A restless, wealthy dilettant, he worked at many professions during his life: writer, actor, painter, draftsman, civil administrator and later, private secretary to Franz Liszt. His irreligious, amoral, unorthodox approach to life appealed to Schubert, perhaps because Schober was the antithesis of Schubert's conservative father. Their platonic friendship was so bonded that they referred to themselves collectively as "Schobert".

Besides Schober, Schubert's other two close friends at that time were Joseph von Spaun (1788-1865), a friend from his seminary days, and Johann Mayrhofer (1787-1836), an amateur poet, law student, and misanthrope who later, in one of his deep depressions, committed suicide by jumping from his office window. Strangely, this passionate liberal was at that time working as a censor for the Emperor's conservative government. Mayrhofer's poetry struck a responsive chord within Schubert, for Mayrhofer was second only to Goethe in the number of poems which Schubert set to music. Mayrhofer recognized the greatness of Schubert's musical settings, saying, "I wrote poetry, he composed what I had written, much of which owes its existence, its development and its popularity to his melodies." He told Grillparzer that his poems seemed good to him only after Schubert had set them to music!

Unfortunately, on the other hand, Johann von Goethe ignored Schubert. Earlier in 1816 Spaun had tried to promote Schubert by sending an album of his settings of Goethe poems to the great poet himself. Spaun nearly groveled at the feet of Goethe, begging his permission to permit Schubert to dedicate to him a planned edition of these songs. Goethe merely returned the music, without comment — a black mark on the poet's perception.

Another rejection which hurt Schubert, but which now has an almost comic overtone, occurred in early 1817 when either Spaun or Schubert sent to the great publishing house Breitkopf and Härtel the newly-composed "*Der Erlkönig*". The publisher, knowing a *different* Franz Schubert (also a composer) in Dresden, returned the work to the wrong Schubert, who wrote to the publisher:

Most Valued Friend,
... I received a valued letter from you in which you enclosed the manuscript of Goethe's 'Erlking' alleged to be set by me. With the greatest astonishment I beg to state that this song was never composed by me. I shall retain the same in my possession in order to learn, if possible, who sent you this sort of trash. ...
    Your most grateful friend
    and brother!!!
    Franz Schubert
    Royal Church Composer[16]

Incredibly, Breitkopf and Härtel rejected Schubert's setting of "*Der Erlkönig*" in 1817 in favor of one by Petersen Grönland. It is worth noting that during Schubert's lifetime this publishing house accepted nothing from Schubert, but at the end of the nineteenth century published his complete works.

Despite such rejections, Schubert was happy and prolifically creative. He enjoyed his new-found freedom and was able to compose for long hours each day. He frequently composed lieder from poetry of his three closest friends, Mayrhofer, Schober and Spaun. The famed "*An die Musik*", "*Der Tod und das Mädchen*" and "*Die Forelle*" were produced in that year.

In 1817 Schubert was twenty years old and unemployed. His three good friends helped him financially and, more importantly, they encouraged him to give direction to his career. He needed a publisher such as Breitkopf & Härtel, an association with a famous name such as Goethe, and/or stable employment as a music teacher. Despite many attempts, he acquired none of these. Undaunted, his friends searched for new avenues to bring to Schubert the fame he deserved. They found in Johann Michael Vogl (1768-1840) the perfect choice: a fine singer to introduce Schubert's lieder to the public. Spaun relates the circumstances:

Schubert, who always had to sing his own songs, now frequently expressed a great desire to find a singer for his songs, and his old wish to get to know the Court opera singer, Vogl, grew stronger and stronger. It was now decided in our little circle that Vogl must be won over for the Schubert songs. The task was a hard one, as Vogl was very difficult to approach.

---

16 *Ibid.*, 76.

Schober's sister, who died young, had been married to the singer Siboni, and Schober still had some connections with the theatre, which made an approach to Vogl easier for him [Schober]. He told Vogl, with glowing enthusiasm, about Schubert's beautiful compositions and invited him to try them out. Vogl replied that he was fed to the teeth with music, that he had been brought up on music and was far more concerned to get free of it than to get to know any new music. He had heard about young geniuses hundreds of times and had always been disappointed, and this was certain to be the case with Schubert too. He wanted to be left in peace and wished to hear nothing more about it. — This refusal upset us all deeply, all except Schubert, who said he had expected just such an answer and found it perfectly understandable.

Meanwhile Vogl was approached repeatedly by Schober, and by others as well, and finally he promised to come to Schober's one evening to see what it was all about, as he put it.

He made his appearance at Schober's at the appointed hour, quite majestically, and when the small, insignificant Schubert made a somewhat awkward bow and, in his embarrassment, stammered some incoherent words about the honor of the acquaintance, Vogl turned up his nose rather contemptuously and the beginning of the acquaintance seemed to us to portend disaster. Finally Vogl said, "Let's see what you have got there; accompany me," and thereupon he took up the nearest sheet of music, containing Mayrhofer's poem "*Augenlied*", a pretty, very melodious, but not important song. Vogl hummed rather than sang, and then said coldly, "Not bad." When, after that, "*Memnon*", "*Ganymed*", and other songs were accompanied for him, all of which, however, he only sang mezza-voce, he became more and more friendly, though he went away without promising to come again. On leaving he slapped Schubert on the shoulders and said to him, "There is something in you but you are too little of a comedian, too little of a showman; you squander your fine thoughts without making the best of them." To others Vogl expressed himself considerably more favorably about Schubert than he did to the latter and his closest friends. (When the song

Johann Michael Vogl (1768-1840). One of the most famous singers of the Vienna Opera, he performed Schubert's lieder in concert and in Schubertiads until he was over 70. (Historic Museum of the City of Vienna.)

"*Die Dioskuren*" came to his notice he declared it to be a magnificent song and said it was frankly incomprehensible how such depth and maturity could emanate from the little young man.) The impression the songs made on him was an overwhelming one and now he approached our circle again of his own accord, invited Schubert to his home, rehearsed songs with him and when he realized the tremendous, profound impression his performance made on us, on Schubert himself and on every kind of audience, he grew so enthusiastic about the songs that he himself now became Schubert's most ardent admirer, and instead of giving up music, as he had previously intended, his enthusiasm for it was kindled anew.[17]

Vogl, who had been a star of the Vienna Court Opera for some twenty years singing Orestes in Gluck's *Iphigénie* and Pizarro in *Fidelio*, was now the leading interpreter of Schubert's lieder. The two set out giving exciting programs in the homes of the educated people of Vienna and in nearby towns. Vogl, who was a voracious reader of philosophy, studying

17   O. E. Deutsch, *Schubert: Memoirs by His Friends*, 131-132.

Marcus Aurelius, Homer and Plato, became a father figure to Schubert.

Schubert's music was at last receiving the recognition it deserved. In addition to the lieder, he devoted much of 1817 to the composition of piano sonatas. The wide variety of styles and the use of unusual key schemes indicate that Schubert was experimenting with both form and tonality. His harmonies became more complex and his melodies were more lyrical and often exuberant. His music was developing a wonderful spontaneity, which resulted from his acquiring self-confidence.

Unfortunately, Schubert's stay at Schober's home had to end, because in August 1817 it became necessary for Schober to travel to France to help his ailing brother Axel, and to bring him home. Schubert therefore vacated the room he had occupied, writing a poem of farewell (somewhat overstated, since Schubert and Schober would continue to live in the same city):

FAREWELL — For the Album of a Friend.

Fare thee well, my dearest friend!
Going to a distant land,
Hold true friendship's hallowed band
In a firm and faithful hand!
Fare thee well, my dearest friend!

Fare thee well, my dearest friend!
Hark, how in a plangent song,
My heart's beats together throng,
Mourning sadly, loud and long.
Fare thee well, my dearest friend!

Fare thee well, my dearest friend!
"Parting" is a bitter word:
Woe to us, for thou hast heard
Calls from where thou art preferred.
Fare thee well, my dearest friend!

Fare thee well, my dearest friend!

If this song may touch thy heart,
Friend, thy shadow, where thou art,
Music will to me impart.
Fare thee well, my dearest friend!
[Franz Schubert][18]

Axel died before Schober arrived in France, but in the meantime Schubert had moved back to his father's home, accepting the harsh condition that he again work as an assistant teacher. This time, however, Schubert was not as unhappy as before because he had made so many friends. His social life was a pleasant diversion from his daytime responsibilities.

As previously stated, Schubert's father had remarried in 1813, and the family had four more children in four years' time. In December 1817 Schubert's father was appointed master of a school in the adjoining district of Rossau. The entire family then moved to new and larger living quarters — a welcome turn of events considering their growing numbers. Franz continued to reside with them.

At about this same time, Schubert made two arrangements for piano duet. These two overtures were not included in the Henle collection of original duets because they are arrangements of orchestral pieces, but they are published by Bärenreiter. We include them here because they were arranged by Schubert himself and because of their historical significance.

THE DUETS OF 1817.

OVERTURE "IM ITALIENISCHEN STILE" IN D, D 592 ¤ ¤ ¤ ¤ ¤ ¤ ¤ ¤

Arranged from the *Italian Overture in D*
    for orchestra ca. November 1817.
Manuscript: lost
First publication: J. P. Gotthard, 1872

This duet was composed for orchestra and arranged for four hands at about the same time as the *Overture in C.* The slow introduction has been elongated by five measures in the duet, as compared to the orchestra version. These overtures were similar to those

OVERTURE "IM ITALIENISCHEN STILE" IN D, D 592

composed by Rossini; the sobriquet ". . . in Italian Style" was given them by Ferdinand Schubert.

OVERTURE "IM ITALIENISCHEN STILE" IN C, D 597 ¤ ¤ ¤ ¤ ¤ ¤ ¤ ¤ ¤

Arranged from the *Italian Overture in C*
    for orchestra, ca. December 1817
    or early 1818.
Manuscript: Stadtbibliothek, Vienna
First publication: J. P. Gotthard, 1872

Between the completion of the *Fantasy in C minor,* (1813) which was the last duet of Schubert's first period of duet composition, and the overtures in D and C for piano duet, Schubert wrote more than five hundred fifty compositions including songs, sonatas for various instruments, symphonies, et cetera. It would seem that he had deserted the duet medium temporarily, perhaps for the reason that he had little time for social life prior to living with Schober. (We have already noted that he was prompted to write duets for amateur music making.) His friends Spaun, Johann Senn, Mayrhofer, and Schober were all more interested in literature, poetry and the theatre than in music; they were certainly not pianists with whom Schubert could have performed piano duets.

Beginning in 1817, Schubert's friendship with Ignaz von Sonnleithner and his son, Leopold, provided motivation to resume writing duets. The Sonnleithners were ardent music lovers who held concerts twice every month in their home, the "*Gundelhof*". Leopold von Sonnleithner wrote concerning these musical evenings:

> For a number of years evening musical parties were held once a fortnight, on Fridays, for invited friends, at the house of my father, the Imperial Councillor Dr. Ignaz Edler von Sonn-leithner (Barrister and Imperial Professor), and for the arrangement and direction of these I had sole responsibility. The most distinguished local amateurs and artists took part in them and artists from outside were glad to be asked to perform. The number of listeners always amounted to one hundred twenty or more

and we had difficulty in warding off the crush of people.[19]

It was through the influential guests at the Friday musicals at the Sonnleithners' that Schubert became well-known in Vienna. The younger Sonnleithner recalled, in his memoirs of 1862, how Schubert was encouraged to write for these musical evenings. The guests formed a symphony orchestra which performed, among several other compositions, Schubert's *Overture in C in Italian Style.* Eduard Jaëll, a well-known conductor, was so pleased by the performance of this overture that he arranged to have it played at a public concert in the "*Zum römischen Kaiser*" inn. This performance on March 1, 1818 was the first public performance of any Schubert work other than the *Mass in F,* performed at the Liechtental Church in 1814, and a cantata performed at an orphanage in 1817. The overture was apparently a success, because on March 12, 1818 an arrangement of it for two pianos, eight hands was performed at the "*Zum römischen Kaiser*" inn. Since only his one-piano, four-hand version is extant, and no trace of an eight-hand version survives, the work performed was most likely the same duet arrangement, with two people playing each part.

There were several favorable reviews of the orchestra concert, most notably one from Dresden, Germany, which was, in effect, Schubert's first "foreign" critique. In the Vienna *Theaterzeitung,* March 14, 1818 we read: "The second part began with a wondrously lovely overture by the young composer Herr Franz

OVERTURE "IM ITALIENISCHEN STILE"
IN C, D 597

Adagio

Allegro giusto

Schubert, a pupil of our much-venerated Salieri, who has learnt already how to touch and excite all hearts. Although the theme was surprisingly simple, a wealth of the most astonishing and agreeable ideas developed from it, worked out with vigour and skill. It is to be wished that this artist will quite soon delight us with a new gift" [Franz von Schlechta].[20]

---

20   O. E. Deutsch, *The Schubert Reader*, 87.

CHAPTER III

The First Important Piano Duet Year (1818)

By 1818 Schubert had written more than 350 lieder. His diligence had finally paid off; his song "*Am Erlafsee*" was published in a little guidebook which had the fanciful title *Picturesque Pocket Book for Friends of Remarkable Localities, Points of Interest of Nature and Art in the Austrian Monarchy.* This book with its expensive price of six florins contained Schubert's first publication (February 6, 1818). There is no record of remuneration to Schubert, but at least his music was in print. The song was a setting of a poem by his friend Johann Mayrhofer, who was most likely instrumental in arranging for its publication. The editor of the book was Dr. Franz Satori, who was Mayrhofer's superior as head of the Central Book Censorship Office.

As mentioned in the previous chapter, both of Schubert's overtures "in the Italian Style" had been performed in public in their orchestral versions and had received excellent reviews. The orchestral *Overture in C* was performed on March 1, 1818 and the *Overture in D* was performed on May 17, 1818. On March 12 Schubert made his first public appearance as a pianist by participating in an eight-hand performance of his arrangement of the *Overture in C*, probably the duet version, doubled at the second piano. The review from the *Theaterzeitung* of March 24, 1818 singled Schubert out for special praise:

> A beginning was made with an overture for two pianos, eight hands by Franz Schubert, performed by Fräulein Therese and Babette Kunz and Herren Schubert and Hüttenbrenner. The reviewer regards it as his duty to draw special attention to the young artist, Herr Schubert, since he has several times had an opportunity to admire his rich gifts. Profound feeling, disciplined yet spontaneous force and appealing charm mark his every work, large and small, ... they will without a doubt find their favored place

among the productions of the day. The performance too deserved all praise. [Franz von Schlechta].[21]

Public performances of piano duets were very popular during this time. At this same concert, a Rondo for four hands by Moscheles was also performed.

Despite Schubert's growing reputation, he seemed distracted and uninspired in early 1818. In the previous year he had written over 65 lieder but in 1818 only fifteen. His sixth symphony was completed in February. Although it was technically advanced, it is not generally considered to be an exciting work. He sketched a symphony in D and a sonata in C for solo piano but left them unfinished. Did the quality and quantity of his music decline because he was too depressed by living at home, or was it because he spent too much time socializing with friends?

Anselm Hüttenbrenner (1794-1868), a fellow student of Salieri, became a close friend of Schubert, and shortly thereafter Anselm's younger brother Josef (1796-1882) was also brought into the Schubert circle. Schubert often stayed overnight at Anselm's room and frequently drank large amounts of red Hungarian wine. One night Schubert copied the score of "*Die Forelle*" ("The Trout") for Josef and sent it to him with the note:

> Dearest Friend, It gives me extraordinary pleasure to know you like my songs. As proof of my most devoted friendship, I am sending you another, which I have just now written at Anselm Hüttenbrenner's at midnight. I trust that I may become closer friends with you over a glass of punch.
>
> Just as, in my haste, I was going to send the thing, I rather sleepily took up the ink-well and poured it quite calmly over it. What a disaster![22]

---

21   O. E. Deutsch, *The Schubert Reader,* 87-88.

22   *Ibid.,* 86.

Schubert had intended to pick up the sandbox (it was the custom to use sand to blot the ink) and had mistakenly gotten hold of the ink. This letter was obviously written by a slightly tipsy or very sleepy person. Schubert calls Josef "Dearest Friend" (*teuerster Freund*) but then says that he would like to "become closer friends." He had not "just now written" the song, but only copied it. Schubert often copied his works for his friends, making slight alterations. "The Trout," for example, exists in five different versions.

On March 14, perhaps after seeing the excellent review of his concert, Schubert was in a lighthearted mood. He made a copy of a waltz for Anselm and in the dedication teased him about his expensive living quarters: "Written down for my coffee, wine and punch [-drinking] brother Anselm Hüttenbrenner, world famous composer. Vienna, 14 March in the year of our Lord 1818, in his own most impressive diggings at 30 florins V.C."[23]

The Hüttenbrenner brothers did little to further Schubert's career; carelessly, they even lost some of his works. In later years Anselm's servant used Schubert's opera *Claudine von Villa Bella* to light fires. One of life's ironies is that Anselm had publishers clamoring for his trite compositions while Schubert could find no publisher.

THE DUETS OF 1818.

RONDO IN D, Opus 138, D 608
("*Notre amitié est invariable*") ¤ ¤ ¤ ¤ ¤

VERSION A   *Composed:* January 1818
             Manuscript: Nationalbibliothek
             [National Library], Vienna
             First publication: Henle 1960

VERSION B   *Composed:* ca. 1818
             Manuscript: lost
             First publication: Diabelli & Co. 1835

RONDO IN D, Opus 138, D 608
Allegretto

Aside from the two duet arrangements of the overtures in C and D, the first original duet work after 1813 was the *Rondo in D*. The rondo was dated in Schubert's own hand "January 1818."

The manuscript (version A) of the *Rondo in D* was purchased by the *Nationalbibliothek* in Vienna from the estate of Diabelli's son-in-law, Josef Greipel, in 1897, which would lead us to assume that this was the same manuscript from which the Diabelli publication was made. If this is the case, Diabelli took greater liberties in editing this composition than with any other Schubert duet. However, we must consider the possibility that there were two different manuscripts, since the existing one is a sketch, and not Schubert's final copy. For this reason performers must choose between the Henle edition (version A), which corresponds almost exactly to the existing manuscript, and all other editions, which are taken from Diabelli's first edition (version B). While the Henle's adherence to the existing manuscript recommends it, Diabelli's alterations (if they were his) might be justified on the following grounds: he contributed to the composition's inner consistency (both formal and in details); he improved its pianistic qualities (compare, for instance, measure 278 in the Henle edition to the corresponding measure in the Diabelli edition); and he provided a more satisfactory ending, lengthening the piece by three measures.

The writers personally believe that Diabelli had two manuscripts of this rondo, and did not himself make major changes in the score. Version B is now lost, but perhaps someday it will reappear; Schubert is unique among composers in that examples of his musical autographs are found every few years. The number of works which Schubert composed was staggering, amounting to more than forty volumes in the *Gesamtausgabe* (first collected works). When O. E. Deutsch published his thematic catalog of Schubert's works, the composer's output seemed even more impressive. The number of entries was only two short of a thousand. When one takes into account that many of these single entries comprise several items (e.g., D 783 includes sixteen German Dances and two Écossaises), the quantity is amazing. In view of this prodigious output it is not surprising that at Schubert's death his manuscripts were to be found all over Austria. They were further scattered throughout the

---

23 *Ibid.*, 88.

world during the 19th century. Some were forgotten, some irretrievably lost, and there were some whose existence had never been suspected. Many of these manuscripts were cataloged by Deutsch as having been lost. More and more of these "lost" works have been found, along with those that had been previously unknown. Often the newly discovered manuscripts cause us to revise what had been viewed as standard performance scores. It is because Diabelli's edition is so superior to the existent manuscript that we suspect his source to have been a finished complete score which has since been lost.

In version A (Henle) the writers disagree with the G in measure 31 (primo), believing it to be A. This note is almost illegible in the manuscript. Since both hands are in octaves, in addition to the fact that this passage appears several times in the composition, it would normally be easy to determine the correct note. In this instance, however, Schubert wrote only the right hand and indicated that the left hand should play one octave lower; each time the principal theme (which contains the note in question) returns, he writes "Repeat the first 39 measures."

In measure 51 of the Henle edition there is the indication "*pp*"; however, this mark appears at the edge of Schubert's manuscript, not within any measure. Since he had written "cresc." in the previous measure, obviously building to measure 52, the writers omit the "*pp*". In performance, in measure 66 (secondo left hand) the G on the third beat should be omitted since it is not in the manuscript and does not correspond to analogous measures. There is an indistinguishable mark near this point in the manuscript, but it is not a note.

The subtitle "*Notre amitié est invariable [Our friendship is constant]*" and the requirement of crossing the hands at the close of the piece may have been contributed by Diabelli; it has long been assumed by musicologists that the inscription was a dedication to Joseph von Gahy (1793-1864), whom Schubert considered his favorite duet partner, and that the crossing of hands symbolized their friendship. Documents and letters frequently mention the duet playing of Gahy and Schubert, but none mention the *Rondo in D*. Because of the importance of Gahy in connection with the duets, his affection for Schubert merits our attention. Gahy related ca. 1860 to Kreissle von Hellborn, the first biographer of Schubert:

The hours I spent making music together with Schubert are among the richest enjoyments of my life and I cannot think of those days without being most deeply moved. It was not only that, on such occasions, I learnt much that was new but the clear, fluent playing, the individual conception, the manner of performance, sometimes delicate and sometimes full of fire and energy, of my small, plump partner afforded me great pleasure; this was still further enhanced because it was just on these occasions that Schubert's genial nature was displayed in its full radiance and he used to characterize the various compositions by humorous interpolations, which sometimes included sarcastic, though always pertinent, remarks. My friendly relationship with Schubert (with whom I was on terms of the intimate "Du") remained unclouded until his death.[24]

The form of the *Rondo in D* is: A (repeated) B A C A plus coda. The repeat is indicated in the manuscript and in the Henle edition, but not in other editions. The Diabelli (version B) is abbreviated in the second and third A sections by forty-seven measures. For an example of another "cut," the reader may wish to compare the shorter (Diabelli) version of the coda (Peters Vol. III, p. 69) with the Henle version (Vol. 1, p. 113). The F major passage (measures 262-266) is omitted entirely in the Peters edition; the omission does not weaken the harmonic scheme. In the existing manuscript, Schubert sketched a section of entirely new material (section D, as it were) which was to be inserted between the final A section and the coda. This sketch is incomplete and has been omitted entirely in all editions.

Although the subtitle "*Notre amitié est invariable*" is probably not Schubert's own, it truly captures the style of the piece. Good humor prevails through simple, straightforward harmony and through liberal use of grace notes sweeping upward, as in the opening measure. Schubert has given the secondo part real importance, not only in accompaniment figures of fresh and original character (see measure 41) but also as a conversational participant. In the primo part, beginning with measure 45 in the B section, we find one of the most successful of Schubert's devices, well described by Maurice J. E. Brown:

_____

24 O. E. Deutsch, *Schubert: Memoirs by His Friends*, 176-177.

A difficult feature to define, but one which cannot be missed when we hear his melodies, is the strongly characteristic "finger-print" in his melodic use of the minor mode. It is compounded of a fondness for decorating the dominant of the key with semitones above and below it. . . . The tendency is, naturally, closely related to his partiality for the chord known as the "Neapolitan" sixth. This chord is based on the semitone above the key note.[25]

The *Rondo in D* and most of Schubert's other duet compositions prior to 1822 reflect joy and optimism; for this reason lightness of character is the primary concern in performance. All of the grace notes are delicate and fall before the beat.

In the summer of 1818 Schubert became the house pianist for Count Johann Esterházy. Schubert had become bored with Vienna and, on the recommendation of Johann Unger (the father of the celebrated singer Caroline Unger-Sabatier), he accepted a position with the Esterházys, who were a musical family living in Vienna during the winter months and at Zseliz on the river Gran, in Hungary (now Czechoslovakia) during the summer. Schubert went there by stagecoach in the early days of July, 1818. Because he had spent all of his life in Vienna, there are few letters in his own handwriting up to then; during the summer at Zseliz, however, letters to and from his family and friends give a vivid description of his activities.

Karl von Schönstein (1797-1876), an amateur musician and a friend of both the Esterházy family and Schubert, wrote to Ferdinand Luib (b. 1811), an early Schubertian biographer, in January, 1857:

> In 1818 Schubert was engaged by Count Johann Karl Esterházy to act during the summer as music master to the Count's family on his estate of Zseliz in Hungary. The two daughters of the Count, Marie and Karoline, were already very good pianists when Schubert went there.... Schubert's task was more one of coaching than teaching.... he became a favorite of the family, remaining with them as music master during the winter in Vienna.[26]

Countess Karoline Esterházy (1805-1851) was tutored by Schubert in Zseliz in 1818 and 1824. He referred to her as "a certain attractive star", which partially fostered the rumor that she was Schubert's secret love. He dedicated the *Fantasy in F minor* (page 71, below) to her. This portrait is from a lost watercolor of 1828 by Josef Teltscher.

His activity as music teacher of the Count's two daughters was surely at least one of the reasons for Schubert's suddenly returning interest in piano duets.

Schubert was very happy for the first few weeks at Zseliz and wrote to Franz von Schober in August, 1818, "I hope that you are happy and in the best of health, as I am. Thank God I live at last, and it is high time, otherwise I should have become nothing but a frustrated musician."[27] But, Schubert's happiness began to fade as the summer wore on. He was one hundred miles from home and missed his devoted family and friends. He longed to return to Vienna even though the hot, uncomfortable journey took several days and fourteen stage coaches. He was treated well at Zseliz but, as was then appropriate for a house musician, he lodged and took his meals in the servants' quarters. On September 8, 1818 Schubert wrote to his friend Schober:

---

25   M. J. E. Brown, *Schubert: A Critical Biography* (London, 1961), 215.

26   O. E. Deutsch, *Schubert: Memoirs by His Friends*, 100.

27   O. E. Deutsch, *The Schubert Reader*, 96.

At Zseliz I am obliged to rely wholly on myself. I have to be composer, author, audience, and goodness knows what else. Not a soul here has any feeling for true art, or at most the countess now and again (unless I am wrong). So I am alone with my beloved [music] and have to hide her in my room, in my pianoforte and in my bosom. Although this often makes me sad, on the other hand it elevates me the more. Have no fear, then, that I shall stay away longer than is absolutely necessary.[28]

In a letter to his brother Ferdinand, written on October 29, 1818, he expresses his loneliness among the people at Zseliz and declares, "My longing for Vienna grows daily. We shall be off by the middle of November."[29]

FOUR POLONAISES, Opus 75, D 599 ¤ ¤ ¤

Composed: July? 1818
Manuscript: lost
First publication: Diabelli & Co. 1827

In the Houghton Library at Harvard University there are sketches of several melodies in Schubert's hand, and among them are the themes for the second, third and fourth of the *Four Polonaises*. The sketches (D 618a, published by Bärenreiter in 1972) are dated July, 1818. We may therefore assume that the *Polonaises* were completed at around that time.

In addition to the Harvard sketches, there is also a version of these *Polonaises* which we will

refer to as the Kremsmünster version because it is in the Benedictine monastery at Kremsmünster in upper Austria. Schubert had a close relationship with this monastery, having visited it three times; many of Schubert's friends, including Johann Michael Vogl, had studied there. This Kremsmünster version is very

FOUR POLONAISES, Opus 75, D 599

---

28   *Ibid.,* 99.
29   *Ibid.,* 109.

close to the Harvard sketch, but is not in Schubert's own hand. The title on the Kremsmünster version reads: *IV Polonaises for the Pianoforte for Four Hands by Franz Schubert*. For some unknown reason the number "VI" had been pasted over the number IV.

Christa Landon, editor of the *Schubert: Neue Ausgabe*, published by Bärenreiter, has made a scholarly comparison among the Harvard sketch, the Kremsmünster sketch, and the first edition. She concluded that since these three are so different from each other, there can be no single "correct" or "authentic" version.

These are charming dances, full of varied melodies, and almost Chopinesque. Robert Schumann described these polonaises (or possibly the *Polonaises* Op 61) as "purely and simply thunderstorms breaking forth, with romantic rainbows over a sublimely slumbering universe."[30] Typical of the authentic polonaise, they are in moderate triple meter, and should be played with vigorous rhythm

appropriate to the dance. The form of each is A B trio A B. The A sections consist of eight measures, the B sections, sixteen; the lyrical trios, varying somewhat in length, frequently employ imitation and are very effectively written. The trio of the second polonaise is especially remarkable, hovering between D major and D minor and including third-related chords and diminished sevenths.

Notable errors in all editions except the Bärenreiter are: *Polonaise No. 1* — the accents in primo measures 1, 2, 5, 6, 17, 18, 19 and 20 should be on the third beat, not the second beat; *Polonaise No. 3* — the turns in the trio, primo measures 18 and 20, should be after the second beat, not on it; *Polonaise No. 4* — in the primo left hand of m. 14 of the trio the note is C, not E on the first sixteenth-note, and in m. 24 the primo left hand should play F, not E on the fourth sixteenth-note.

THREE HEROIC MARCHES, Opus 27, D 602 ¤ ¤ ¤

Composed: July? 1818
Manuscript: lost
First publication: Sauer and Leidesdorf, 1824

At approximately the same time that Schubert wrote the *Four Polonaises*, D 599, he turned his attention to the march form, of which he was later to compose a total of seventeen for piano duet. The first group, *Three Heroic Marches*, D 602, is generally attributed to the year 1818, although the material of the first march had been used in 1816 as an introduction to a sketch of a cantata, *Die Schlacht* (The Battle), with words by Schiller. These and later marches for piano duet, all with titles given by publishers, were repeatedly orchestrated after Schubert's death.

The first march, in B minor, is characterized by two devices: the ascending fourth in the melodic

THREE HEROIC MARCHES, Opus 27, D 602

No. 1. **Allegro moderato**

TRIO

No. 2. **Maestoso**

TRIO

No. 3. **Moderato**

TRIO

30 *Ibid.*, 800.

line and the rhythmic pattern ♩ ♩. ♪|♩ with which each section begins. The form of this march, as well as the other two, is A B Trio A B. One generally expects a march to have four- or eight-measure phrases; however, a notable feature of Schubert's marches is the occurrence of five-, six-, seven-, and ten-measure phrases. The A theme of the first march is ten measures long rather than eight. Other "irregular" phrase lengths are found in the march section of the *Fantasy in G* and in the *Three Military Marches.* Although the first march is far less significant than its two more mature companion pieces, it does have much harmonic interest, particularly in the B section.

The second march, in C major, follows the form of the first, but each section has been greatly expanded. The A and B sections are closely related; the rhythms of the first four measures of each section are identical. Yet, the contrast between AB and the trio is far greater than in the first march. Although the march in C major is marked "maestoso," exuberance abounds. It includes a few simple imitations (measures 8 and 9) but only between the right and left hands of the primo. Significant conversation between the players is yet to come.

The third march, in D major, is an unpretentious little composition, again characterized by its dotted rhythms throughout the A and B sections. In the trio the primo again makes an attempt at canonic imitation, but promptly relapses into the dotted rhythm.

The first edition of the *Three Heroic Marches*, from the publishing house Sauer and Leidesdorf, was republished by Diabelli around 1830 in exactly the same guise. The Henle edition is faithful to the original publication, although the editor of the Henle has added a few dynamic marks and accents, carefully placing them in brackets to indicate that they are not original. He has also filled in staccatos and slurs for the left hands of both primo and secondo, where both hands are playing in unison, *et cetera*. As is usually the case, the Peters edition has been marked with longer, and probably more logical slurs.

In the Bärenreiter edition, the interpretive marks of all parallel passages are alike. Notable errors which have been corrected in the Bärenreiter (March II) are:

¶M. 21 and 24, the first quarter-note should be changed to ♪ ⁊ to correspond to the secondo.

¶M. 39 and 41, the secondo right-hand rhythm should be changed to ♩.. ♪ to match the primo m. 43.

¶M. 21 of the trio, ♩ ♩ ♩ ♩ should be changed to ♪ ♪⁊ ♪⁊ ♪⁊ to match m. 5.

All three marches are most effective when played in a simple, straightforward manner.

INTRODUCTION AND VARIATIONS ON AN ORIGINAL THEME IN B Flat, Opus 82 No. 2, D 603 (D 968a) ¤ ¤ ¤ ¤ ¤ ¤ ¤ ¤ ¤ ¤ ¤ ¤ ¤

Composed: July? 1818
Manuscript: lost
First publication: Schuberth and Co., 1860

Except for his "Gastein" symphony, no composition of Schubert has as mysterious a history as the *Introduction and Variations on an Original Theme in B Flat.* In no preserved writings by Schubert or his friends do we find these variations mentioned. Many years ago a few musicologists questioned their authenticity because they were not found until 1860. In that year, Julius Schuberth and Company (Hamburg and Leipzig) re-issued Schubert's *Variations on a Theme from Hérold's "Marie"*, Op. 82, No. 1 (D 908) for piano duet, which had been quite successful, and they included with its publication the *Introduction and Variations...* as Op. 82, No. 2. No one seems to know how the manuscript reached Schuberth and Company or where it had been during the forty or so years between its composition and publication. Kreissle von Hellborn, the first biographer of Schubert, believed that the manuscript was bought in a purchase of

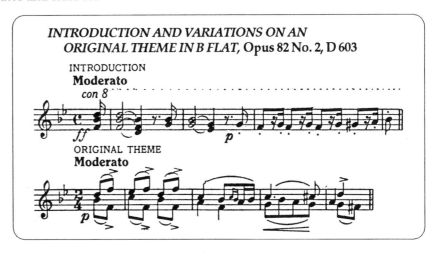

INTRODUCTION AND VARIATIONS ON AN ORIGINAL THEME IN B FLAT, Opus 82 No. 2, D 603

Ex. 4. Schubert, *Introduction and Variations...*, D 603, (Finale) m. 5-12.

Schubert, *Sonata in B Major*, Opus 147, (Finale) m. 1-8.

other Schubert compositions by Haslinger and Company, along with Op. 82, No. 1.

Since Alfred Einstein states that the *Introduction and Variations...* is not a composition of Schubert,[31] and Maurice J. E. Brown states that it is,[32] we must examine their reasoning. Einstein believed that the work was beyond Schubert's ability in 1818, the date which Deutsch believed to be accurate, and that Schubert never would have contented himself to write an introduction with only four variations and a finale. Einstein's arguments seem invalid, for the duet sonata, Opus 30 (D 617) is equally mature and was composed in 1818. To say that he would never have written as few as four variations is without foundation, for the *Andantino varié* has only four variations and is certainly a work of Schubert. We believe the *Introduction and Variations...* to be Schubert's because it has much in common with Schubert's other compositions of this period. An appropriate example of this can be found in the *Sonata in B Major* for piano solo written in August 1817. Both the first movement of this sonata and the introduction to the variations are in dotted rhythms. Both employ pedal points while the upper voices are staccato. The most striking similarity, in Brown's opinion, is shown in our Ex. 4 (above).[33] The composition is Schubertian in smaller details as well, as in measure 10 where the G is flatted.

Once the authenticity of a work is questioned, confusion seems to persist. In the revised edition of *Franz Schubert: Thematic Catalog of His Works in Chronological Order* by O. E. Deutsch (1978) the Deutsch number of the *Introduction and Variations...* has been changed from D 603 to D 968a. This is not a true Deutsch-number, since the change was made by the editors of the revised catalog after his death. We believe such changes to be unnecessary and confusing; the Deutsch number 603 was historically well-established. To the casual observer the higher Deutsch number may imply that it is a late work, rather than to denote a work which cannot be dated with certainty. The dates of many of Schubert's works are open to question.

The words "on an Original Theme" appear in the title, even though the "originality" might be questioned considering the great similarity between this theme and that of Beethoven's *Variations in A Major* on a Russian dance from the ballet *Das Waldmädchen* for piano solo. The original ballet music was composed by Paul Wranitzky (1756-1808) who moved to Vienna when he was twenty years old and whose music was very popular throughout Austria and Germany. It seems unlikely that Schubert did not know Wranitzky's ballet and Beethoven's variations; hence, the similarity of his theme to its predecessors seems more than coincidental (see Ex. 5, next page).

Schubert might have regarded the *Introduction and Variations...* as an exercise in the variation form, deliberately choosing a theme similar to Beethoven's and studying his methods of thematic elaboration. It is also possible, of course, that the word "original" was given by the publisher.

The introduction to the variations is an announcement which seems, at first glance, to be flip-

31   A. Einstein, *Schubert: A Musical Portrait* (New York, 1951), 152.

32   M. J. E. Brown, *Schubert's Variations* (London, 1954), 40.

33   *Ibid.*, 40.

Ex. 5. Schubert, *Introduction and Variations...*, D 603, m. 35-41.

Moderato

Beethoven, *Variations in A Major*, m. 1-6.

Allegretto

pant—an inappropriate prologue to the material which follows. Care must be taken, therefore, to "place" the staccatos carefully and to play the entire section with breadth and deliberation. Since all editions have had to rely on the Schuberth edition for interpretive markings, there are no significant differences among the various editions. They all have accent marks on the weak beats of the theme. We may assume that Schubert placed accents on the second and fourth beats for compensatory emphasis—to make them equal to the first and third beats, which are naturally stronger. If these irregular accents are played roughly the result will be inappropriate and unmusical. A convincing interpretation of such irregular accents must, therefore, be preceded by thoughtful experimentation. The staccatos which appear throughout the composition should be light, in keeping with the character of the theme. From the theme through the third variation the basic note values are progressively shortened. The theme is in eighth-notes, the second variation is in thirty-second notes, and the third is in triplet thirty-second notes. The fourth variation, "più lento", is a re-statement of the theme, with the secondo player sharing the melody. After a "grand pause" and a one-measure cadenza the finale begins. This "vivace" movement in 3/8 meter is as unrelated to the theme and variations as is the introduction, but it has considerably more originality and verve.

At measure 32 the secondo's right hand has whole notes which should be B^b and D, not G and B^b as in the Henle edition. At measure 277 and again at measure 293 the Breitkopf and Härtel and the Henle

editions follow the first edition in having a G^b in the secondo left hand. The Peters edition has changed this to an A^b. We believe A^b to be correct because it is obviously a part of a chromatic scale (F, $F^\#$, G, A^b, A-natural, B^b). There is an unexpected ending, accomplished by a diminuendo and ritard to the point of "andante", followed by a sudden "presto" flourish.

GRAND SONATA IN B Flat, Opus 30, D 617 ¤ ¤ ¤ ¤ ¤ ¤ ¤ ¤ ¤ ¤

Composed: August? 1818
Manuscript: lost
First publication: Sauer and Leidesdorf, 1823
Dedication: Count Ferdinand Pálffy d'Erdöd

In the *Wiener Zeitung* of October 27, 1823 there appeared an announcement which stated, "In the press, and to appear next week: Franz Schubert, first *Grand Sonata for Pianoforte Duet*, Opus 30."[34] This work, Schubert's first duet sonata, did not appear "next week" as announced, but was published two months later in December, 1823. Most sources agree that Anton Schindler, in his 1867 *Memoirs of Schubert*, was correct when he dated the sonata 1818. This composition had been erroneously dated 1824 in the Gustav Nottebohm catalog because it was confused with the second duet sonata in C major. The *Grand Sonata in B Flat* is an example of some of Schubert's most imaginative writing. It abounds with highly original melodies and modulations, as well as imitative mo-

34 O. E. Deutsch, *The Schubert Reader*, 294.

tives shared between the players. The work deserves to be placed high in the standard duet repertoire.

The first movement of the *Grand Sonata in B Flat* begins with a three-measure introduction in which the primo has running sixteenth-notes outlining and embellishing the dominant seventh chord. The form of the movement is traditional: Introduction A Transition B Closing Development A Transition B Closing. The A theme is Mozartian in character. Schubert has made effective use of appoggiaturas, specifically on the first beats of measures 5, 7, 9 and 10. Here is an early example of one of Schubert's favorite devices: the theme appears first as a single melodic line, and is repeated immediately afterward in octaves. The transitional theme (m. 20) serves to modulate into the secondary theme which is in D^b in the exposition and in G^b in the recapitulation. These modulations into third-related keys are frequently used at this stage of Schubert's development, more so than in his previous work. The B theme (m. 33) begins in the secondo part, after which the primo "develops" it by means of a sequential pattern. The closing theme (m. 53) is rhythmically akin to the transitional theme; the organic unity thus achieved proves that Schubert's writing was already far more mature in this sonata than in the earlier, shorter duets of 1818. The first part of the development section uses materials from the transitional theme (measures 69-86). Beethoven's influence upon Schubert is apparent in the placement of a new theme in the midst of the development section, as in the first movement of Beethoven's Symphony No. 3, "*Eroica*".

Since the second movement ("Andante con moto") begins with a simple, stately theme of two eight-measure phrases, both of which are repeated, one would expect the movement to be in variation form. It is, however, in ternary form although it is easy to see that Schubert was not primarily concerned with form in this movement. There are at least three new themes in the middle section, all in major although the opening theme is in minor. Schubert then returns to the A section, but it too appears this time in major, with unanticipated brightness. The irregular accents which appear in the first sixteen measures and in analogous places should receive gentle emphasis.

The third movement, a sprightly "Allegretto" in B^b major, begins on a major III chord, the same notes as the final chord of the previous movement (D-F#-A). Schubert evidently wished to "pivot" from one movement to the next, which would seem to indicate that he was already beginning to work toward the unification of sonata movements, a device which he perfected later. The "Allegretto" is moderately fast, energetic, and gives the secondo player important material in the middle section, including chromatic sixteenth-note passages. The key scheme is built on third relations: B^b major, G^b major, D minor, B^b major, C^b major, and ending in B^b major.

Since the manuscript of the *Sonata in B Flat* is lost, we must rely on the first edition of Sauer and Leidesdorf for comparisons. This first editor omitted the turns at measure 110; the error was later corrected in the *Gesamtausgabe* edition to correspond to the same passage in the exposition (m. 8). The *Gesamtausgabe*, Peters and Henle editions generally follow all the marks of the first edition except for a few longer slurs in the Peters edition.

GERMAN DANCE WITH TWO TRIOS AND TWO LÄNDLER, D 618 ¤ ¤

Composed: August? 1818
Manuscript: Stadtbibliothek, Vienna
First publication: Festschrift für Hugo Riemann, 1909

The title of this manuscript is *Deutscher mit 2 Trio für piano forte zu 4 Hände*. This shows that Schubert intended to write one *Deutscher* only; he eventually added another one which he wrote down as two separate Dan-

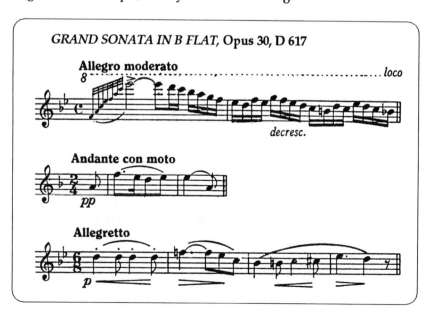

GRAND SONATA IN B FLAT, Opus 30, D 617

Allegro moderato

loco

decresc.

Andante con moto

pp

Allegretto

p

ces, numbered 1 and 2. But since number 1 has to be repeated after number 2, it is clear that the second is in fact a trio; together they comprise one *Ländler*, not two dances as indicated by Deutsch and Henle. Nevertheless, we have retained here the traditional title.

Schubert had an affinity for dance forms, even though he himself could not dance. Leopold von Sonnleithner wrote in 1857: "He sometimes went to private balls at the houses of families he was intimate with; he never danced but was always ready to sit down at the piano, where for hours he improvised the most beautiful waltzes; those he liked he repeated in order to remember them and write them out afterwards."[35] Joseph von Spaun wrote similarly: "From time to time he surprised us dancing enthusiasts with the most beautiful German dances which were the fashion of the day."[36]

The original manuscript of the *German Dances...* caught the attention of Brahms in 1872 in Stuttgart. There are only three current publications of this dance group: it is included in the Henle collection, a Bärenreiter volume, and is also published separately by J. Curwen & Sons, Ltd., London (available through G. Schirmer in the U.S.). The Henle and Bärenreiter editions are generally faithful to the original manuscript in every detail, except for a few phrase marks, which are not clear in the original. The editor of the Curwen publication, Jack Werner, has inserted phrasings, supplemented the dynamic marks and provided fingerings and pedalings, all of which make it a fine piece for teaching children, except for a few note errors in the melodies. In measures 3, 11, 67 and 75, primo right hand, the second note should be an F$^\#$, not D$^\#$; in measures 55 and 63, left hand, the final note should be B, not G$^\#$.

The "*gemütlich*" popular dance music of Vienna has changed very little since 1818. This music is characterized by drone basses seldom venturing beyond the dominant and tonic chords, disjunct melodies (resembling yodeling) alternating with conjunct, ornamented lines, and accents either on the first or third beat of the measure. The *Ländler* are generally more lyrical and less rhythmic than the *Deutscher* (German dances), a contrast which should be kept in mind in performance.

It is well known that Schubert often wrote his dances in two ways—for both piano duet and for piano solo. For example, Trio I of *German Dance*, D 618 is almost identical to *Ländler No. 7*, D 366. Schubert's dances for both solo and duet numbered more than four hundred. Considering how he and his friends made

GERMAN DANCE WITH TWO TRIOS AND TWO LÄNDLER, D 618

35 O. E. Deutsch, *Schubert: Memoirs by His Friends*, 121.

36 *Ibid.*, 133.

numerous copies, paying no attention to order, title or key, one can see that organizing these dances into any logical order is a musicologist's nightmare.

EIGHT VARIATIONS ON A FRENCH SONG IN E MINOR, Opus 10, D 624 ¤ ¤ ¤ ¤ ¤ ¤ ¤ ¤ ¤ ¤ ¤ ¤ ¤ ¤ ¤

Composed: September, 1818
Manuscript: Fair (finished) copy, lost
First draft: Theme, Var. I, part of Var. II in photo-copy in Nationalbibliothek, Vienna. Remainder of Var. II, Var. III and part of Var. IV, Sibley Music Library, Univ. of Rochester, N. Y. Twelve measures of Var. VII and seven measures of Var. VIII, Bibliothèque Nationale, Paris. Fragment of end of Var. VIII, University Library, Leningrad.
First publication: Cappi, Diabelli and Co., 1822
Dedication: Ludwig van Beethoven

The *Eight Variations on a French Song,* dedicated to Beethoven by his "admirer and worshipper, Franz Schubert," has caused one of the great controversies in musical biography. Did Schubert meet Beethoven in 1822 and present him with the variations? Schubert's friends relate conflicting stories. Joseph Hüttenbrenner wrote on December 26, 1857:

> Schubert took an engraved copy of the varia-tions [Opus 10] to Beethoven, but the latter was not home. Both Karl Beethoven [the nephew] and Herr Schindler, however, told me repeatedly that they [the variations] received Beethoven's approval for, over a period of a few months, Beethoven played them almost every day with his nephew. Otherwise, Schubert never came into per-sonal touch with Beethoven except, for the first and last time, with Anselm, Teltscher and

me, at Beethoven's death-bed, where we were taken by Schindler.[37]

Hüttenbrenner's account may not be reliable, for Beethoven was deaf at that time, so it is questionable whether or not he would have played the piano for enjoyment then. Schindler relates a different story of this 1822 visit:

> Schubert fared badly in 1822, on the occasion of presenting his variations for pianoforte duet, which were dedicated to the master [Beethoven]. The shy and, at the same time, silent artist showed himself in an un-favourable light, in spite of the fact that Diabelli accompanied him and, when he was presented, interpreted his feelings to the master. His courage, which he had preserved intact until reaching the house, left him com-pletely in the presence of this artistic majesty. And when Beethoven expressed the wish that Schubert should write down the answers to his questions himself, his hand was para-lysed. Beethoven ran through the copy . . . and came across a mistake in the harmony. With gentle words he drew the young man's attention to it, immediately adding, however, that it was by no means a deadly sin; meanwhile Schubert, perhaps just because of this kindly remark, completely lost control of himself. Only when he was out of the house did he pull himself together again and abuse himself roundly. He never again had the courage to present himself to the master.[38]

Schubert's close friend Spaun read this account by Schindler, whose information was sometimes unreli-able, and in 1864 disputed the latter's statement by writing: "Schindler's story of Schubert's visit to Beethoven is completely incorrect. Schubert often la-mented, and especially at the time of Beethoven's death, how much he regretted that the latter had been so inaccessible and that he had never spoken to Beethoven."[39]

Schubert used as his theme the French song "*Le bon Chevalier*", said to be a work by Queen Hortense of

EIGHT VARIATIONS ON A FRENCH SONG IN E MINOR, Opus 10, D 624

37 *Ibid.,* 75.
38 *Ibid.* 325.
39 *Ibid.* 366.

Holland (1783-1837) or more likely by her house musician, Louis Drouet. It was a favorite air of the Esterházy family. On the manuscript of the sketches of the *Polonaises,* D 599, there is a hurriedly written sketch of this song. (It is slightly different from the original.) The sketch is dated "July, 1818." The duet manuscript also appears to have been written in some haste; the marking *"simile"* has been used frequently in place of the left-hand notes when the left hand doubles the right, particularly at the beginning of Variation II. This has caused some scholars to believe that there was an additional fair copy, which has now been lost, used for publication. Some believe that the existing (scattered) manuscript is only a rough draft, but there are no clear-cut answers.

Schubert has indicated rather clearly that the theme is to be phrased with contrasts of staccato and legato; the variations, however, are sparsely marked. Those phrasings that exist in the present editions are largely the work of editors. Either the first publisher took great liberties in changing certain notes of Schubert's manuscript, or he had a different manuscript than the one that survives today. According to the manuscript, the primo left hand at measure 14 should have a C, not B. The C corresponds to the same harmony in Variation I, measure 30. In Variation I, measure 18, the notes in the primo right hand should be

as in the manuscript, in order to correspond to the same pattern at measure 20. In the last measure of Variation I (secondo) the manuscript has repeated chords

Since the first publisher may have exercised freedom in these instances, the writers believe that there are other "wrong" notes in present editions, although the portions of manuscript in which they would appear are lost: in Variation VI, measure 122 (primo, left hand) the writer prefers a C# rather than C double-sharp, which is out-of-key; in Variation VII, measure 143, third beat, the primo should have D-naturals rather than D#s, to correspond to the D-naturals in the secondo part. One wonders whether this might be the "mistake in harmony" which Beethoven found, according to Schindler's account. The indication "Das

Title page of *Variations on a French Song,* composed for Pianoforte, 4 Hands, and dedicated to Herr Ludwig van Beethoven by his Worshipper and Admirer Franz Schubert, 1822. Note that Beethoven's name appears more prominently than Schubert's.

1te Mal piano, das 2te Mal forte" at Variation II is not found in the manuscript.

The theme, in its original statement, is in minor except for the second four-measure phrase. It lends itself well to harmonic reinterpretation and this Schubert has done with success. The composition gains intensity through progressively quicker note values but not through thicker texture; whatever intensity is developed in the course of the piece must be gained by the performers' sensitivity to contrasting qualities implied in the variations—lyrical, martial, *et cetera*. The staccatos which alternate with short legato phrases throughout the theme are to be played lightly, but not too short. The writers suggest that the quarter-notes be given one half their value, with separate pedalings for each staccato note to cushion the abruptness. The primo player should emphasize the legato phrases for an appropriate contrast.

Variation I, in the original key, is quiet and delicate with the melody transformed into triplet figures. Variation II is martial; the primo has the theme basically in its original form, while the secondo moves throughout in steady, staccato eighth-notes. Variation III (in major) has a brighter quality, but there are few other deviations from the original theme. In Variation IV the secondo carries the theme while the primo has scale-like patterns of running sixteenth-notes. Variation V in the key of E, the parallel major, is Mozartian in style, with chords broken into triplet accompaniment figures and frequent trills and grace notes in the melody. In Variation VI Schubert has tossed the melody back and forth between the two players. Here again we find highly effective use of minor scales, in this instance very robust and decisive. While the composition as a whole is restrained, this variation enhances its surroundings with its energy and contrast. Variation VII, "più lento," has a buoyant and pianistic descant.

In the final variation (VIII) Schubert crowns the composition with what may be his most sophisticated writing to date. He begins in E major (m. 166) and after a brief venture into other related keys the key signature is changed to A^b major at measure 223, an example of third-relation. He returns to E major very briefly and modulates then to B^b major, which is a tritone away from the previous key—a daring move in 1818! The harmonic richness of the *Eight Variations on a French Song* causes one to understand why the young Schubert dared to dedicate it (and, possibly, to present it personally) to Beethoven.

Possibly the most notable feature of Schubert's 1818 style of duet writing is the growing importance of the secondo part. In the larger works of this period the secondo is no longer merely an accompaniment to the primo. It has become a participant in the melodic fabric.

The duets discussed in this chapter were composed for public performance, for social gatherings at the Sonnleithners', and for teaching the Esterházy daughters. We know from documents of Karl von Schönstein that Schubert continued to teach Marie and Karoline Esterházy in Vienna after their return from Zseliz in November, 1818. The lessons most likely continued until May of 1819; however, there were no duets written during that time. Schubert did not return to his post as a school teacher even though he was officially listed by the City Chief Inspectorate for several years as "School Assistant in the Rossau".

Ferdinand Schubert (1794-1859), the composer's brother, the director of a teachers' training school in Vienna; after Schubert's death this brother sold most of the former's manuscripts to Diabelli. (Historic Museum of the City of Vienna.)

A woodcut engraving of Franz Schubert, used by Kreissle von Hellborn in his biography of 1865. From a drawing by Leopold Kupelwieser of July 10, 1821.

CHAPTER IV

Music for the Theater (1819-1823)

With regard to Schubert's compositions we can associate the years 1815-1816 with songs, 1817 with sonatas, and 1818 with piano duets. For the next five years, 1819-1823, Schubert turned his attention almost exclusively to music for the theater. He did not completely abandon other forms, however, continuing to write lieder, piano pieces and chamber works, but in terms of time and sheer volume, music for the stage consumed most of his energy.

Concerts and recitals at that time were generally private affairs held in the homes of the wealthy, so public exposure for young composers through such channels was minimal. One path to recognition, popularity and wide acceptance was through public performances of opera. The Viennese at this time adored opera, Rossini being a favorite, but they were less enthusiastic about German opera. When Schubert returned from Zseliz in late 1818 Vogl introduced him to the director of the Kärntnertor Theater (the official court theater). He was granted a commission to write a one-act comic singspiel (operetta), *Die Zwillings-brüder* (The Twin Brothers) in which Vogl would play the parts of both brothers; this was no easy feat since both brothers had to be on stage simultaneously in the final scene! A performance by Vogl usually assured critical success, but unfortunately for Schubert, Rossini himself arrived in Vienna at that time and the opera houses featured almost nothing but the celebrated Italian composer's works.

Schubert's opera was postponed for over a year. The impatient young Schubert wrote to Anselm Hüttenbrenner in May 1819: "instead of my operetta they do other rot, enough to make your hair stand on end."[42]

After a frustrating spring trying to get his opera performed, Schubert took a relaxing vacation for almost three months with Vogl at the singer's home in Steyr. This picturesque town some 90 miles west of Vienna lifted his spirits. There were endless parties, outings and music-making. Schubert wrote to his brother Ferdinand: "At the house where I lodge there are eight girls, nearly all pretty. Plenty to see and do."[43] His interest in the "eight girls" is somewhat surprising, because he had confided to friends that he was in love with his long-time friend Therese Grob. He was not, however, able to take on the financial responsibility of a wife. Documents tell us almost nothing about the relationship with Therese, but from the Liechtental Parish Register we find that on November 21, 1820, she married Johann Bergmann, master baker. Schubert never had a lasting romantic attachment after Therese, except for a nebulous, secret love for Karoline Esterházy.

In Steyr he was introduced to several music patrons and was commissioned to write a quintet for Sylvester Paumgartner and his circle of friends. The result of this commission was the "Trout" quintet, whose lighthearted spirit is a reflection of Schubert's happy summer.

In September 1819 Schubert returned to Vienna and continued living with Mayrhofer. (He had moved in with Mayrhofer in November 1818 after returning from Zseliz.) Joseph von Spaun tells us that they lived "for a few years in the same room, under the care of the excellent widow [Anna] Sanssouci, who tried to keep things reasonably tidy for the two somewhat impractical gentlemen." Mayrhofer, who has been described as sensitive, introspective, pessimistic, and morbid, was a man who suffered ill health and hypochondria. He made life miserable for himself and everyone around him. Schubert, by contrast, was sociable, fun-loving, and sometimes self-indulgent. His habit was to work from mid-morning through early afternoon, and then to meet with friends for coffee, conversation and a walk. The early evenings were filled with concerts or casual music-making with friends, and the day was completed with a late-night supper.

---

42 O. E. Deutsch, *The Schubert Reader*, 117.
43 *Ibid.*, 121.

Therese Grob in later life. Schubert's first love
(see preceding page), she married a baker in
1820. By several reports she had a fine voice.
(Historic Museum of the City of Vienna.)

Here are contrasting versions of Schubert's typical
day according to his friends Hüttenbrenner and
Sonnleithner.

Hüttenbrenner:

While Schubert and Mayrhofer were living
together in the Wipplingerstrasse, the former
every day at 6 o'clock in the morning would
seat himself at his writing-desk and compose
without a break until one in the afternoon,
smoking a few small pipes.[44]

Sonnleithner:

Schubert was extraordinarily fertile and in-
dustrious in composing. He had no use for
everything else that goes by the name of
work. Seldom going to the theatre or into
fashionable society, he loved to spend the evening at an inn, in the company of lively
friends, and on such occasions midnight often
passed unnoticed and pleasure was indulged
in to excess. As a result of this he acquired the

habit of staying in bed in the morning until
10 or 11 o'clock; and as this was the time
when he felt the greatest urge to compose, the
morning hours passed in this way, and the
best time for earning some money by teaching
was thus lost.[45]

Sonnleithner was a wealthy, puritanical conservative, whose view of Schubert was rather judgmental.
It should be noted that Sonnleithner was not one of
Schubert's intimate friends; there was a formal
reserve between them which caused Sonnleithner to
complain that Schubert "never dropped by my house
for a visit." Schubert probably sensed that he was
seen in a somewhat disapproving light, thus keeping
some distance between them. At any rate, it is interesting to see how many contrasting views there are
concerning Schubert's life-style. Apparently his complex personality had both a lofty, spiritual side and
an earthy, sensual aspect.

In the autumn of 1819 the director of the Theater
an der Wien commissioned Schubert to write incidental music for a "magic play" in three acts called
Die Zauberharfe (the Magic Harp), no doubt hoping to
repeat the great success of Mozart's Die Zauberflöte.
"Magic plays" were popular with the Viennese because no matter how complicated and unbelievable
the plot became, a benevolent deity or possessor of
magical powers would always set things right in the
end.

In the summer of 1820 Die Zwillingsbrüder and Die
Zauberharfe were premiered. In June Die Zwillingsbrüder was performed at the Kärntnertor Theater to
mixed reviews. Schubert's friends were all present to
cheer, which seemed to annoy the other people who
attended, among them Josef Rosenbaum, who
worked for the Esterházy family, and who wrote in
his diary (June 14, 1820) "The operetta has nothing to
recommend it, yet Schubert's friends made a lot of
noise while the opposition hissed—at the close there
was a fuss until Vogl appeared and said: 'Schubert is
not present. I thank you in his name.'"[46] Schubert
was, in fact, in the gallery with Anselm Hüttenbrenner but refused to come forward because he was
shabbily dressed and could not be persuaded to exchange his old worn coat for Anselm's evening tail-

44   O. E. Deutsch, Schubert: Memoirs by His Friends, 182.
45   Ibid., 109.
46   O. E. Deutsch, The Schubert Reader, 135.

coat. With unfavorable reviews, the operetta closed after six performances.

In August the Theater an der Wien staged the premiere of *Die Zauberharfe*. The mixed reviews closed the play after eight performances. Part of the criticism was that the actors did not know their parts; in fact, the prompter was often heard by the audience first. The story of the play was considered shallow, dull and boring, but the music was greeted favorably. In the Vienna *Conversationsblatt* a critic wrote "What a pity that Schubert's wonderfully beautiful music has not found a worthier subject...."[47]

Schubert was not devastated by these failures. He wrote sixteen works for the theater with only three ever being publicly performed, none with success. There have been various theories as to why Schubert's works for the theater (including his operas) always failed. It is generally agreed that the stories and dialogue were weak. We submit that another possible reason for these failures was a police record which Schubert had received in March. Austria was a police state at this time, so critics would have believed it dangerous to praise anyone considered by the government to be controversial, as Schubert had become. Some background for this is in order.

Prince Metternich, councillor to Emperor Franz, was gaining more and more power in his determination to keep Austria under his control. He was ruthless in his persecution of any element perceived to be dangerous to the throne. All communications were censored—books, songs, plays, newspapers, even tombstone inscriptions. After the writer August von Kotzebue was assassinated in Mannheim (1819) by a "revolutionary" student, Metternich used this event as an excuse to tighten his stranglehold on the University. Censors were placed in classrooms to monitor every word. Competitive sports such as swimming and gymnastics were banned because the assembly of spectators might cause trouble. No one was exempt from the censorship. Franz Grillparzer, Austria's greatest poet, could not get his drama *King Ottokar's Fortune and End* admitted to the theater because it depicted the downfall of a king. Friedrich von Schiller's *Maria Stuart* and *Wilhelm Tell* remained permanently forbidden. No royalty, high government official, priest, or general could be portrayed as a villain. Spies and informers were so prevalent that a

friend wrote in one of Beethoven's notebooks, "Now the Assembly is working on a law which prescribes how high the birds are permitted to fly and how fast the rabbits can run."

Schubert's friends ranged from conservatives such as Vogl and Spaun to liberals such as Franz Bruchmann (1798-1867) and Johann Senn (1795-1857), who had been a fellow student with Schubert at the Seminary. Senn studied law at the University of Vienna but soon turned his attention to poetry. This charismatic young man attracted a wide circle of friends including Schubert, Bruchmann, Kupelwieser, Mayrhofer, and others. These were not revolutionaries handing out pamphlets or making public speeches against the government; rather, they were intellectuals who wanted the freedom to read and discuss any subject they chose. The police were informed about this group of liberals, and one night in March 1820 came to Senn's room and arrested him and four of his friends, including Schubert. The police reported that Senn had said he "did not care a hang about the police" and that the "government was too stupid to be able to penetrate into his secrets." He was sentenced to fourteen months in prison and banished to his birthplace in Tyrol, never to return to Vienna. His career was ruined and he died in poverty.

Schubert was only reprimanded, but now had a blot on his record. He was becoming well known; his listing as a subversive probably damaged the chances of his two theater works being accepted by the critics. The police never forgot nor forgave anyone who had a record. In 1829 when it was proposed that Franz' father, Franz Theodor, be given a "Civil Gold Medal of Honor" for service to the Austrian educational system, this high distinction was denied him because the same chief of police, Count Josef Sedlnitzky, who earlier had interrogated Schubert, requested that the Emperor withdraw the honor. In 1844, after Franz Theodor's death, the question was raised a second time, but the medal was withheld again.

In late 1820, Schubert's friends began to gather two or three times a week to play and sing his music. Since these gatherings were almost exclusively devoted to Schubert's music they were referred to as "Schubertiads". Such musicals were held in the homes of Sonnleithner, Bruchmann, Schober and others. Spaun had earlier (1817) sent Schubert's song "*Der Erlkönig*" to Breitkopf & Härtel for publication, but

47 *Ibid.*, 148.

Eduard von Bauernfeld (1802-1890). Viennese
dramatist and amateur musician — a frequent
piano duet partner with Schubert.
(Historic Museum of the City of Vienna.)

Franz Grillparzer (1791-1872). A portrait of the
great Austrian poet and dramatist, painted by
Ferdinand Georg Waldmüller in 1844. Grillparzer
met Schubert ca. 1820, followed his career very
closely, and was chosen to write the inscription
on the composer's tombstone. (Historic
Museum of the City of Vienna.)

without success. Now, members of the Schubert
group decided it was time to try again. This is detailed
in an account by Sonnleithner:

> Suddenly Schubert's name was talked of in all
> the musical circles and people were asking
> why his songs were not published.
> Meanwhile, through a personal friend of
> Schubert's (Herr Josef Hüttenbrenner), I had
> become better acquainted with the former's
> conditions of life and had discovered that his
> financial situation was far from satisfactory.
> We resolved, therefore, to look for a publisher
> for his works, a task for which Schubert him-
> self, with his naive simplicity, was quite un-
> suited. I offered the *Erlkönig* to the art dealers
> Tobias Haslinger and Anton Diabelli; but
> both refused to publish it (even without fee)
> as they expected no financial success because
> the composer was unknown and because of
> the difficulty of the pianoforte accompani-
> ment. Hurt by this refusal, we decided our-

selves to arrange its publication for Schubert's
benefit. I, Hüttenbrenner and 2 other
artlovers combined to meet the costs of the
first volume out of our own pockets and, in
February 1821, we had the *Erlkönig* engraved.
When my father announced, at one of our
soirées, that the *Erlkönig* was available, almost
100 copies were bought that same evening by
those present and the expenses of the 2nd
volume were covered. So we had the first 12
works engraved at our own expense and sold
on commission at Anton Diabelli's. From the
abundant proceeds we paid Schubert's debts,
namely his rent, his shoemaker's and tailor's
accounts and his debts at the tavern and the
coffeehouse, and handed over to him, in addition, a considerable sum in cash; unfortunately some guardianship, such as this, was necessary, for he had no idea of domestic economy
and was often led by his tavern friends (mostly painters or poets and only a few musicians)
into useless expenditure from which the
others benefited more than he did himself.[48]

With three hundred copies sold within eighteen
months, success opened doors for other publications.

At about this time, Schubert's friend Joseph von
Spaun then moved to Linz and Anselm
Hüttenbrenner moved to Graz, but new friends took
their places. Between late 1820 and 1822 Schubert became close to the four Fröhlich sisters, Anna, Barbara,

---

48 O. E. Deutsch, *Schubert: Memoirs by His Friends*, 108.

Kathi and Josefine, who introduced him to the poet Franz Grillparzer. The painters Moritz von Schwind and Leopold Kupelwieser and the playwright Eduard von Bauernfeld also joined the group.

In early 1821 Schubert felt himself able to afford a room of his own, so he moved from Mayrhofer's to a place by himself. In the summer he went for the second time with Schober to Atzenbrugg, 20 miles northwest of Vienna. Schober's uncle managed a small castle there and allowed Schober and his guest to occupy it for a while in the summer. These days at Atzenbrugg were filled with parties, dancing, singing, and charades.

In August, Schubert and Schober returned to Vienna whereupon the two decided to collaborate on a "grand" opera (the only such effort on Schubert's part) which was to be called *Alfonso und Estrella*. The opera had not been commissioned; Schober would supply the libretto and Schubert the music. Finding Vienna too filled with distractions, they returned to Atzenbrugg and nearby St. Pölten, where another of Schober's uncles was the Bishop. With great enthusiasm Schubert wrote to Spaun "We have high hopes for it."[49] Sadly, there was a change in the administration of the Kärntnertor Theater and Vogl resigned, leaving Schubert with no personal contacts there. The opera was never performed.

In 1823 Schubert wrote the opera *Fierrabras* with the librettist Josef Kupelwieser (Leopold's brother). This score is considered to be much more attractive than that of *Alfonso und Estrella*. It is notable that in *Fierrabras* Schubert used a device later to be known as "*leitmotif*" and associated with Wagner. Unfortunately, the libretto was again poor, which made it unworthy of production. At the end of 1823 Schubert was commissioned to write incidental music for a new play, *Rosamunde*, by Helmina von Chézy (the librettist of Weber's *Euryanthe*). The text does not survive, but Schubert's music has remained popular. It was premiered at the Theater an der Wien on December 20, 1823 and closed after two performances. Later, in 1827, he sketched an opera *Der Graf von Gleichen*

with the libretto by Bauernfeld, but it soon became obvious that he had given up hope of writing for the theater.

After Schubert and Schober had returned from Atzenbrugg in 1821, Schubert moved in with the Schober family. He remained there until the summer of 1823 (except for a short time with his family). Schober's promiscuity began to cause gossip within the Schubert circle, and apparently it was thought that Schubert's own behavior was being influenced by Schober's. Schubert's old Seminary friend Anton Holzapfel wrote (February 22, 1822): "I rarely see him [Schubert] nor do we hit it off very well, his world being a very different one [from mine]."[50] Bauernfeld later wrote: "in Schubert there slumbered a dual nature. The Austrian element, uncouth and sensual, revealed itself both in his life and in his art."[51] Schober's negative influence temporarily caused a rift between Vogl and Schubert. Anton von Spaun (brother of Josef) wrote in July 1822: "Vogl is much embittered against Schober, for whose sake Schubert behaved most ungratefully toward Vogl.... Schubert is surely on the wrong road."[52] Joseph Kenner, a Seminary friend, wrote in 1858: "Anyone who knew Schubert knows how he was made of two natures, foreign to each other, how powerful the craving for pleasure dragged his soul down to the slough of moral degradation, and how highly he valued the utterances of friends [Schober in particular]."[53] Kenner further spoke of Schober's "deep moral depravity." Wilhelm von Chézy (the son of the *Rosamunde* author, Helmina) wrote in 1863: "Unfortunately Schubert's thirst for life lured him into the byways from which there is usually no return, at least no healthy return."[54]

At the end of 1822, or early in 1823, Schubert contracted syphilis. Eric Sams, the noted British scholar, wrote a detailed article for the *London Musical Times* in 1980 entitled "Schubert's Illness Re-examined" in which he studied all documents that make any reference to his illness. Armed with present-day knowledge about the three stages of syphilis, he care-

---

49 O. E. Deutsch, *The Schubert Reader*, 194.

50 *Ibid.*, 211.

51 O. E. Deutsch, *Schubert: Memoirs by His Friends*, 233-34.

52 O. E. Deutsch, *The Schubert Reader*, 230.

53 O. E. Deutsch, *Schubert: Memoirs by His Friends*, 86.

54 *Ibid.*, 261.

fully traced the disease's development. Documents give evidence of the first stage when Schubert remained confined to his room. The second stage is signaled by evidence of having rashes, sore throat, anemia and fever. The third stage, characterized by aching bones and sore muscles, occurred in 1827 and 1828, the year of his death. The actual cause of his death was typhoid fever, but his body was in a weakened condition from syphilis.

On August 14, 1823, Schubert wrote to Schober: "Whether I shall ever quite recover, I am inclined to doubt."[55] As Schubert's illness caused him to be absent from many of the "Schubertiads", the group gradually evolved into one with lesser artistic tastes and aspirations. Schubert complained that they spoke of "nothing but riding, fencing, horses and hounds," later adding that "if it goes on like this, I don't suppose I shall stand it for long among them."[56] This "rough chorus of beer-drinkers and sausage-eaters," as Schubert called them, contributed nothing any longer to art.

THE DUETS OF 1819-1823.

OVERTURE IN G MINOR, D 668 ¤ ¤ ¤

Composed: October 1819
Manuscript: Stadtbibliothek, Vienna
First publication: Gesamtausgabe, 1897

The *Overture in G minor* is dated October, 1819. It was not mentioned in documents during Schubert's lifetime; therefore, we must rely upon Maurice J. E. Brown who, in his book *Schubert: A Critical Biography,* says that this overture was unknown until 1896 when some papers of a deceased friend of Ferdinand Schubert were found, among them the *Overture in G minor.*[57] The nineteenth-century musicologist Eusebius Mandyczewski, in his critical notes for the *Gesamtausgabe,* expressed his belief that this overture is an arrangement of an orchestral composition of which the original manuscript has been destroyed. The duet manuscript ends with a three measure pause which suggests that something more is to follow. Perhaps this was the overture to the stage work *Adrast* (D 137) which is possibly of the same period.

This piece exists only in the Bärenreiter edition and the *Gesamtausgabe.* As a piano piece it is of minimal interest to the present writers; perhaps it would have been more effective with orchestral color.

OVERTURE IN F,
Opus 34, D 675 ¤ ¤ ¤

Composed: November 1819
Manuscript: lost
First publication: Cappi and
     Company, 1825

The *Overture in F* was composed one month later, in November, 1819. Maurice Brown believed that the reason that the *Overture in F* was published instead of the *Overture in G minor,* which he (Brown)

OVERTURE IN G MINOR, D 668

---

55   O. E. Deutsch, *The Schubert Reader,* 286.

56   *Ibid.,* 301.

57   M. J. E. Brown, *Schubert: A Critical Biography,* 89.

considered to be musically superior, was that the latter was in the hands of friends and temporarily mislaid.[58] This idea, although reasonable, is not supported by evidence.

There is a story which stems from Joseph Hüttenbrenner that Schubert composed the *Overture in F* in three hours. He claimed that the composer wrote in the manuscript, "Written in November, in Herr Joseph Hüttenbrenner's room at the 'Citizen's Hostel', within three hours, and lunch neglected over it."[59] Since the manuscript is lost, we cannot prove or disprove the above quotation, but it would seem to be impossible even for Schubert to have written this work of more than twelve pages' length in three hours.

The romantic overture was generally a programmatic orchestral composition. The *Overture in F* is notable for two reasons: 1) it is one of the few original works in this form for keyboard and 2) it is "absolute" music, not programmatic. The form, Introduction AB Closing AB Closing Coda, is a departure from the traditional sonata-allegro form of a "regular" overture. Schubert has used here an effective key scheme based upon third-relations. The introduction is in F minor and the work progresses through F major, A^b major and C major. Schubert's fondness for the Neapolitan sixth chord is evidenced again by the chromatic shift from C major to D^b major for the B theme. After a characteristic "grand pause" a coda in 6/8 brings the work to a close.

Even though the *Overture in F* is an original four-hand work, Schubert's approach is that of a symphonist. The frequent use of the tremolo bass, repeated chords, and dynamic contrast attest to the composer's symphonic intent.

The *Gesamtausgabe*, the Peters, the Henle, and the Bärenreiter editions all follow the first edition except for one notable difference: the Henle and the Bärenreiter editors have corrected an obvious mistake at measure 207 by delaying the *8va* until measure 209. The wedge-shaped staccato marks (▼) in the first three measures of the al-

legro section, secondo part, raise an interpretive question. Today one generally uses a dot for a "normal" staccato and a wedge for a note of even shorter duration—*staccatissimo*. The wedge had a somewhat different meaning in earlier times. In Leopold Mozart's *Treatise on the Fundamental Principles of Violin Playing*, 1756, he indicated that a stroke or wedge should be strongly accented and separated from the other notes;[60] this made it a combination of accent and staccato. Mozart and Haydn used this stroke to indicate staccato, accent, or both,[61] and this interpretation was still held in Schubert's time. Since the strokes in the "Allegro" involve quarter-notes and half-notes, Schubert probably wanted them to be played more "*marcato*" than "*staccato*".

For the first time since the early fantasies we find a broken-octave left-hand figure beginning at measure 107 and again at measure 205. At measure 118 and in analogous measures Schubert interrupts this tremolo effect by repeated octaves rather than continuing in broken octaves. Considering that the allegro should move quickly, the fast repeated sixteenth-notes are likely to become indistinct and overly thick. In order to alleviate the problem, the writers suggest substituting broken octaves, i.e., continuing the tremolo already begun.

OVERTURE IN F, Opus 34, D 675

---

58 *Ibid.*, 89.

59 O. E. Deutsch, *Schubert: Memoirs by His Friends*, 126.

60 W. Apel, *Harvard Dictionary of Music* (Cambridge, 1955), 708.

61 H. Ferguson, *Style and Interpretation* Vol. III (London, 1964), 10.

THREE MARCHES MILITAIRES,
Opus 51, D 733 ¤ ¤ ¤ ¤ ¤ ¤ ¤ ¤ ¤ ¤ ¤ ¤

Composed: ca. 1822 (1818?)
Manuscript: lost
First publication: Diabelli and Co., 1826

Schubert's duet marches, polonaises, German dances and *Ländler* cannot be listed in a definite chronological order because of the vagueness of references to these pieces.

Among the marches, only the *Kindermarsch* (Children's March), D 928, can be dated with certainty. When a march is mentioned in a letter or diary, the comments might be referring to a published march, or one still unpublished, since the latter were frequently played within Schubert's circle of friends. For example, a letter dated April 28, 1821 from Anton Ottenwalt to Josef von Spaun offers this information: "Next to me, Marie [Ottenwalt, née von Spaun] is practicing the march of Schubert. Although it is only the bass [secondo]... still it is hard for me to escape the charming distraction."[62] This is the earliest known mention of Schubert's four-hand marches. It cannot be a reference to a published opus, since the first marches, Opus 27, D 602, did not appear in print until December 1824; it merely establishes that Schubert did compose marches for four hands by 1821.

The *Military Marches* were dated by Dr. Deutsch as ca. 1822. This date was most likely assigned because the publishing firm Cappi & Diabelli had purchased the rights to all of Schubert's music up to April 1823. At that time Schubert broke relations with the firm and requested that they return all of his music. They did not return these marches, and published them in 1826.

Of the seventeen duet marches of Schubert, the one most frequently heard is the first, in D major, from the group of *Three Military Marches*, Opus 51. During the nineteenth century these popular marches were frequently arranged for many different media. Ferdinand Schubert titled the potpourri which he assembled in 1836 "*Schubertine [Schubert'sche] Lyra, the Cycle of Favorite Compositions by Schubert, Arranged for Orchestra*", which starts with the first *Military March*, Opus 51.

All three marches include trios in the sub-dominant; the "da capo" creates an overall ABA. While all three are unified by the rhythm of the introduction

their forms differ:

1. Introduction ABA Trio Introduction ABA
2. A A1 A2 A1 Codetta Trio A A1 A2 A1 Codetta
3. Introduction ABA Codetta Trio Introduction ABA Codetta

THREE MARCHES MILITAIRES, Opus 51, D 733

62 O. E. Deutsch, *The Schubert Reader*, 175-176.

Although the *Military Marches* are probably not of sufficient interest (except for the first) to merit inclusion in a concert program, they are far superior to the military marches of the French and Viennese army bands of that period. Their harmonic structure is richer, their modulations bolder, and their rhythms are more varied.

The first march deserves its reputation as the "favorite." Its charm is enhanced by a performance which is somewhat slower than the usual M.M. 120 for marches. The slower tempo permits strong emphasis upon such phrases as

and greater freedom for nuances.

The second march has little variety in melodic material; it is both "*gemütlich*" and undistinguished, especially the trio. Although one might find the third march charming in virtue of its very simplicity, the melodic materials and the harmonic structure are of little interest. These marches are suitable sight-reading material and exercises in ensemble playing for intermediate-level students. The present-day editions include corrections of some notes and dynamics which had not been present in the first edition.

OVERTURE TO "ALFON-SO UND ESTRELLA", Opus 69, D 773 ¤ ¤ ¤ ¤

Composed (arranged): 1823
Manuscript: lost
First publication: Sauer and Leidesdorf, 1826
Dedication: Anna Hönig

OVERTURE TO "FIER-RABRAS", D 798

Composed (arranged): 1824-1827
Manuscript: Paris Conservatoire
First publication: Gesamtaus-gabe, 1897

Schubert's two major operas, *Alfonso and Estrella* and *Fierrabras*, were never performed during his lifetime. Perhaps it was because of this frustration that he made arran-

gements for piano duet of the overtures of both operas. The *Overture to "Alfonso and Estrella"*, of which he thought very highly, was arranged by him for piano duet in 1823 and published in 1826 as Opus 52, later corrected to Opus 69. The duet is dedicated to Anna Hönig, who was, at one time, the fiancée of Schubert's friend Moritz von Schwind. In regard to the date of Schubert's arrangement of *Fierrabras*, some authorities disagree with the earlier date because of the type of paper he used. Some claim that this type of paper was not available until September, 1826.

In summary, during this period of five years (1819 through 1823) Schubert composed comparatively little for piano duet. His creative interest during this time was in music for the theater (incidental music for *Die Zauberharfe* and *Rosamunde*) and opera (*Alfonso and Estrella* and *Fierrabras*). The *Overture in F* and the second and third *Military Marches* do not seem to be as inspired as the duets of the previous period and of Schubert's later years. Only the first *Military March* is likely to be performed in concert.

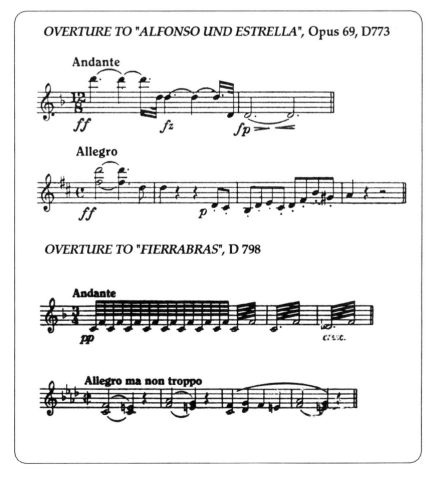

OVERTURE TO "ALFONSO UND ESTRELLA", Opus 69, D773

OVERTURE TO "FIERRABRAS", D 798

"Charade Party at Atzenbrugg". This aquarelle by Leopold Kupelwieser was commissioned by Franz von Schober, who described the game and identified the guests in a letter: some members of the party are miming the second syllable of "Rheinfall", a charming district near the Atzenbrugg Castle; they are depicting the Fall of Man, Eve handing an apple to Adam as they stand beneath the Tree of Knowledge (Kupelwieser himself); the serpent (Franz von Schober) looks through the branches while Almighty God (Josef von Gahy) stands on the stove with a broom as sceptre; the angel with a flaming sword stands at the door to banish Adam and Eve from the garden; Schubert is seated at the piano; underneath the piano is Kupelwieser's dog Drago. (Schubert Museum, Vienna.)

"Excursion to Aumühl" — aquarelle by Leopold Kupelwieser, 1820. This scene depicts Schubert's friends traveling from Atzenbrugg (see above) to Aumühl. Note Spaun's concern as the wagon wheel rolls over his hat! (Historic Museum of the City of Vienna.)

CHAPTER V

The Return to Zseliz (1824)

Because of Schubert's advancing syphilitic condition, his moods shifted drastically from time to time. There were some days when he felt well and became optimistic about his future and other days when he felt ill and in total despair.

The new year, 1824, was ushered in with a party at which Schubert's friends drank a toast to all members of the Schubert circle who were absent. As the evening progressed, they began to drink to "everybody's sweetheart". In the midst of the fun, Schubert and his physician, Dr. Josef Bernhardt, had a target-shooting contest and Schubert, obviously tipsy, broke a windowpane! The party did not end until 4:30 a.m.; Schubert was in good spirits.[63] On January 7 a friend wrote to Schober: "Schubert is almost completely well and is in nearly constant communication with Dr. Bernhardt and Maximilian Leidesdorf [his new publisher]."[64]

In February, after a two-week fast and confinement to his home, Schubert was again seen in public. Schwind tells us (February 22, 1824) that "Schubert is quite well. He has given up his wig...."[65] Due to syphilis his hair either fell out or was shaved because of the rash that accompanied the disease.

Schubert was plagued by frustrations and disappointments even in his last years. The five years which he had devoted to music for the stage represented a significant portion of his productive life, but with little positive effect. He, like most people of uncommon ability, had his share of jealous enemies. After the failure of the play *Rosamunde* the editor of the *Theaterzeitung* sent a copy of a vitriolic review to the composer Karl Maria von Weber and asked him to pass it on to the *Dresden Abendzeitung* for re-publication. Weber responded, "He probably thought this would give me pleasure, but it only brought me embarrassment."

Problems with publishers also continued to trouble Schubert. In 1821 his friends paid Diabelli to publish Opp. 1-7 and 12-14. The composer did not trust the publisher, so he marked the back of each copy with "Sch" or "Schbt" in order to control the number of copies which Diabelli engraved, and to prevent unauthorized copies. (Only signed copies were legitimate.) Schubert was correct in his mistrust of Diabelli. At a low point in Schubert's failing health, with mounting hospital and medical bills, the publisher had persuaded the composer to sell all rights to the ten songs held by the firm. Schubert agreed to this in spite of warnings from his friends, especially Sonnleithner. Schubert later accused Diabelli of overcharging for copy work, withholding copies of music to which he was entitled, and keeping his manuscripts. He then entered a new relationship with the publishers Sauer and Leidesdorf, but fared no better with them. Leidesdorf, who was as poor a businessman as Schubert, was an artistic dreamer, always on the brink of bankruptcy. Schubert later had to return to Cappi and Diabelli, but with no improvement in the relationship. He eventually tried a half-dozen more publishers.

The publishing business, which was quite new to Vienna, was very different from that of today. Publishers at that time also served as retail outlets for their publications; they sold to the general public only what their own firms produced. There was no music retailer from whom to purchase works of various publishers. Since all music was hand-engraved, there was little financial advantage, as there is nowadays, in printing great numbers of copies. Therefore, publishers usually issued about 200-300 copies. Compared with today's prices of mass-produced scores, music at that time was quite expensive. Then, as now, firms usually preferred easier, shorter works. Scores were carelessly edited and cheaply printed, and they included numerous errors. Beethoven called his publishers "hell hounds,"

---

63   O. E. Deutsch, *The Schubert Reader*, 319.

64   *Ibid.*, 319.

65   *Ibid.*, 330.

and Schubert declared that "The artist shall remain for all time the slave of every miserable peddler."

One possibility as to why Schubert was so shabbily treated by his publishers was that he was not in favor with the government (see Chapter 3); Sauer and Leidesforf were "suppliers to the court." They preferred the compositions of Salieri, who had a clean political reputation.

Schubert had finished the song cycle *Die schöne Müllerin* in November, 1823, and was now in the process of having Sauer and Leidesdorf publish it. The piece was historically significant because it was the first song cycle ever written—a form which became so popular in the nineteenth century. Because the original Schubertiad partipants (Schober, Spaun, Hüttenbrenner and Kupelwieser) had scattered and Schubert's friendship with Mayrhofer was strained, Schubertiads were seldom held. Fortunately, there were new friends to replace the absent ones. Moritz von Schwind and Eduard von Bauernfeld were now good friends of the composer. In the 1850s, years after the composer's death, Bauernfeld wrote his recollections of their good times together:

> Then came Schubert evenings, known as *"Schubertiaden"*, when the wine flowed in buckets, the excellent Vogl served up wonderful songs and poor Schubert had to accompany him for so long a stretch with his short, fat fingers that they hardly obeyed him. It was worse when we gave a dance—we called them "sausage dances" in those simple days— when pretty women and young girls were present. Our "Bertel," as he was tenderly nicknamed, had to play his latest waltz, and play it again and again, while they formed a cotillion. The corpulent little man, dripping sweat, had to wait until a frugal supper was served before he could relax. No wonder that he sometimes failed us and that more than one *Schubertiade* took place without Schubert, especially when he was not feeling sociable or didn't like some of the guests.[66]

At this time two new acquaintances influenced Schubert's life. The first was Ignaz Schuppanzigh, who was the leading violinist in the city and had the finest string quartet. This violinist, whom Beethoven also considered a friend, had great renown. He inspired Schubert to compose two string quartets—one

Moritz von Schwind (1804-1871). The foremost Germanic painter of fairy tales and legends. A devoted friend of Schubert. (Historic Museum of the City of Vienna.)

in A minor (Op. 29, No. 1) and one in D minor (*"Der Tod und das Mädchen"*). The Schuppanzigh Quartet introduced the A minor quartet with great success. The theme which is associated with *Rosamunde* was used for the slow movement (and also, later, in the solo piano *Impromptu*, Op. 142, No. 3). Contrary to the commonly held belief that *Rosamunde* preceded the A minor quartet, Mr. Brown was of the opinion that the quartet had been composed, or at least sketched, before *Rosamunde*, probably in November 1823. Pressed for time, Schubert used for his *Rosamunde* music several compositions which he had made or sketched before. Thus, the so-called *"Rosamunde"* theme would in fact come from the second movement of his string quartet, and not vice-versa.

The second new acquaintance was Count Ferdinand Troyer, a fine clarinettist who was the "chief steward" to Archduke Rudolf. Count Ferdinand commissioned Schubert to write a work "exactly like Beethoven's Septet." Schubert did nearly as the Count requested, except that it was an octet. Both the *Septet* and *Octet* had six movements; where Beethoven placed an adagio, Schubert has one too;

---

66 O. E. Deutsch, *Schubert: Memoirs by His Friends*, 229.

both include an Andante and Variations; the keys are identical. Aside from these factors, Schubert's work has all of his own musical characteristics.

A letter from Schwind to Schober on 6 March 1824 describes Schubert's activity at that time:

> Schubert is pretty well already. He says that after a few days of the new treatment he felt how his complaint broke up and everything was different. He still lives one day on panada [bread pudding] and the next on cutlets, and lavishly drinks tea, goes bathing a good deal besides and is superhumanly industrious. A new Quartet is to be performed at Schuppanzigh's, who is quite enthusiastic and is said to have rehearsed particularly well. He has now long been at work on an Octet, with the greatest zeal. If you go to see him [Schubert] during the day, he says, "Hello, how are you? — Good!" and goes on writing, whereupon you depart.[67]

There was excitement in Vienna in the spring of 1824 over the fact that Beethoven's ninth symphony was to be performed. After all, it had been ten years since the premiere of his eighth symphony. The Viennese had heard that the ninth would be a gigantic work, even employing a choir in the final movement. Schubert happily looked forward to the concert, which he attended.

Leopold Kupelwieser had gone to Rome to paint illustrations of landscapes, buildings, and folk costumes for a book which was to be published. His friend Johann Smirsch, an amateur painter, went to visit Kupelwieser, carrying with him a letter from Schubert (March 31, 1824), who sums up his innermost feelings about his health and informs Kupelwieser about current happenings in Vienna:

A rare drawing of Schubert by Josef Teltscher, who became acquainted with Schubert during the Schubertiads in the early 1820s. Their friendship deepened during the years 1825-1827. (Historic Museum of the City of Vienna.)

Dear Kupelwieser,

For a long time I have felt the urge to write to you, but I never knew where to turn. Now, however, Smirsch offers me an opportunity, and at last I can once again wholly pour out my soul to someone. For you are so good and honest, you will be sure to forgive many things which others might misunderstand in me. In a word, I feel myself to be the most unhappy and dejected creature in the world. Imagine a man whose health will never be right

67   O. E. Deutsch, *The Schubert Reader*, 331.

again, and who in sheer despair over this always makes things worse and worse, instead of better; imagine a man, I say, whose most brilliant hopes have perished, to whom the felicity of love and friendship have nothing to offer but pain, at best, whom enthusiasm (at least of the stimulating kind) for all things beautiful threatens to forsake, and I ask you, is he not a miserable, unhappy being? "My peace is gone, my heart is sore, I shall find it never and nevermore" I may well sing every day now, for each night, on retiring to bed, I hope I may not wake again, and each morning but recalls yesterday's grief. Thus, joyless and friendless I would pass my days, if Schwind did not visit me now and again and turn on me a ray of those sweet days of the past. Our society (reading circle), as you probably know already, has done itself to death due to a reinforcement of that rough chorus of beer-drinkers and sausage-eaters, for its dissolution is due in a couple of days, though I had hardly visited it myself since your departure. Leidesdorf, with whom I have become quite well acquainted, is in fact a truly thoughtful and good fellow, but so hugely melancholy that I am almost afraid I owe him more than enough in that respect; besides, my affairs and his do badly, so that we never have any money. The opera by your brother (who did not do any too well in leaving the theatre) has been declared unusable, and thus no claim has been made on my music. Castelli's opera, "The Conspirators" [*Die Verschworenen*], has been set in Berlin by a local composer and received with acclamation. In this way I seem once again to have composed two operas for nothing. Of songs, I have not written many new ones, but I have tried my hand at several instrumental works, for I wrote two Quartets for violins, viola and violoncello and an Octet, and I want to write another quartet, in fact I intend to pave my way towards a grand symphony in that manner. The latest in Vienna is that Beethoven is to give a concert at which he is to produce his new Symphony, three movements from the new Mass and a new Overture. God willing, I too am thinking of giving a similar concert

next year. I will close now, so as not to use too much paper, and kiss you 1,000 times. If you were to write to me about your present enthusiastic mood and about your life in general, nothing could more greatly please
Your
faithful Friend
Frz. Schubert.[68]

From a letter which Johanna Lutz (Sonnleithner's cousin) wrote to Leopold Kupelwieser from Vienna on May 26, 1824, we learn of Schubert's second departure for Zseliz: "Your letter found Schubert still here but he must have gone by now."[69] Moritz von Schwind also wrote to Kupelwieser on the same day: "Schubert has left for Count Esterházy's in Hungary... he has resolved to write a symphony."[70]

Zseliz was physically and spiritually healing for Schubert. Not only were the fresh air and regular living habits beneficial, but his status as music master was rewarded with a considerable pay increase and a room in the castle instead of the servants' quarters. On the whole, he seemed fairly content and well, according to the letters which he wrote to his family and friends. The Count's two daughters were now mature young ladies with considerable pianistic ability; this probably gave Schubert the incentive to return again to the piano duet medium.

THE PIANO DUETS OF 1824.

SONATA IN C ("GRAND DUO"), Opus 140, D 812 ¤ ¤ ¤ ¤ ¤ ¤ ¤ ¤ ¤ ¤ ¤

Composed: June, 1824
Manuscript: Bodleian Library, Oxford
First publication: Diabelli & Company, 1838
Dedication: (by publisher) Clara Wieck

The *Sonata in C ("Grand Duo")* was mentioned by Schubert in letters from Zseliz. On July 18, 1824 he wrote to his brother Ferdinand, "I am better able now to find happiness and peace in myself.... A *Grand Sonata* and variations on a theme of my own, both for four hands, which I have already written, shall serve you as proof."[71] This sonata holds an unusual place

68   *Ibid.*, 338-40.
69   *Ibid.*, 347.
70   *Ibid.*, 347-48.
71   *Ibid.*, 363.

Ex. 6. Schubert, *Sonata in C*, Opus 140, m. 1-4 and 50-53.

among all of Schubert's works, for there has been a controversy ever since Robert Schumann's early writings concerning the connection between it and the lost "Gastein" symphony. There was a theory that Schubert often wrote for one piano, four hands because he had no orchestra at his disposal, and that duets, with their independent voicing and wide tessitura, were his substitute. Some nineteenth-century scholars believed that this sonata, with its symphonic style, was a duet version of a symphony which we know he intended to write, but which was never found.

Robert Schumann, even after seeing the manuscript in Schubert's own hand, inscribed "Sonata for four hands," was not convinced: "in spite of Schubert's manuscript, I still hold to my own opinion respecting the duo. One who wrote as much as Schubert docs not trouble too much about titles, and thus he probably hastily entitled his work 'Sonata' while 'Symphony' was what he had in mind."[72] Schumann, of course, did not know of the letters which were written in July and August of 1824 wherein Schubert continued to call his work a sonata; this evidence refutes Schumann's theory that the title was added in haste and by mistake. Donald Tovey in his book *Essays in Musical Analysis*, Vol. 1, suggests that the sonata is a reduction of a symphony because the score was so

successfully orchestrated by Joseph Joachim in 1855.[73] Although the sonata looks like a piano reduction because of its long melodic whole notes and thick texture, many other duets share these characteristics.

This Sonata is the longest of Schubert's four-hand works and one of the most powerful. It is far more serious in mood than its predecessor, the *Grand Sonata*, Opus 30, D 617. The *Grand Sonata*, Opus 30 is

---

72 R. Schumann, *On Music and Musicians* (New York, 1946), 116.

73 D. Tovey, *Essays in Musical Analysis* Vol. I (London, 1943), 215.

Ex. 7. Schumann, *Piano Concerto in A minor*, m. 12-15; 54-57.

Ex. 8. Schubert, *Sonata in C*, Opus 140, 2nd movt., m. 6-8.

Schumann, *"Seit ich ihn gesehen"*, m. 26-27.

more typical of the late classical keyboard sonatas whereas the *Sonata in C*, Opus 140, D 812, foreshadows the romantic symphony. There are at least two similarities between the first movement of the *Sonata in C* and the first movement of the "Unfinished" Symphony, which had been composed two years earlier. Both introduce the B theme in a low register (the secondo part in the sonata and the 'cello in the symphony). Both have a "false development" of the B theme (duet measures 66-116) before the real development begins, i.e., the B theme is broken into motives which undergo alterations and modulations and which are alternately shared by the two players. Unlike the "Unfinished" Symphony, the central development section elaborates on both the A and B themes.

The most notable feature of the first movement of the *Sonata in C* is its thematic cohesion. The B theme

seems almost to be an extension or alteration of the A theme since both are based on the same rhythm (see Ex. 6, preceding page).

Since Robert Schumann had the highest regard for Schubert's work, this similarity between the themes might have influenced him. Just three years after the publication of the *Sonata in C,* the first movement of Schumann's *Piano Concerto in A minor* was completed. In this concerto Schumann went a step further toward unification of the whole work. Whereas Schubert's two themes shared the same rhythm, Schumann's themes are alike in rhythm and melody; their difference lies in the shift from minor to major. Such unification foreshadows the "thematic transformation" in the tone poems of Franz Liszt. (See Ex. 7, above.)

The chief characteristics of the second movement of the *Sonata in C* are its very long melodic lines and

Ex. 9. Schubert, *Sonata in C*, Opus 140, 4th movt., m. 407-12.

cato phrases alternate with sforzando chords until the trio begins at measure 165. Here the mood changes abruptly; the primo melody is in dotted half-notes and the secondo accompaniment provides an underlying rhythm:

This movement, Schubert's only scherzo for piano duet, is full of syncopation, energetic motion and bustling humor. It should be performed at a rapid pace, emphasizing its playful nature by making abrupt contrasts between the "*sforzandi*" and "*pianos*". The quiet trio should be played very legato in contrast to the boisterous outer sections. In the manuscript, the bass notes in measures 84 and 88 are not tied; these notes are tied in all available editions except the Bärenreiter. The writers prefer to repeat the notes in accordance with the manuscript, to ensure that the pedal point is heard throughout.

deceptive cadences. There are three themes: the first is lyrical; the second has an aggressive quality — *staccato*, *forte*, and with *sforzandi*; the third is introduced in the secondo part, again lyrical but incorporating a pizzicato effect both in the melody and in the accompaniment. The form is:

A	B	C	A	B
A^b Maj.	E Maj.	E^b Maj.	A^b Maj.	C Maj.

C	Coda
A^b Maj.	A^b (modul.)

One finds features within the first few lines which might well have influenced both Schumann and Brahms. Ex. 8, preceding page, shows a remarkable similarity between Schubert and Schumann in both melody and harmony. Shortly after this passage (Schubert measures 22-25) we find a Brahmsian hemiola, not previously found in Schubert's four-hand works.

After a typically Schubertian "grand pause" the coda, which derives from a fragment of the A theme, proceeds through a succession of brief modulations and enharmonic changes (measures 233 and 238-39).

There are two errors in the Henle edition: at measure 34, primo part, the key signature should have four sharps rather than four flats, and at measure 137, secondo part, the upper E^b note (which clashes with the E-naturals in the primo) should be omitted because this flat does not appear in like passages.

The form of the third movement is scherzo–trio–scherzo. There is an incessant onrush as quick stac-

The fourth movement has a loosely constructed sonata-allegro form which has three themes in the exposition and recapitulation instead of the usual two. Schubert further obscures the form by using closely related themes, which cadence in foreign keys. This constant shifting of keys gives the entire movement a freedom akin to a development section. The unique characteristic of the first statement of the fourth movement of the *Sonata in C* is that there are three key-feelings within the first line: initially we hear an octave E played *sforzando* and held seven counts, then the theme begins in A minor and ends in C major (measure 12). The metric regularity of the movement is often interrupted by long tied notes that tend to obscure the bar-lines. Ex. 9 (above) foreshadows the pointillistic techniques of the twentieth century.

Because of its length, approximately forty minutes, the *Sonata in C* is difficult to program; it is also formidably difficult to perform. Among the challenges are the frequent sharing of the same note by the two players and pedaling for a legato melody and non-legato or pizzicato accompaniment simultaneously, as in the first movement, B theme. There are a few other orchestral effects which require experimentation. For example, at measure 144, first movement, all editions except the Bärenreiter have a tied whole-note in the bass. Here again the note is not tied in the

Ex. 10. Schubert, *Variations*, Opus 35, m. 173-76.

manuscript, and the repeated form of pedal-point is far more practical. In the last movement the tempo changes at measure 425 (*più lento*), 468 (*tempo I*) and 532 (*più mosso*) were added in pencil by an editor and are not by Schubert.

VARIATIONS ON AN ORIGINAL THEME IN A Flat, Opus 35, D 813 ¤ ¤

Composed: July 1824
Manuscript: lost
First publication: Sauer & Leidesdorf, 1825
Dedication: Count Anton Berchtold

One of the great masterpieces among Schubert's compositions is his Opus 35 *Variations on an Original Theme in A Flat*, D 813, written in June or July of 1824. Schubert was, at that time, studying *The Well-Tempered Clavier* and teaching Bach fugues to Marie and Karoline Esterházy. One finds herein the influence of Bach, including some canonic imitation. It is obvious that Schubert had no trouble publishing this work, because it was in the hands of Sauer and Leidesdorf in Vienna shortly after his return from

Zseliz in October of 1824 and published a few months later on February 9, 1825. The work gained immediate popularity. After Schwind had heard the variations at a Schubertiad he wrote to Franz von Schober:

> The new variations for four hands are something quite extraordinary. The theme is as grandiose as it is free and noble. In eight variations, these pages are quite independently and vitally developed and yet each again seems to reveal the theme.[74]

Since the work was dedicated to Count Anton Berchtold, who was not one of Schubert's friends, we may assume that this dedication was financially inspired.

The *Variations*, Opus 35, D 813, can be compared to Schubert's earlier *Variations on a French Song*, Opus 10, D 624, and to the *Introduction and Variations on an Original Theme*, Opus 82, No. 2, D 603. All three follow a basic pattern: the theme is in a moderate tempo; the variations gain rhythmic intensity by diminution of the note values. In each set the last variation is the longest and ends in a *tour de force*. The *Variations on a French Song* may well have been the model for the *Variations on an Original Theme*, Opus 35. In comparing these two sets of variations, we see that both of the themes begin with an anacrusis (c ♩ ♪♩); both of the "Variations 1" have triplets as the basic unit; both of the "Variations 2" have an unflagging secondo accompaniment figure; in both, the quieter variations (3, 5, and 7) are alternated with the more agitated ones (4, 6 and 8). On the other hand, the comparison reveals considerable growth in Schubert's variation style between 1818 and 1824. Among his first three sets of duet variations, Opus 35 may be the first to be built upon a truly original theme; of the previous two sets, one was built upon "*Le bon Chevalier*" and the other closely resembled the theme from Wranitzky's ballet music *Das Waldmädchen*.

VARIATIONS ON AN ORIGINAL THEME IN A Flat,
Opus 35, D 813

THEME
Allegretto

---

74   O. E. Deutsch, *The Schubert Reader*, 401.

The theme of the *Variations on an Original Theme*, Opus 35, D 813 consists of three eight-measure phrases (A B A') instead of the more usual binary structure. The writing is technically demanding; the primo and secondo parts are of nearly equal importance. The harmonic language is more complex (see measures 170-171, Var. 7); there is generous use of chromaticism, notably in the modulatory sections (measures 235-236 and 256-257). Nearly every variation includes canonic imitation at the beginning of the B section of the theme, although Bach's influence is most strongly felt in Variation 4.

The beauty of Variation 7, "*Più lento*", defies description. The dissonant harmonies (triads with added seconds, fourths, sixths and sevenths), floating through various tonalities, reveal Schubert as a colorist who anticipated impressionism by half a century (Ex. 10, preceding page). The vagueness of tonality and the irregular and fragmentary structure of the phrases create an atmospheric aura. The final variation is a highly-spirited *Siciliano* whose relentless rhythm is highly effective.

In Variation 2 (m. 49), the writers believe that the primo right hand should have a G-flat added above the E-flat on the third beat to make it consistent with all analogous passages.

FOUR LÄNDLER, D 814 ¤ ¤ ¤ ¤ ¤ ¤ ¤

Composed: July 1824
Manuscript: lost
First publication: J. P. Gotthard, 1869

The *Four Ländler*, D 814, composed in July, 1824, were first published in 1869 in a collection of twenty *Ländler*, the first sixteen of which Brahms had transcribed for piano duet from pre-existing solos by Schubert. These *Four Ländler*, D 814, appearing as numbers seventeen through twenty, were already duets of Schubert. Subsequent editions are all exactly like the Gotthard edition. The writers assume that the phrasing in the four-hand publication was added, at least partially, by Brahms.

These simple *Ländler* are typical of the charm of the Biedermeier

style. Their brevity would lead us to believe that Schubert intended them for the ballroom rather than for concert performance; it was the custom to repeat each section many times. The title "*Ländler*" gives us no clue as to performance practice, since these pieces were also called "*Allemandes*" and "*Waltzes*" in certain publications. (Schubert arranged *Ländler No. 1* for piano solo and entitled it "*Allemande*".) However, *Ländler* were generally slower than waltzes. The *Four Ländler*, D 814 are of little importance as compared to other compositions of this period. Each is only sixteen measures in length and in binary form. They are so easy that two hands could play all the notes almost as well as four.

SIXTEEN GERMAN DANCES AND TWO ÉCOSSAISES, Opus 33, D 783a

Composed: July, 1824
Manuscript: lost
First publication: Cappi & Company, 1825

Of all of Schubert's compositions, the history of his dance music is the most tangled and puzzling. He often made copies for friends, with slight changes in harmony or melody, and seemingly without interest in any specific numerical order. Schubert also confused the issue by his indifference to formal categories of the dances. For example, he called a piece "*Ländler*" in one manuscript, "*Deutscher*" in another,

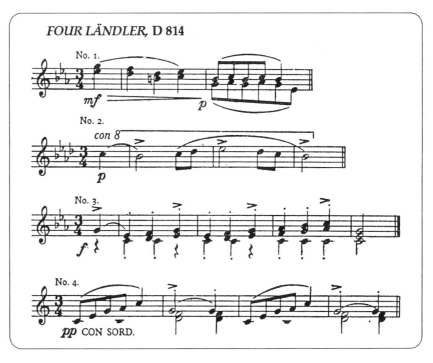

and it was published as "*Walzer*". After his death publishers selected at random various dances (published and unpublished) and changed the titles from "*Deutscher*" to "*Ländler*" or "*Walzer*", transposed some to new keys, and substituted one trio for another.

Schubert often wrote these dances for both piano solo and piano duet. For the following reasons, the writers believe the duet arrangements of the *German Dances and Écossaises* to be Schubert's own, and not arrangements by another person. Schubert wrote these pieces for four hands, probably in July 1824 (the duet manuscript of numbers 8 and 9 are so dated), and gave them to the publishing firm of Cappi & Co. They were advertised in the *Wiener Zeitung* on 11 February 1825 for sale both as solos and duets. Since the manuscripts of two of the dances (Nos. 8 and 9) in Schubert's own hand were known to exist and are well-documented, one could assume that the others in the collection are also authentic. The manuscripts of dances 8 and 9 were auctioned off in August 1928

in Berlin and their whereabouts are unknown today. Since Schubert wrote with such ease it would be unlikely for him (or the publisher) to have left such an assignment to an "arranger". The duet manuscripts were evidently among some other Schubert manuscripts when Cappi & Co. sold their firm to Joseph Czerny (unrelated to Karl Czerny) in 1828; some years later Czerny sold the firm to A. O. Witzendorf who reissued these four-hand pieces ca. 1860. The *German Dances and Écossaises* were republished in 1983 by the Neil A. Kjos Music Company.

The late Christa Landon and O. E. Deutsch both questioned the authenticity of these dances. It is true that there are some differences between the manuscripts of Nos. 8 and 9 and the printed version of 1825, but this is not surprising since Schubert often altered versions of his works. The question of whether these were arranged by Schubert himself or someone else cannot at the present time be answered with certainty.

SIX GRAND MARCHES AND TRIOS, Opus 40, D 819 ¤ ¤ ¤ ¤ ¤ ¤ ¤ ¤ ¤

Composed: ca. Oct. 1824
Manuscript: lost
First publication: Sauer & Leidesdorf, 1825
Dedication: J. Bernhardt

According to O. E. Deutsch's *Schubert: Thematic Catalog of All His Works*, the last duets which Schubert composed at Zseliz were the *Six Grand Marches and Trios*, Opus 40, D 819. This dating is questionable, as it is based on Josef von Spaun, who did not differentiate between Schubert's two visits to Zseliz (1818 and 1824). These Marches were dedicated by Schubert to the physician who cared for him during his serious illness of 1823. All of these marches were immediately popular, and Schubert was frequently requested to participate in their performance. Spaun, on a trip through Galicia (in southeastern Poland), heard them in an arrangement for wind

SIXTEEN GERMAN DANCES AND TWO ÉCOSSAISES, Opus 33, D 783a

instruments, played in a parade. In 1859-60 Franz Liszt arranged numbers 3 and 5 for orchestra, the latter called *Funeral March*.

One might reasonably assume that Schubert intended these pieces for social occasions and perhaps for teaching; he was teaching the Esterházy daughters at this time. There is no unifying element among the six marches except that they are in the usual AB Trio AB, da capo form and in duple or quadruple meter. Marches 1, 4 and 6 are in major; marches 2, 3 and 5 are in minor.

Schubert often constructs his melodic lines in two-measure or four-measure phrase units which are immediately repeated (see Ex. 11, next page). This practice gives balance and continuity, but its frequent recurrence can become tiresome, especially when the material is simple. For this reason, and because a few of the marches are similar, one should not attempt to perform them as a group.

Two of the most appealing marches are numbers five and six. Franz von Hartmann, in his diary dated December 15, 1826, stated, "I was moved almost to tears... by the trio of the fifth March, which always reminds me of my dear, good mother."[75] From this remark, March No. 5 in E-flat minor is now known as the *"Trauermarsch"*. It is marked *Andante* and begins with a sighing melody punctuated by a detached, pulsating secondo reminiscent of the *"Crucifixus"* in Schubert's *Mass in G*. Following a climactic B-flat major chord is a resolution to G major at measure 98-99. The first chord of the third-related harmonies is *fortissimo* and contrasts effectively with the subsequent *pianissimo*.

In contrast to the *"Trauermarsch"*, March No. 6 is a jaunty *Allegro con brio*. It would be difficult to imagine anything jollier than the B theme (Ex. 12, next page). The pervasive dotted rhythm of the march section effectively sets off the quiet and graceful trio.

The first edition of the *Six Grand Marches and Trios* had numerous inconsistencies; all present day editions have perpetuated these inconsistencies except the Bärenreiter, where they have been corrected.

DIVERTISSEMENT À LA HONGROISE, Opus 54, D 818 ¤ ¤ ¤ ¤ ¤ ¤ ¤ ¤ ¤ ¤ ¤

Composed: ca. Autumn 1824
Manuscript: lost
First publication: Matthias Artaria & Co., 1826
Dedication: Katherina von Lászny

Baron von Schönstein, an amateur musician and a house guest of the Esterházys, related the following:

SIXTEEN GERMAN DANCES AND TWO ÉCOSSAISES, Opus 33, D 783a (CONTINUED)

75 *Ibid.*, 571.

Ex. 11. Schubert, *Grand March No. 6*, Opus 10, m.6-9.

Ex. 12. Schubert, *Grand March No. 6*, Opus 10, m. 29-32.

The theme of the *Divertissement à la hongroise*, which is dedicated to Frau von Lászny, née Buchwiesner, is an Hungarian song, which Schubert picked up in Count Esterházy's kitchen at Zseliz; an Hungarian kitchen-maid was singing it and Schubert, who was just returning home with me from a walk, heard it as we passed. We listened for a considerable time to the singing; Schubert had obviously taken a liking to the song, continued humming it to himself for a long time as he went on his way and lo and behold! the next winter it appeared as the theme of the above mentioned Opus 54, one of his grandest pieces.[76]

The work has three sections: *Andante*, which is based on the Hungarian folk-tune mentioned above, *March*, later orchestrated by Franz Liszt, and *Allegretto*, originally composed as a piano solo and entitled "*Ungarische Melodie*". In 1846 Liszt made a transcription of the complete *Divertissement* for piano solo.

76 O. E. Deutsch, *Schubert: Memoirs by His Friends*, 103.

Katherina von Lászny, to whom the work was dedicated, was an actress of "ill repute", the wife of a Hungarian, and the hostess for many of the Schubertiads. The *Divertissement*, with its Hungarian theme, dramatic tremolos, appoggiaturas, and improvisatory style, was meant as a compliment to Katherina.

In the nineteenth century the three sections were often performed separately in arrangements. Robert Schumann observed in his diary on October 9, 1836, that "Mendelssohn stamped his feet impatiently over the work."[77] Wagner found it trivial. Their dislike may have been due to the numerous repeats. The present writers consider the *Divertissement* to be more enjoyable when the repeats are omitted (except for the *march da capo*).

Schubert used tremolos of the broken octave type for dramatic and/or orchestral effect ever since his first duet of 1810. Now we find for the first time a cadential, triadic tremolo in imitation of the Hungarian cimbalom. In the *Divertissement* these tremolos are usually major triads which conclude minor sections. The typical Hungarian rhythm

is also frequently used at section endings. This conclusion was also used by Liszt in his *Hungarian Rhapsodies*. Many other Hungarian characteristics (syncopation, cadenzas, melodic embellishment, vacillation between major and minor) are found in the *Divertissement*, but one Hungarian cliché is notably absent—the *"alla Zoppa"* (limping) rhythm:

The first section begins with a slow, introspective statement which re-appears midway through the section and which also serves

as its closing, referred to here as "A".

Section I
A   B   A   C   A
min. Maj. min. Maj. min.

The B and C themes form the main body of the section and should be played at approximately M.M. 76 (to the quarter-note). Section II, the march, is most effective at approximately M.M. 72, but four beats per measure should be felt rather than two. The trio, which is in major, is sometimes played slightly faster than the march. The third section is in a rather free form, but its broad outlines are like Section I:

SIX GRAND MARCHES AND TRIOS, Opus 40, D 819
(CONTINUED)

No. 4. Allegro maestoso

TRIO

No. 5. Andante

TRIO

No. 6. Allegro con brio

TRIO

77 M. J. E. Brown, *Schubert: A Critical Biography*, 160.

Section III

A   B   A   C   A
min.   min.   min.   Maj.   min.

The tempo will change from one theme to another in keeping with the gypsy character, and the rubato required in this composition presents a major challenge for good ensemble.

In comparing the compositions of this Zseliz period with those of the 1818 visit, we see several changes in Schubert's style. There are more languid, pensive melodies; phrases are longer and less regular and the forms are expanded. The "grand manner" of the mature romantic requires more space in which to develop, yet in spite of the greater length the themes are more interrelated. Because of the more integrated form as found in the *Sonata in C* and in the *Divertissement à la hongroise* the listener needs some prior knowledge of the form in order to enjoy Schubert's mature duets to the fullest. Except for the *Ländler* and a few of the marches, the duets of this period are technically more demanding than those of the previous period.

The *Divertissement à la hongroise* deserves special notice as one of the earliest examples of the romantic treatment of folk music. Composers before Schubert had employed folk melodies in their compositions but these were usually treated in a stylized manner. Haydn, for example, used a Croatian folk tune for the last movement of his Symphony No. 104 but this melody, with its balanced four-measure phrases, was treated in a refined manner and within a classical form. In the *Divertissement*, however, Schubert foreshadowed later romantics by using the melody in a pure and unsophisticated manner.

Schubert returned to Vienna with Baron von Schönstein on October 17. As was so often the case, the Baron was annoyed with Schubert. He wrote to Esterházy: "I nearly forgot to tell you that on the second day of our caravan we suffered the most appalling cold. Schmetterling [his dog] nearly froze to death... the lackadaisical Schubert managed to smash the window at the back of the coach as soon as we were out of Diószeg, whereby the ghastliest of cold winds was given free play about our ears."[78]

Schubert moved back to the Rossau district with his family. He was mentally and physically improved for having spent those quiet summer months at Zseliz. Schwind wrote to Schober (November 8, 1824): "Schubert is here, well and divinely happy, rejuvenated by joy and pain and a pleasant life."[79] The struggle for wider recognition was to continue. Schober wrote to Schubert (December 2, 1824): "If only you could secure a few noisy drummers among the reviewers to talk incessantly about you in the papers, it would be easy enough. I know some quite unimportant people who have become famous and popular in that way, so why should not the one who most deserves this have recourse to such methods?"[80]

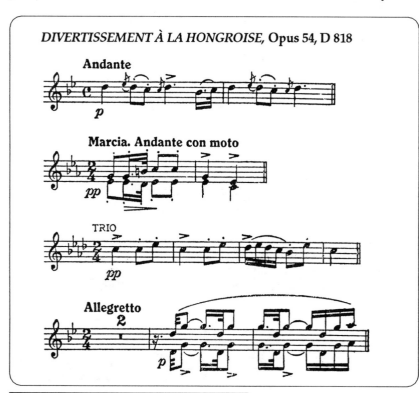

DIVERTISSEMENT À LA HONGROISE, Opus 54, D 818

Andante

Marcia. Andante con moto

TRIO

Allegretto

78   O. E. Deutsch, *The Schubert Reader*, 380.

79   *Ibid.*, 383.

80   *Ibid.*, 386.

CHAPTER VI

A Reputation Is Established (1825-1827)

Schubert's reputation grew steadily from 1825 through 1827. His compositions were performed more frequently, more works were published, and the Schubertiads became more popular than ever. In February 1825 he moved from his father's house to a room next to the Karlskirche in order to be close to his friend Moritz von Schwind, who lived next door. He remained there for eighteen months, except during the summer when he traveled with Vogl. It was in February, too, that Schubert became a close friend of Eduard von Bauernfeld (1802-1890). Bauernfeld, who was twenty-three (five years younger than Schubert), became a well-known playwright and translator of Shakespeare. Bauernfeld and Schubert had met earlier (see illustration, page 34), but in this year their friendship became constant. Later, Bauernfeld's writings became a fertile source of information for Schubert scholars. He describes their meeting and friendship:

> I was sitting thus in my den, one evening in February 1825, when my boyhood friend, Schwind, brought Schubert to see me, who meanwhile had already become famous or, at least, well known. We were soon on intimate terms with one another. At Schwind's request I had to recite some crazy youthful poems of mine; we then went to the piano, where Schubert sang and we also played duets, and later to an inn till far into the night. The bond was sealed, the three friends remained inseparable from that day on. But others too grouped themselves round us, mostly painters and musicians, a circle of people, with a zest for life and with similar aims and ideas, who shared together their joys and sorrows....
>
> How often did we three wander about until the small hours, accompanying one another home — but as we could not bring ourselves to part, it was not uncommon for us all to spend the night together, at one or another's lodgings. We were not very particular about comfort on these occasions! If necessary, friend Moritz would throw himself down on the bare floor boards, wrapped only in a feather coverlet....
>
> In the matter of property, a common-ownership attitude prevailed; hats, boots, neckerchiefs, even coats and certain other articles of clothing too, if they but chanced to fit, were common property; but gradually, through manifold use, as a result of which a certain partiality for the object always ensue[d], they passed into undisputed private possession. Whoever was flush at the moment paid for the other, or for the others.[81]

A lithograph of Schubert by Josef Teltscher, finished in late 1825. Teltscher (1801-1837) was a gifted portrait painter whose life was cut short by drowning. (Nationalbibliothek, Vienna.)

---

81   O. E. Deutsch, *Schubert: Memoirs by His Friends*, 227-228.

A watercolor of Schubert by Wilhelm August Rieder, May 1825. This is the best known and most popular of the Schubert portraits. It owes its existence to a sudden rainstorm in Vienna from which Rieder sought shelter in Schubert's apartment next to the Karlskirche. (That house was demolished in 1961.) While there, Rieder began the portrait. A copper engraving of it was immediately made by Johann Passini and reproductions were available for purchase in Vienna in December 1825.
(Historic Museum of the City of Vienna.)

In early summer Schubert again tried to earn the respect of Goethe by sending him some settings of his (Goethe's) poems. Schubert wrote: "If I should succeed in giving evidence of my unbounded veneration of Your Excellency by the dedication of these compositions of your poems, and possibly in gaining some recognition of my insignificant self, I should regard the favorable fulfillment of this wish as the fairest event of my career."[82]

For this presentation to Goethe, Schubert had gone to the added trouble of having the titles printed in gold, on satin paper. This letter too, like Spaun's

letter of 1816, remained unanswered. Goethe apparently preferred the simple settings of his poems as composed by Zelter and Reichardt.

Although Schubert was enjoying his friendship with Schwind and Bauernfeld, the relationships were time-consuming; therefore, when Vogl proposed that he and Schubert should make a *musical* journey to Steyr in 1825 (as they had in 1819), Schubert was enthusiastic. In May they traveled to Steyr, and from there to Linz, Gmunden, Salzburg and Bad Gastein, where they presented lieder recitals and Schubert, with new friends, performed im-

---

82   O. E. Deutsch, *The Schubert Reader*, 420.

promptu piano duet programs. Schubert wrote a long letter to his parents in which he said: "In upper Austria I find my compositions everywhere, especially in the monasteries of St. Florian and Kremsmünster where with the aid of a gallant pianoforte player I performed my four-hand variations [Opus 35] and marches [probably Opus 40] with notable success."[83] His partner for this performance was Father Heinrich Hassak, dean of the monastery.

This four-month period was a supremely happy part of Schubert's life, but on October 3 he had to leave his many admirers and friends and return to Vienna. His favorite duet partner, Josef von Gahy (one of the figures in Leopold Kupelwieser's aquarelle - page 40, top), returned with him. Awaiting Schubert were not only Schwind and Bauernfeld, but also Schober, who had returned from Breslau, and Kupelwieser from Italy. They proceeded to enjoy comradeship and frequent parties together.

At the end of the year, December 9, 1825, the *Wiener Zeitung* announced an engraving by Passini of Wilhelm Rieder's watercolor portrait of Schubert: "The composer of genius, sufficiently well known to the musical world, who so often enchanted his hearers with his vocal compositions in particular, appears here, engraved in copper by Herr Passini's cunning hand, as a perfect likeness, and we therefore believe we have presented Schubert's numerous friends and admirers with a welcome gift."[84] This great honor and recognition ended Schubert's year 1825 on a triumphant note.

In addition to his early association with the publisher Diabelli, he began to publish increasingly with the firms Sauer & Leidesdorf, Cappi & Company, and A. Pennauer. In 1826 the publishers Artaria and Thaddäus Weigl would be added.

In April of 1826 Schubert sought the position of Vice-Director of the Imperial Court Chapel.[85] Even though his income had increased, he stated in his letter to the Emperor that his desire for the position was partially due to financial need. His old friend and teacher Salieri, who had been the court Kapellmeister, had died the previous May, so there was no representative of the court to intercede on Schubert's behalf.

Once again, Schubert was denied a position of steady employment. He seemed to be restless,

moving from the south part of Vienna to the north side (Währing) in late spring. Schwind and Schober lived with him intermittently. After a few months he moved with Schober back to the inner city. This living arrangement lasted only a few weeks until he moved near the city park, where he lived alone. His illness was playing hide-and-seek, and his emotions were at times turbulent. Bauernfeld gives us an insight into an aspect of Schubert's personality which is seldom seen:

> It was on a summer's afternoon and, with Franz Lachner and others, we had strolled over to Grinzing for the "*Heuriger*" [new wine], to which Schubert was especially partial, though I was quite unable to acquire a taste for its acute tartness. We sat over our wine, indulging in lively conversation, and it was not until the dusk of the evening that we walked back; I wanted to go straight home, as I was living in an outlying suburb at that time, but Schubert dragged me forcibly to an inn and I was not even spared the coffee-house afterwards, at which he was in the habit of winding up the evening, or rather the late hours of the night. It was already one o'clock and an extremely lively musical discussion had arisen over the hot punch. Schubert emptied glass after glass and had reached a sort of elated state in which, more eloquent than usual, he was expounding to Lachner and me all his plans for the future. At this point a singular misfortune had to bring a couple of professional artists, celebrated members of the Opera House orchestra, into the coffee-house. As these people came in Schubert stopped short in the middle of his impassioned discourse; his brow puckered, his small grey eyes gleamed out fiercely from behind his spectacles, which he pushed restlessly to and fro. But scarcely had the musicians caught sight of the master when they rushed up to him, grasped him by the hands, paid him a thousand compliments and almost smothered him with flattery. Finally it transpired that they were extremely anxious to have a new composition for their concert, with solo passages for their particular instru-

---

83   *Ibid.*, 435-36.

84   *Ibid.*, 477-78.

85   *Ibid.*, 520-21.

ments, and they were sure that *Meister* Schubert would prove accommodating, etc.

But the master turned out to be anything but accommodating; he remained silent. After repeated entreaties he said suddenly: "No! For you I will write nothing."

"Nothing for us?" asked the men, taken aback.

"No! Not on any account."

"And why not, Herr Schubert?" came the rejoinder, in a rather nettled tone. "I think we are just as much artists as you are! No better ones are to be found in the whole of Vienna."

"Artists!" cried Schubert, hurriedly draining his last glass of punch and getting up from the table. Then the little man pulled his hat down over his ear and faced the *virtuosi*, one of whom was tall of stature, and the other more inclined to stoutness, as though threatening them. "Artists?" he repeated. "Musical hacks are what you are! Nothing else! One of you bites at the brass mouthpiece of his wooden stick and the other blows out his cheeks on the horn! Do you call that art? It's a trade, a knack that earns money, and nothing more! — You, artists! Don't you know what the great Lessing says? — How can anyone spend his whole life doing nothing but bite on a piece of wood with holes in it? — That's what he said — (turning to me) or something of the kind! Didn't he? (Once more to the *virtuosi*): You call yourselves artists? Blowers and fiddlers are what you are, the whole lot of you! I am an artist, I! I am Schubert, Franz Schubert, whom everybody knows and recognizes! Who has written great things and beautiful things, that you don't begin to understand! And who is going to write still more beautiful things — (to Lachner): that is so, my friend, isn't it? — the most beautiful things! Cantatas and quartets, operas and symphonies! Because I am not just a composer of *Ländler*, as the stupid newspapers say and as the stupid people repeat — I am Schubert! Franz Schubert! And don't you forget it! And if the word art is mentioned, it is *me* they are talking about, not you worms and insects, who demand solos for yourselves that I shall never write for you — and I know very well why! You crawling, gnawing worms that ought to be crushed

Zum grünen Anker (The Green Anchor). This tavern still stands on the Grünanger-gasse and is still managed by the same family who served Schubert.

under my foot — the foot of the man who is reaching to the stars — *Sublimi feriam sidera vertice*[86] (to me): translate that for them! — To the stars I say, while you poor, puffing worms wriggle in the dust and with the dust are scattered like dust and rot!!"[87]

The Schubert circle expanded in 1826 despite the fact that Vogl and Kupelwieser married, and were therefore not as frequent in attending the Schubertiads. Fritz and Franz von Hartmann, friends of Spaun, moved to Vienna in late 1826 and attended the Schubertiads until mid-August of 1828. Their diaries have been a valuable source of information concerning Schubert. Both brothers were law students but they had a strong interest in music, and became loyal friends of the composer. From their diaries we learn of frequent Schubertiads and endless parties at *The Green Anchor Inn, Bogner's Café,* and *Castle of Eisenstadt Tavern.* One can assume from the late hours Schubert kept that his disease was in a dormant state and that he was comparatively healthy.

---

86   My brow will touch the stars. (Horace)
87   O. E. Deutsch, *Schubert: Memoirs by His Friends,* 230-232.

There have been several references in this book to Schubert's relationship with women. The only two to whom he felt an emotional attachment appear to have been Therese Grob and Karoline Esterházy. The former was an adolescent love, but because of his preoccupation with studies and his financial insecurity, their relationship ended in 1820. The latter was of the nobility and, as such, not a realistic prospect for a wife; Schubert knew that his feelings for her should remain at some emotional distance. One begins to hear stories of his "love" for Karoline during his second visit to Zseliz (1824), when she was nineteen years old. It would be interesting to know just what kind of an association Schubert did have with her, because reportedly Karoline was so child-like and immature that, according to Dr. Deutsch, "her mother sent her out to play with her hoop when she was thirty."[88] Later, in 1844, she married a count, but the marriage was soon annulled. In 1824, however, her behavior might not have seemed so strange considering the fact that she was at that time a very young, protected and sheltered girl who would never have had to make decisions or think for herself. Perhaps Schubert's feelings were more an infatuation with the idea of love than love itself.

Schubert's friends hinted more than once that he had a healthy interest in sex. There were rumblings of an affair with a chambermaid named Pepi Pöckelhofer at Zseliz, and he had at least one encounter with an unidentified woman of Vienna from whom he contracted syphilis. There is one bit of historical gossip which bears repeating, and may or may not be factual. In the 1860s Schober (who never wrote his memoirs) related to the journalist Ludwig Frankl that in early 1827 there was a plan to have Schubert marry Auguste Grünwedel, a young dancer from a good Viennese family. Schober related that the two were "in love," but that Schubert was too shy to further their relationship. There are also two mentions of Grünwedel in Hartmann's diary of February 1827, but with no direct connection to Schubert.[89]

In March 1827, Schubert moved to Schober's home near the Graben where he remained (except for a short interim) until two months before his death. He

Schubert, ca. 1827. An oil painting by Willibrord Josef Mähler. Although atypical because Schubert is shown without glasses, Leopold von Sonnleithner considered this to be a very good likeness.

was given two rooms and a "music closet", which was the largest living space he had ever enjoyed.

In the previous month Beethoven had looked at the song cycle *Die schöne Müllerin* and the lied "*Die junge Nonne*" and had stated, according to Anton Schindler, "truly, there is in Schubert a divine spark."[90] By early March all of Vienna knew of Beethoven's illness. Friends and admirers began to bring food and *Gumpoldskirchner*, Beethoven's favorite wine. Josef Hüttenbrenner wrote that in March, a few days before Beethoven died, he, his brother Amselm, Schindler, the painter Teltscher and Schubert visited Beethoven.[91] If this is true, then for the first and last time these two great musical geniuses, who lived at the same time in Vienna without ever meeting, finally spoke a few words together. (Many years later Spaun claimed that Schubert and Beethoven never met.)[92]

88   O. E. Deutsch, *The Schubert Reader*, 364.

89   *Ibid.*, 603.

90   O. E. Deutsch, *Schubert: Memoirs by His Friends*, 307.

91   *Ibid.*, 192.

92   *Ibid.*, 366.

On the 26th of March Beethoven died. Two days later his body was placed on view in his bed at the Schwarzspanier Haus. Hartmann described this wake in rather gruesome detail. The next day Beethoven was taken to the Währing cemetery where he was buried. Schubert was given the honor of being one of thirty-six torch-bearers in the funeral procession. The funeral oration was written by the poet Franz Grillparzer and delivered by the actor Heinrich Anschütz. That evening Schubert, Schober, Schwind and Fritz von Hartmann went to the *Castle of Eisenstadt Tavern* where they remained until one o'clock in the morning and "talked of nothing but Beethoven."

Schubert resumed the association with the publisher Diabelli which he had terminated in 1823. His music was being reviewed in the major German cities such as Frankfurt, Leipzig, Berlin, Mainz and Munich. In June he was elected a Representative of the *Gesellschaft der Musikfreunde* of Vienna, an honor which had already been bestowed upon him in Linz and Graz. Dr. Karl Pachler and his wife, Marie, who were prominent in the musical life of Graz, invited Schubert and Johann Jenger to be their house guests in the early fall. Jenger, who was associated with the Styrian Music Society, had been Schubert's friend

since 1825. As a result of this visit with the Pachlers, Schubert wrote the piano duet *Kindermarsch* for Frau Pachler and her young son Faust.

The last three months of 1827 were physically and mentally painful for Schubert. His illness, which had been dormant for a time, was beginning to manifest itself with severe headaches. Numerous social engagements had to be cancelled. As his illness progressed, his musical productivity increased! He completed Book II of *Winterreise*, Opus 89, D 911, *Impromptus*, Opus 142, D 935, *Moments Musicaux*, Opus 94, D 780, *Piano Trio*, Opus 100, D 929, *German Mass*, D 872, several songs, and numerous dances.

THE PIANO DUETS OF 1825-1827.

Music historians have questioned the original relationship between the *Divertissement en forme d'une Marche brillante et raisonnée*, Opus 63, No. 1 and the *Andantino varié et Rondeau brillant*, Opus 84, Nos. 1 and 2. The *Divertissement...*, Opus 63, No. 1 was announced in the *Wiener Zeitung* on June 17, 1826 with the formidable title *Divertissement en forme d'une Marche brillante et raisonnée pour le pianoforte à quatre mains, composé sur des motifs origineaux [sic] français*. The "French original themes," never identified, were most likely of Schubert's own invention.

More than one year later, on July 6, 1827, the same newspaper announced the publication of the *Andantino varié et Rondeau brillant*. Since the manuscripts are lost we can only speculate as to whether Schubert submitted them simultaneously as a three-movement work or whether he submitted the Andantino and Rondeau at a later date as separate compositions. The shorter and simpler of the works published during Schubert's lifetime are by far the most numerous; therefore, if Weigl (the first publisher) did separate the three, he was responding to public demand by doing so. The key arrangement (E minor, B minor, and E minor) points toward a three-movement work. The first of the three works was labeled "Opus 63"; later "Opus 63, No. 1" was added,

Ex. 13. Schubert, *Divertissement...*, Opus 63, m. 1-8; 52-55.

Tempo di marcia

which clearly indicates that there were to be other parts in the opus. It seems that all authorities now believe that Opp. 63 and 84 were meant to be one work, yet the three "movements" are seldom, if ever, performed as a group.

DIVERTISSEMENT EN FORME D'UNE MARCHE BRILLANTE ET RAISONNÉE, Opus 63, No. 1, D 823 ¤

Composed: ca. Autumn, 1825
Manuscript: lost
First publication: Thaddäus Weigl, 1826

The title of this work was probably given by the publisher, since Schubert's own titles were usually simple, avoiding such terms as "*brillante*" and "*raisonnée*"; the latter means "constructed according to the rules of composition". The work is in sonata-allegro form; its primary and secondary themes are reproduced in Ex. 13, above. There is a long development section in which the possibilities of the A theme are thoroughly explored, but the B theme remains essentially the same; a coda incorporates the A theme.

Schubert has displayed in the *Divertissement...* an elegance of style and a fruitful exploitation of four-hand possibilities. It requires of its performers a total awareness of the voicing among all four hands and the ability to subdue the colorful accompaniment figures. The writers suggest that a performance based on a feeling of two beats per measure (M.M. 63 to the half-note) lends grandeur to the piece, while a four-beat pulse may lead to choppiness. The Weigl edition and subsequently the *Gesamtausgabe* and Peters editions show a trill on E and F-natural at measure 26. This is an error, and inconsistent with four parallel

measures; the Henle and Bärenreiter editions correct it to E and F$^\#$. The second theme, which first appears in the left hand of the primo and later in the right hand of the secondo, presents a problem of shared notes (measures 64-66). The performers are confronted with two possibilities: 1) playing the note simultaneously with both fingers (this is not always feasible, but it has the advantage of ensuring uniformity in both patterns) or 2) omitting the accompaniment note.

ANDANTINO VARIÉ, Opus 84, No.1, D 823 ¤ ¤ ¤ ¤ ¤ ¤ ¤ ¤ ¤ ¤ ¤ ¤ ¤ ¤ ¤ ¤

Composed: ca. Autumn 1825
Manuscript: lost
First publication: Thaddäus Weigl, 1827

The *Andantino varié* consists of a sixteen-measure theme followed by four variations and concluded by a restatement of the opening theme. The first edition omitted repeat signs at measure 8; these should be added. The staccato notes of the first and fifth measures of the theme should not be short; rather, they should be played as ♪ ♪ ♪ ♪ ♪ ♪ ♪ ♪ with pedal. When the same four-note figure reappears an octave higher in measure 13, the first edition and the Bärenreiter indicate a legato phrase; the *Gesamtausgabe* and Peters editions indicate a *portato* touch. The writers prefer the original legato phrasing because of the ethereal quality of the higher register and because of the unresolved harmony.

The first variation is a light and unpretentious embellishment of the theme, legato in the primo except for some *staccato* punctuations, and with a very dry accompaniment pattern in the secondo. The original

Ex. 14a. Schubert, *Andantino varié*, Opus 84, No. 1, m. 65-66.

Ex. 14b. Schubert, *Andantino varié*, Opus 84, No. 1, m. 72-73.

tempo is maintained. The counter-melody which begins at measure 28, primo left hand, should be slightly emphasized. The second variation is *staccato* and *pianissimo*, but with heavily accented triplet figures in both parts. Here again the pedal should hardly be touched except to fortify the accents in the climactic measure 45. The third variation is a canon of running sixteenth-notes. The first edition does not indicate whether the sixteenth-notes should be legato or non-legato. While some performers play it non-legato, the writers prefer the variation to be legato, as indicated in the Peters score. A few of the lowest left-hand notes (primo) must be omitted to make room for the secondo part. Maurice Brown states concerning the last variation:

> But the crown of the work, the section which raises it above all its contemporary work in the medium, is the fourth, and final, variation, *un poco più lento*. Schubert wrote nothing else like this variation; the key changes to the tonic major and the music is ethereal, remote, full of a lovely, expansive, melodic flowering that calls for exquisite playing. He asks for *pianissimo* tone (and in one place uses the direction—not very common with him—*ppp*) and above the rich B major harmonies the flute-like, pastoral phrases rise and fall in one streaming song. The music is warm, but passionless; here is, in truth, the "child-like" Schubert, in the best sense of the word.[93]

The final and longest variation is, in fact, a variation within a variation. For example, the first statement is in simple triplets (Ex, 14a). And it is embellished: Ex. 14b. Contrary to what some musicologists say, the writers believe that all

against triplets should be played as written, and not as

(see Rhytnm, Chapter VIII).

RONDEAU BRILLANT, Opus 84, No. 2, D 823 ¤ ¤ ¤ ¤ ¤ ¤ ¤ ¤ ¤ ¤ ¤ ¤ ¤ ¤ ¤ ¤ ¤

Composed: ca. Autumn 1825
Manuscript: lost
First publication: Thaddäus Weigl, 1827

As compared to the *Divertissement en forme d'une marche brillante et raisonnée* and the *Andantino varié,* the *Rondeau brillant* is inferior. Neither the melodies nor the harmonies are of sufficient interest to sustain such a long composition. The almost relentless rhythm

is tiring to the listener and, especially, to the secondo player, who seldom shares a melodic line. The loosely constructed form seems not to show Schubert as a formal innovator; instead, it seems to have been arrived at almost by chance.

---

93 M. J. E. Brown, *Schubert's Variations,* 79.

SIX POLONAISES, Opus 61, D 824 ¤ ¤ ¤

Composed: April to June, 1826
Manuscript: Brussels Conservatoire, Archives
First publication: Cappi and Czerny, 1826

These six polonaises are actually comprised of two manuscripts: the first with polonaises 1 through 4, and the second with numbers 5 and 6. The title on the first page is *"Polonaise à 4 mains"*, which leads one to believe that Schubert originally intended to compose only one single polonaise. However, shortly thereafter (we assume, because the same paper was used), three more polonaises were added to the first, whereupon Schubert wrote the Roman numeral "IV" before the word "Polonaise" on that first title page and dated it April 1826. The second manuscript is again titled *"Polonaise"* (numbers 5 and 6) and written between April and June, 1826. Although the autograph is a rough copy, it is apparently the one used by the publisher, because it has the censor's approval written on the first page and dated June 28, 1826, and some notations made by the publisher. Schubert made some corrections on this manuscript prior to publication. All present day editions are basically alike.

We find no mention of any Schubert polonaise by his immediate circle, but Schumann thought well of them, and reviewed the *Six Polonaises,* Opus 61 in the *Frankfurt Allgemeiner Musikalischer Anzeiger* on April 14, 1827:

> Not polonaises in the true sense of the term should be expected here, but short, most original and for the most part very richly melodious little movements for the pianoforte in polonaise rhythm, which however we should have preferred not to be maintained throughout these two books, this having resulted in undue uniformity, hardly compensated for by the other beauties and peculiarities. The execution is difficult at times on account of the

sometimes surprising and sometimes, it may be said, far-fetched modulations. Thoroughly recommended.[94]

One seldom finds any "far-fetched" modulations, even by the standards of that day. Schumann probably referred to the modulations to third-related keys, which appeared frequently in Schubert's works.

Performers should bear in mind the fact that the polonaises are not folk dances, but courtly ceremonial promenades during which society chose to

SIX POLONAISES, Opus 61, D 824

BOOK I.
No. 1.

TRIO

No. 2.

TRIO

No. 3.

TRIO

---

94   O. E. Deutsch, *The Schubert Reader,* 627-628.

exhibit its splendor. The tempo, therefore, must be dignified—never hurried.

GRANDE MARCHE FUNÈBRE
D'ALEXANDRE I, Opus 55, D 859 ¤ ¤

Composed: December 1825
Manuscript: lost
First publication: A. Pennauer, 1826

GRANDE MARCHE HÉROÏQUE
AU SACRE DE NICHOLAS I,
Opus 66, D 885 ¤ ¤ ¤ ¤ ¤ ¤ ¤ ¤ ¤ ¤ ¤ ¤ ¤

Composed: early 1826
Manuscript: lost (except for m. 79-83, primo part, found on manuscript sketch for the four songs, D 877, Statbibliothek, Vienna)

SIX POLONAISES, Opus 61, D 824 (CONTINUED)

First publication: A. Pennauer, 1826

The two marches, Opp. 55 and 66, which Schubert composed on the occasion of the death of Czar Alexander I of Russia and to celebrate the coronation of Czar Nicholas I, were written in late December, 1825 and early 1826. Alexander I (born 1777) had been Czar of Russia from 1801 until his death on December 1, 1825. All editions of both compositions are accurate, as based upon the first edition.

The *Grande Marche funèbre*... follows the usual form AB-trio-AB. The tempo, *andante sostenuto*, should be an appropriately stately pace with two pulses per measure rather than four. The *Grande Marche héroïque* is actually comprised of two A-minor marches and trios. The first of these marches, a *Maestoso*, is in the form of AB-trio, without da capo. The second march, *Allegro giusto*, has the form AB-trio-AB-Coda. The coda is an alteration of motives from the A theme and the trio of the first march, thus unifying the work. Among Schubert's seventeen duet marches, the *Grande Marche héroïque* is the only one with a somewhat uncommon form.

In the first trio and in the *Allegro giusto* sections of the *Grande Marche héroïque* Schubert alludes to Slavic folk style rather than quoting an existing song as he did in the *Divertissement à la hongroise*. The first trio and the *Allegro giusto* are characterized by frequent accents: see Ex. 15, next page. The *Grande Marche funèbre* and *Grande Marche héroïque* sound somewhat orchestral because of the frequent employment of tremolo effects and pizzicato. Indeed, Rimsky-Korsakov quite successfully orchestrated the *Marche héroïque*, which received a performance under the direction of his fellow Russian composer and "Mighty-Five" member, Balakirev, in 1868.

Since these marches are characterized by heavy accents and their texture is often thick, the performers should emphasize the outer voices (primo right hand and secondo left hand) and subdue the inner voices. Schubert has been very specific in his dynamic indications, which encompass a wide range of effects. In the *Grande Marche funèbre* there are "*fff*"s—a mark rarely used by Schubert. The two marches are based upon the same rhythmic motive:

Ex. 15. Schubert, *Grande Marche héroïque,* Opus 66, m. 50-53 and 84-85.

Maestoso

Allegro giusto

and

The duet version of the *Grande Marche funèbre* — played February 8, 1826 — was apparently very successful. Subsequently, July 14, 1826, the *Wiener Zeitung* announced a piano solo version, also published by A. Pennauer. Since the manuscript for this version is lost, its authenticity is debatable; Dr. Deutsch, for one, credits the arrangement to someone other than Schubert. Christa Landon believed that if someone other than Schubert had made the arrangement, nevertheless it must have been done with Schubert's permission, and perhaps under his supervision. The present writers suggest that since the composer remained in constant contact with his publisher, and was in dire need of money, the most likely possiblitity is that the arrangement is by Schubert himself.

DEUX MARCHES CARACTÉRISTI-QUES, Opus 121, D 886 (968b) ¤ ¤ ¤ ¤

Composed: ca. Spring, 1826
Manuscript: lost
First publication: Diabelli and Company, 1829

Dr. Deutsch based his approximate dating for these marches on a June, 1826 letter from Franz von Schober to Eduard von Bauernfeld, in which Schober reported that "Schubert has written four-hand marches, which are said to be very fine."[95] Since all of Schubert's marches except the *Grand Marche héroïque...* and the *Three Marches militaires* (which had

GRANDE MARCHE FUNÈBRE D'ALEXANDRE,
Opus 55, D 859

95 *Ibid.,* 532.

been in Diabelli's possession for several years) had been published by this time, Deutsch assumed that Schober must have been referring to the *Deux Marches caractéristiques.*

Since the exact date is not known, the revised *Schubert: Thematic Catalogue of All His Works* (1978) unfortunately assigns to these marches a new Deutsch numbering of 968b. This seems regrettable since the original number (886) was historically established, and since no evident purpose is served by changing the number. For that matter, none of Schubert's marches (except the *Kindermarsch*) can be dated with any real certainty.

Of the seventeen marches which Schubert composed for piano duet, the two Opus 121 marches are the only ones in 6/8 meter instead of the usual quadruple. They are in the form March-Trio-March *da capo* with an added coda in the second march. In the first march the incessant rhythm,

at M.M. 112-116 to the dotted quarter, creates an exciting yet hypnotic effect. The accents are frequently displaced to the fourth eighth-note; there are piano *subito* effects.

These devices serve as humorous surprise elements. In the trio, slurs often connect the last beat of a measure to the first beat of the next. This interruption of the otherwise constant *staccato* seems to be tongue-in-cheek.

The second *Marche caractéristique* has the same rhythmic constancy in the secondo as the first march but there is more melodic and rhythmic interest. The first part of the A theme consists of two- and three-note slurs with natural emphasis on the first and fourth beats; the second part of the A theme is syncopated by means of accents on the third and sixth beats (see Ex. 16, next page). The phrase which begins at measure 77 and which seems to be building toward a dramatic peak is brought to a humorous conclusion by an unex-

Ex. 16. Schubert, *Marche caractéristique*, Opus 121, No. 2, m. 23-24.

pectedly pallid resolution. Both *Marches caractéristiques* are better performed without repeats, and they should probably not be programmed together since they are so similar.

All editions are basically alike. In a few places the dynamic marks are missing in either the primo or secondo parts. In the second march, at measures 10 and 174, the secondo final eighth-note should be F, not G, to correspond to measures 90 and 254.

VARIATIONS ON A THEME FROM HÉROLD'S "MARIE", Opus 82, No. 1, D 908 ¤ ¤ ¤ ¤ ¤ ¤ ¤ ¤ ¤ ¤ ¤ ¤ ¤ ¤ ¤ ¤ ¤

Composed: February, 1827
Manuscript: Staatsbibliothek of Prussian Culture, Berlin
First publication: Tobias Haslinger, 1827
Dedication: Kajetan Neuhaus, Prof. of Theoretical and Practical Philosophy at Linz

The *Variations on a Theme from Hérold's "Marie"*, Opus 82, No. 1, lend further support to the assumption that Schubert wrote piano duets for financial gain as well as for more creative reasons. The composer clearly meant to "cash in" on the popularity of a current tune, the miller's song "*Was einst vor Jahren*" from the opera *Marie,* successfully performed in Vienna on December 18, 1826. That Schubert's duet was also very popular can be judged from enthusiastic reviews such as the one by G. W. Fink, who praised it in the *Leipzig Allgemeine Musikalische Zeitung* for February 6, 1828: "we declare the *Variations* to be the best of his [Schubert's] that has so far come our way. The theme is at once very cap-

tivatingly treated, yet with the greatest simplicity."[96] This review was probably read by the Leipzig publisher H. A. Probst, because three days later (February 9) he wrote to Schubert:

> I have further taken delight in several four-hand works, e.g. the *Four Polonaises*, Opus 75, and the *Variations on the Miller's Song,* Opus 82, which convince me more and more that it would be easy to disseminate your name throughout the rest of Germany and the North, in which I will gladly lend a hand, considering talents like yours.[97]

Schubert received another letter from Probst written October 6, 1828 asking for "anything understandable '*à 4 mains*' you might be writing, rather like your variations on the miller's song from *Marie*."[98] The variations continued to be popular and were republished as Opus 82, No. 1 (together with the previously unpublished *Variations on an Original Theme in B Flat,* designated Opus 82, No. 2).

Although the *Variations on a Theme from Hérold's "Marie"* enjoyed almost immediate favor, the piece is no longer much admired. Hérold's theme and its harmonization sound perfunctory to twentieth-century ears, and Schubert's treatment is unimaginative as compared to his greater works. Today it seems full of clichés. However, one must respect what he was able to do with an uninspiring theme—Variations IV, VI, VII and VIII are not without interest. Like Schubert's earlier variations, this composition has eight variations, the eighth being considerably longer than the others. The theme is harmonized by a drone bass sug-

VARIATIONS ON A THEME FROM HÉROLD'S "MARIE", Opus 82, No. 1, D 908

THEME
Allegretto

96 *Ibid.,* 733.
97 *Ibid.,* 735.
98 *Ibid.,* 814.

gesting the miller's wheel which is also present in the opera setting. Schubert himself must have been dissatisfied with the repetitious, sequential theme, for he crossed out four measures of the theme and the parallel measures of every variation except numbers V and VII.

Variations IV and VI are aimed at bravura effects; No. VI incorporates chromatic scales throughout. Variation VII, an *Andantino* in 12/8 meter, was originally marked *Allegretto* in 4/4; Schubert changed the tempo and meter as an afterthought, a fact which should influence the performance tempo. The primo in Variation VII includes difficulties wherein the left hand plays between the first and fifth fingers of the right hand (measures 192-194). Schubert wrote at the end of Variation VII "*Segue subito*", but this indication is omitted in all editions except the Henle. In Variation VIII, measure 238, the first editor changed the F-natural of the right hand primo to F^b, and all editions retained this amendation until the Henle edition restored the F-natural which corresponds to the D-natural at the parallel measure 270. Otherwise, all editions are identical.

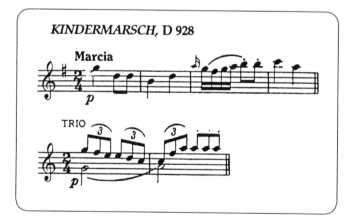

KINDERMARSCH (no opus), D 928 ¤ ¤

Composed: October 11, 1827
Manuscript: Gesellschaft der Musikfreunde [Society of the Friends of Music], Vienna
First publication: J. P. Gotthard, 1870

The *Kindermarsch* was a gift to the small son of Karl Pachler and his wife, Marie, who had entertained him and Johann Baptist Jenger at Graz from September 3 to 20, 1827. Marie Pachler, a friend of Beethoven, had asked Schubert to write a four-hand composition for the occasion of her husband's "feast day" or "name day", November 4, which she intended to play with her son, Faust, who was nearly eight years old. On returning to Vienna Schubert wrote to Frau Pachler: "I shall never forget the friendly lodging... where I have spent the happiest days in a long time."[99] On October 10 Jenger received a letter from young Faust, expressing his wish that Schubert be reminded of his promise to write the duet, since he needed time to practice his part. On October 12, Schubert sent the little piece on to Graz with another letter: "With this I am sending to you the four-hand piece for little Faust.

I fear I shall not earn his applause, since I do not feel that I am exactly made for this kind of composition."[100]

The march has no value of any special significance. Einstein wrote: "Faust Pachler could only manage something very elementary, while the adult player on the left half of the keyboard, in this case his mother, undertook the lion's share."[101] The writers, in fact, find both parts, primo and secondo, nearly alike in simplicity.

The *Kindermarsch* has the traditional form AB trio AB, and the tempo indication is simply "*Marcia*". All editions are faithful to the manuscript.

99 *Ibid.*, 671.
100 *Ibid.*, 679.
101 A. Einstein, *Schubert: A Musical Portrait*, 282.

CHAPTER VII

The Final Year (1828)

At the stroke of midnight the writer Eduard von Bauernfeld interrupted a New Year's Eve party that was being held at Franz von Schober's dwelling, where most of the Schubert circle had gathered. A poem which Bauernfeld had written to be read aloud for the occasion was prophetic; he wrote, "Yet youth must at last succumb to old age." The eighth verse seems to allude to Schubert and his circle of friends as he writes:

> The spells of the poet, the pleasures of
>   singing,
> They too will be gone, be they true as they
>   may;
> No longer will songs in our party be ringing,
> For the singer too will be called away.
> The waters from source to the sea must
>   throng,
> The singer at last will be lost in his song.[103]

At the beginning of the new year most of the friends were back in Vienna. Even Mayrhofer, who had been estranged from the group, came to some of the functions. The reading (literature) parties which had been discontinued resumed with the reading of Romantic writers such as Tieck, Kleist, Goethe and Heine. The Schubertiads continued with ever increasing popularity. Spaun announced his engagement and a Schubertiad was held in honor of the future bride. Like Kupelwieser, Spaun distanced himself from the circle not long after the marriage. He had never approved of the free lifestyle of Schober, and may have felt some relief to be leaving the group.

On February 9 two publishers, Probst of Leipzig and Schott and Sons of Mainz, wrote to Schubert inquiring about the possibility of publishing his works. One of the envelopes was addressed simply to "Franz Schubert, Esq., Famous Composer in Vienna."[104]

As his illness progressed Schubert worked more intensely than ever. He no longer took extended holidays from his beloved city, nor from his all-consuming work. Masterpiece followed masterpiece at a staggering rate; his creative powers were soaring to new heights. In March his *Symphony in C*, later called "The Great", was completed, although it is generally agreed that most of it was written between March 1825 and October 1826. This was Schubert's ninth symphony, and as with Beethoven, his ninth was to be his last. For Schubert it was a period of brilliance in writing for one piano, four hands: the superb *Fantasy in F minor*, Opus 103 was begun in January and completed in April; in May the passionate *Allegro in A Minor* (Opus 144, D 947), called *"Lebensstürme"*, was finished; in June the *Rondo in A Major* (Opus 107, D 951) was completed. He was occupied for the remainder of the summer with the song cycle *Schwanengesang*. In September he composed three solo piano sonatas and in October, sacred music.

One of Schubert's last works was the song *"Der Hirt auf dem Felsen"* for voice, piano and clarinet. It is joyful music, yet it hints that Schubert's greatest suffering was perhaps that he was not really understood, even by his best friends. Fr. Reinhard writes: "The middle section of *'Der Hirt auf dem Felsen'* seems to me very dramatic in describing his utter loneliness, *'ich hier so einsam bin!'* (words which may have been added to the poem by Schubert himself). But then, as in the *Winterreise* his optimism takes over, and the last section reveals his unbroken belief in a better life hereafter, which is also certified by his religious works, which he composed during the same period. *'Der Frühling will kommen!'* [Spring will come!]"[105]

For some time Schubert's friends had encouraged him to present a concert of his own compositions. Bauernfeld had said earlier:

---

103 O. E. Deutsch, *The Schubert Reader*, 703.

104 *Ibid.*, 736.

105 R. van Hoorickx, in a personal letter written to the authors, 1988.

Do you want my advice? Your name is on everybody's lips and each new song of yours is an event! You have also composed the most glorious string quartets and trios—not to mention symphonies! Your friends are delighted with them, but for the moment, no music dealer wants to buy them and the public still has no idea of the beauty and charm which lie hidden in these works. So make an effort, conquer your laziness, give a concert next winter—just your own things, of course.[106]

A request was made of the *Gesellschaft der Musikfreunde* to use their small concert hall on March 21. By some strange coincidence the date was changed to the 26th, which was the first anniversary of Beethoven's death. An effusive announcement was made in the *Theaterzeitung* (March 25, 1828):

Franz Schubert, whose powerfully intellectual, enchantingly lovely and original works have made him the favorite of the entire music public, and which may well secure their creator a more than ephemeral, no, an imperishable name by their genuine artistic value, will perform on 26 March at a private concert.[107]

The concert was not only a great financial success but, for the composer's admirers filling the room, an artistic triumph as well. Franz von Hartmann wrote that evening in his diary "I shall never forget how glorious that was."[108] Bauernfeld wrote, "On the 26th was Schubert's concert. Enormous applause, good receipts."[109]

Schubert and his friends waited for weeks for the newspaper reviews; not one Viennese paper managed to review the concert. Their attention went instead to the astonishing violinist Paganini, who had arrived on March 16 and performed on the 29th, remaining in Vienna for four months. As the *Dresden Abendzeitung* observed:

One hears but one voice within our walls [Vienna], and that shouts "Hear Paganini"....

[At] a private concert given by the favorite composer Schubert... there was unquestionably much that was good... but the minor stars [i.e. Schubert and collaborators] paled before the radiance of this comet [Paganini] in the musical heavens.[110]

The proceeds from the concert and sale of his *Piano Trio*, Opus 100, improved Schubert's financial situation, and ironically, he was able to purchase two very expensive tickets to Paganini's recital for himself and Bauernfeld. However he soon ran short of funds again, and was forced to cancel plans to return to the Pachlers' home in Graz.

Meanwhile, with Kupelwieser and Vogl having married in 1826, Spaun and Sonnleithner about to marry in the spring of 1828, Bauernfeld becoming more involved with his own work, and the Hartmann brothers moving away from Vienna, Schubert's circle had begun to break apart; one of their last outings together was to hear the young Johann Strauss (Sr.) perform at the *Oak Tree Inn*.

On September 1, on the advice of his physician, Ernst Rinna, Schubert changed his residence from Schober's home to the house of his brother Ferdinand, in the Neue Wieden suburb. Apparently Schubert did not intend the move to be permanent, since he left all of his music at Schober's apartment. Ferdinand's house was newly built, and the plaster was not quite dry, which caused the house to be damp—less than ideal conditions for the ill Schubert. On September 5 he attended the first performance of Bauernfeld's comedy *Der Brautwerber* (The Suitor). After the play Schubert, Schwind, Schober, Grillparzer and others went to an inn where they waited for Bauernfeld to join them, but he never arrived—his play having been such a failure that he walked the streets alone until after midnight.

On Saturday, September 27 a large party was given at which Baron von Schönstein sang several Schubert songs, and the composer performed the three new piano (solo) sonatas which were to be his last. At the beginning of October, Schubert, Ferdinand and two friends set out on a walking trip where they visited Eisenstadt some 25 miles from Vienna! Schubert went

---

106 O. E. Deutsch, *Schubert: Memoirs by His Friends*, 237.

107 O. E. Deutsch, *The Schubert Reader*, 751.

108 *Ibid.*, 754.

109 *Ibid.*, 754.

110 *Ibid.*, 756-57.

to Haydn's grave and stood there in silence for quite some time.

Schwind moved to Munich where he was to work as a painter at the Art Academy. This was, no doubt, a great loss to Schubert, who was never to see him again. With Schubert's health rapidly deteriorating, he and his brother made a nostalgic return to the Himmelpfortgrund district where the composer had been born. They ate at the *Rotes Kreuz Inn,* which was a favorite of the Schubert family; there Schubert fell ill.

For the next week the composer's health was stable. He attended a requiem composed by Ferdinand, after which they took a three-hour walk. Schubert, who had been studying Bach fugues and Handel's contrapuntal style, enrolled in a class taught by Vienna's foremost authority on polyphonic writing, Simon Sechter (1788-1867). He had only one lesson before he was finally bedridden.

In the weakened condition caused by syphilis, Schubert now contracted typhoid fever, the same disease which had killed his mother in 1812. Typhoid fever followed a three-week course in three stages: in the first week the patient experienced headaches and extreme shifts in mood; in the second stage the disease would be characterized by rapid physical deterioration; in the third, the patient became delirious, and often died.

At the beginning of the second stage Schubert wrote the last letter he would ever write. This letter, to his dear friend Schober, confided: "Rinna is treating me. If ever I take anything, I bring it up again at once."[111] The letter asked for something to read by the American novelist James Fennimore Cooper. Dr. Rinna, himself, had become ill and so two other doctors were brought in, one an expert on syphilitic care. Schubert also had two nurses and several family members to care for him.

His last hours during the third stage of typhoid fever were made more comfortable by affectionate family members and friends. Spaun visited him on November 16, and Bauernfeld and Lachner the following day. His fever was so high that he became delirious and had hallucinations. He

believed he was already underground; Ferdinand tried to assure him he was still in his bed. Schubert replied "No, it's not true. Beethoven does not lie here." Because of this statement, Ferdinand believed that his brother wanted to be buried next to Beethoven—which was done. Schubert remained unconscious, but at three o'clock on Wednesday, November 19, the composer turned toward the wall and feebly said his last words, "Here, here is my end." He was thirty-one years old.

THE PIANO DUETS OF 1828.

FANTASY IN F MINOR, Opus 103, D 940 ¤ ¤ ¤ ¤ ¤ ¤ ¤ ¤ ¤ ¤ ¤ ¤ ¤ ¤ ¤ ¤

Composed: April, 1828
Manuscript: Nationalbibliothek, Vienna
First publication: Diabelli & Co., March, 1829
Dedication: Karoline Esterházy

In January, 1828, the first sketch of the *Fantasy in F minor,* Opus 103, was begun. This incomplete draft is owned by the Frederick R. Koch Foundation in New York. The *Fantasy* was completed in April of 1828.

FANTASY IN F MINOR, Opus 103, D 940

111 *Ibid.,* 819-20.

Kreissle von Hellborn, the first biographer of Schubert, believed that Diabelli and Company had "arranged" the dedication to Karoline Esterházy; however, a letter to the publisher Schott, written by Schubert, stated that his *Fantasy* was to be dedicated to her.[112] Eduard von Bauernfeld stated in his memoirs (1869) that "[Schubert] was, in fact, head over ears in love with one of his pupils, a young Countess Esterházy, to whom he also dedicated one of his most beautiful piano pieces, the *Fantasy in F minor* for piano duet."[113]

Eduard von Bauernfeld in his diary, dated May 9, 1828, mentioned hearing the first performance of the work by Schubert and Franz Lachner. It made such an impression that neither Bauernfeld nor Lachner ever forgot the first hearing. Years later at a dedication of the statue of Schubert in City Park, Vienna, on May 15, 1872, Lachner asked Bauernfeld, "Do you still remember how Schubert and I played you his new Fantasie for piano duet for the first time?"[114]

Schubert was the first composer to fuse the compound four-movement sonata into a continuous work. The *Fantasy in F minor* is comprised of four movements; each of its sections corresponds to a movement in the traditional sonata-allegro form. The *Fantasy* represents a continuation and further development of Beethoven's innovations of structure; he (Beethoven) had already expanded the development sections and codas of his sonatas and symphonies and brought the movements into close relationship by means of cyclic devices. The themes of Beethoven's later works were more lyrical than the jagged motives characteristic of his early works; he increasingly used fugal techniques in sections of sonata movements. The frequent tempo changes within the movements suggest that Beethoven's concept of the sonata form became more and more similar to that of a fantasy. The cyclic form later culminated in Franz Liszt's tone poems and in his *Piano Sonata in B minor*. The difference between Schubert's use of cyclic form and that of Liszt is that Schubert retained the theme in its original form throughout, while Liszt transformed the theme continuously.

The unifying factor in the *Fantasy in F minor* is the interval of an ascending fourth. Not only does the interval appear in the opening theme, but also in the B theme, the transitional theme, the opening theme of

section II, the opening theme of section III, and most insistently in both the principal and secondary subjects of the fugal section IV. A list of the themes and their formal organization follows (see facing page for musical illustrations — Ex. 17):

I. Allegro molto moderato
  A A[1] A B A B A transitional theme
II. Largo
  C D C
III. Allegro vivace
  E F E
IV. Tempo I
  A A[1] A B (Fugue) A

The opening theme should be played at approximately M.M. 104-108 to the quarter-note, although one often hears much slower performances. This faster tempo contributes to a feeling of forward motion and gives more intensity to the upper notes in the melody; it also prevents a heavy-handedness in the secondo part. After the dramatic pause at measure 37 the tempo could be subtly increased as a means of accentuating the brighter quality of the A theme in major. The altered tempo further serves to bridge the contrast between the quiet, leisurely opening and the more agitated B theme.

There are certain passages which cannot be played without adaptation. At measures 58-61 and 84-87 only the Henle edition is faithful to the manuscript. In all

[TEXT CONTINUED PAGE 77]

ILLUSTRATION PAGE 74: the first sketch of the *Fantasy in F minor*, Op. 103, January 1828. This incomplete draft is located at The Pierpont Morgan Library in New York.

ILLUSTRATIONS PAGES 75-76: these are pages (primo and secondo) from the completed manuscript of the *Fantasy in F minor*, Op. 103. At the beginning of the fugal section one can see that Schubert orginally wrote *"Più mosso"*, but later crossed it out. (Nationalbibliothek, Vienna)

---

112 *Ibid.*, 739.

113 O. E. Deutsch, *Schubert: Memoirs by His Friends*, 233.

114 *Ibid.*, 242.

Ex. 17. Schubert, *Fantasy in F minor*, Opus 103, D 940

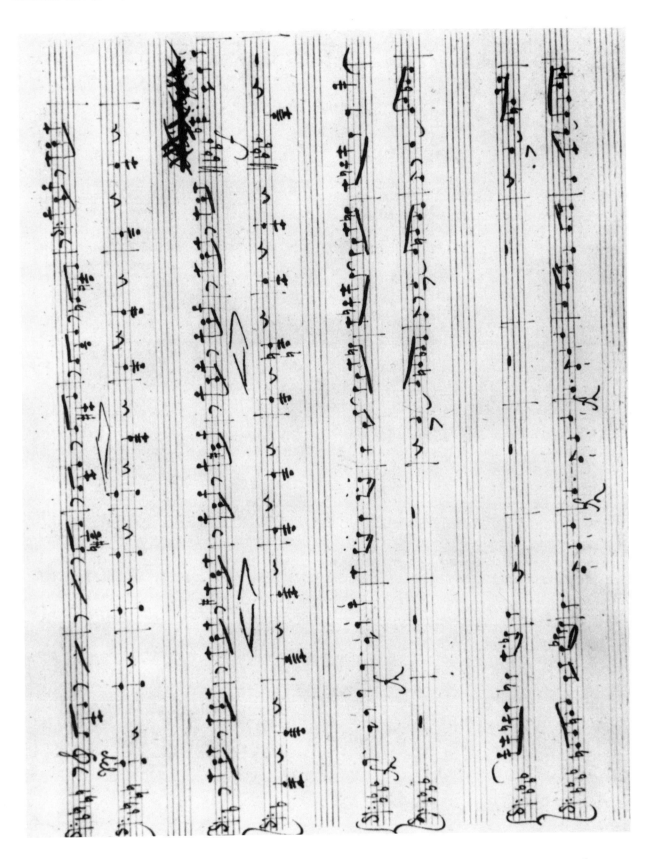

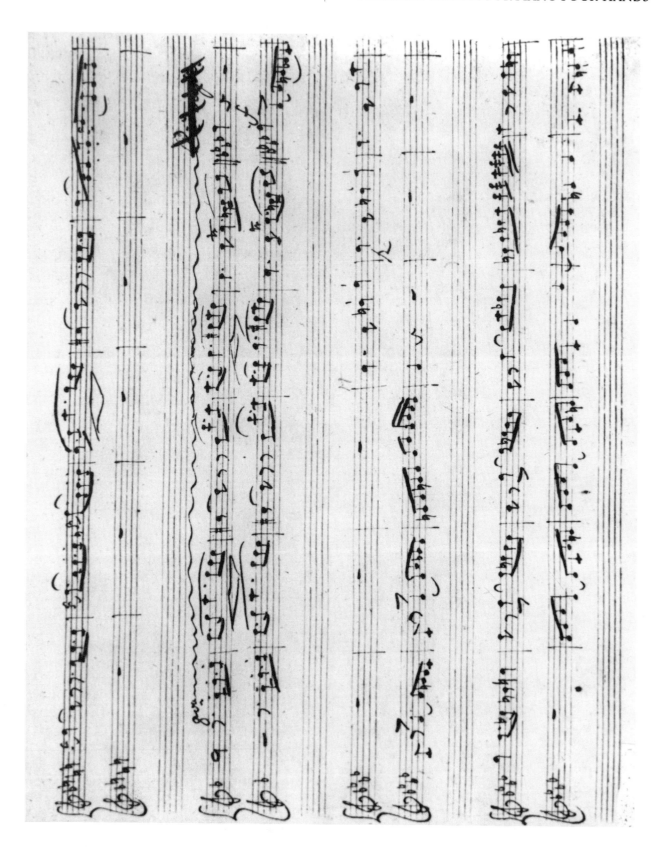

other publications the eighth-notes in the primo part, left hand have been omitted:

This was done because the secondo right hand pattern interferes, sharing the same F. Since this motive is taken directly from the B theme it should remain intact. The secondo right hand pattern (measure 57) should begin on the lower F rather than the upper (as Schubert originally intended, according to his sketch), thus minimizing the problem of the shared note. The secondo player should execute these measures non-legato and with a very low wrist in order to accommodate the left hand of the primo player.

In examining the sketch of January, 1828 and the completed manuscript of April (see illustrations, pages 74-76), one finds justification for a tempo which is slightly faster than that of most performances today, particularly in section II in which the Largo should be regarded in its literal sense, meaning "broad" rather than "extremely slow". In the sketch Schubert first marked the tempo "Andante molto," later crossing out the "molto". He also changed the rhythm from

in the sketch to

in the final manuscript. One must choose a tempo which is appropriate for both the C theme and the D theme.

The early sketch of section III was marked *"Allegro"* (later changed to *"Allegro vivace"*); it included a middle section, *"Tempo di marcia"*. In the final manuscript the march was discarded and the *"con delicatezza"* remained as a trio. The tempo of section III may be interpreted as being quite fast with one basic pulse per measure, or it may be played as a robust *Ländler* with a definite three-beat feeling. The writers prefer a moderate M.M. 80 (to the dotted half-note). At measures 206-207 and 355-356 all editions except the Henle have changed the secondo right hand to

but it should be

which is according to the manuscript and parallel to the other appearances of the E theme. The primo left hand must be altered to accommodate the upper F; the writers suggest:

The entire fugue of section IV seems to press forward with ever-increasing intensity (with the exception of a *piano subito* in the seventeenth measure of the movement). While it is effective to play the beginning of the fugue in a stately manner, the numerous appearances of the subject may become labored and pedantic if a steady tempo is maintained throughout. Schubert's increasing use of chromatic triplet figures in both hands of the primo and secondo seems to warrant an increase in speed. This natural tendency to accelerate is also supported by the fact that in the final manuscript Schubert marked the fugue *"più mosso"*, but this mark was later crossed out.

The first edition, by Diabelli, is faithful to Schubert's final manuscript throughout.

DUO IN A MINOR ("LEBENSSTÜRME"), Opus 144, D 947 ¤ ¤ ¤ ¤ ¤ ¤ ¤ ¤ ¤ ¤ ¤

Composed: May, 1828
Manuscript: lost
First publication: Diabelli & Company, 1840

One month after the completion of the *Fantasy in F minor* Schubert wrote a one-movement piece in sonata-allegro form. It has been believed that he intended it to be the first movement of a sonata; the

DUO IN A MINOR ("LEBENSSTÜRME"),
Opus 144, D 947

Allegro ma non troppo

Ex. 18. Schubert, *Duo in A minor,* m. 1-4.

Ex. 19. Schubert, *Duo in A minor,* m. 12-17.

Ex. 20. Schubert, *Duo in A minor,* m. 89-95.

Ex. 21. Schubert, *Duo in A minor*, m. 104-08.

Ex. 22. Schubert, *Duo in A minor,* m. 138-41.

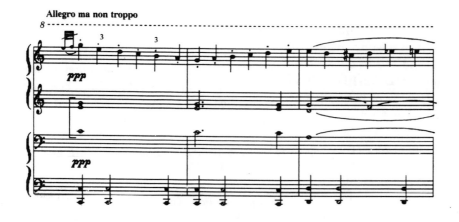

[Example completed on page 82, below.]

Rondo in A, which will be discussed later in this chapter, might have been the final movement. This "first movement", the *Duo in A minor*, was published by Diabelli with the title *"Lebensstürme—Characteristisches Allegro"*, which is probably editorial. The *Gesamtausgabe* retained the title *"Lebensstürme"*; the Peters edition calls it *"Allegro"*; Dr. Deutsch referred to it as a *Sonata Movement for Piano Duet*; Ferdinand Schubert's listing of his brother's works refers to it as *Duo in A minor*, as do the Henle and the present writers.

The *Duo in A minor* is a monumental work—the culmination of Schubert's compositional techniques. It contains wide use of Neapolitan sixth chords, third relations, chromatic shifts, rhythms of two-against-three, et cetera. Dramatic effects are achieved through repeated chords, tremolos, and "grand pauses".

The most distinguishing aspect of the *Duo in A minor* is Schubert's new approach to sonata-allegro form. He has discarded the established bi-thematic exposition and has replaced it with principal and secondary theme groups, each having two themes. The opening theme, which has great breadth and nobility, is introductory in style (see Ex. 18, previous page). It is followed by the lyrical theme of Ex. 19. The second theme group begins at measure 89 with sustained chords over a pulsating bass (Ex. 20), and is followed by a theme derived from the 12th measure (Ex. 21). An expanded codetta (beginning at measure 183) recalls motives from the first theme group and concludes with an entirely new theme (measure 231). The vigorous development section (beginning at measure 260) utilizes only the first theme group. The recapitulation (measure 347) is slightly abbreviated; it is followed by a coda (measure 577). This is the first duet composed of theme groups; Schubert had previously used this technique in the *Symphony in C Major*, D 944, and in the *Piano Trio in E^b,* Opus 100, D 929. This form was later used by most of the Romantic composers.

The *Duo in A minor* is one of the most difficult four-hand compositions but one of the most rewarding to perform. Both parts are of equal importance; themes and theme fragments are distributed evenly among the four hands. In measure 115 the turn *(Doppelschlag)* in the primo should be on the second beat, in accordance with the first edition, not on the third beat, as in the Henle and the Peters editions. All editions have been well marked with regard to dynamics. The second "theme group" is *ppp*, a mark which was seldom used and which should be carefully heeded. The writers suggest that at measures 138-152 and again at measures 458-472 the secondo right hand play the chords of the primo left hand; this allows for greater agogic freedom and avoids ensemble problems. (See Ex. 22, preceding page.)

FUGUE IN E MINOR for Piano or Organ, Opus 152, D 952 ¤ ¤ ¤ ¤ ¤ ¤ ¤ ¤ ¤ ¤

Composed: June 3 (or November), 1828
Manuscript: Paris Conservatoire
First publication: Diabelli & Company, ca. 1844

One month before Schubert's death, Josef Lanz (a Viennese piano teacher) and Schubert called upon the renowned theorist and teacher of counterpoint Simon Sechter to arrange for Schubert to study counterpoint. A lesson time was agreed upon and Friedrich Wilhelm Marpurg's "Dissertation on Fugue" was chosen as a text. Due to Schubert's failing health the study project was barely begun. Because Schubert wrote only one independent fugue and because of his desire to study with Sechter it was concluded that Schubert felt deficient in contrapuntal technique. It must be remembered, however, that the *"Unfinished"* Symphony, the *"Wanderer"* Fantasy, and the four-hand *Fantasy in F minor* contain very fine contrapuntal sections. The fact that Schubert, when he was already an established composer, sought formal study is a credit to his musical integrity.

The *Fugue in E minor* for Piano or Organ was reported to have been composed at Baden near Vienna on June 3, 1828. Dr. Deutsch accepted without question the inscription "3 June 1828" by an unknown hand (Franz Lachner's?) on the manuscript. Lachner related this story of the fugue in or around 1835:

FUGUE IN E MINOR for Piano or Organ, **Opus 152, D 952**

Allegro moderato

Ex. 23. Schubert, *Fugue in E minor*, m. 85-87.

[*Example completed on page 82, below.*]

In the year 1828, on 3 June, Schubert and I were invited by the editor of the *Modezeitung*, Herr Schickh, on an excursion to Baden near Vienna; in the evening Schickh said to us: we will go to Heiligenkreuz first thing tomorrow morning in order to hear the famous organ there; perhaps you could compose some little thing and perform it there? Schubert proposed that we each compose a fugue, and towards midnight we had both finished. The next day—at 6 o'clock in the morning—we drove to Heiligenkreuz, where both fugues were performed in the presence of several monks from the monastery.[115]

The music historian Robert Winter has suggested that the fugue was written earlier than 1828, because this manuscript shares a type of paper with seventeen other manuscripts written by Schubert between September 1826 and May 1827. Fr. Reinhard has discovered that this fugue subject appears twice in exercises connected with Schubert's study of fugue and counterpoint with Sechter; he is of the opinion that "this fugue was, in fact, Schubert's first (and last!) exercise which he made for Sechter in the beginning of November 1828, and it would therefore also be his very last composition!"[116] The phrase "for Piano or Organ" was added by the first publisher; Schubert's manuscript gives no indication as to which instrument he preferred. Lachner's letter and the inclusion of long pedal points substantiate the fact that the *Fugue in E minor* is, indeed, an organ composition. It is Schubert's only work for the organ and his only independent fugue. It has been included in publications of Schubert's piano, four-hand works as a matter of tradition which began with Diabelli (Diabelli identified the work as "for piano or organ"; subsequent publishers may have included it among the "complete duets" thinking of works for keyboard and not just for piano).

There is a passage near the end of the composition which is remarkable for its advanced chromaticism (see Ex. 23, above).

The Diabelli, *Gesamtausgabe*, Peters, and Henle editions are generally in agreement. All have the tempo indication *Allegro moderato*; the manuscript has no such indication, nor any phrase or dynamic marks.

---

115 *Ibid.*, 195-96.

116 R. van Hoorickx, "Fugue and Counterpoint in Schubert's Piano Music", *Piano Quarterly* (Spring, 1979), p. 51.

RONDO IN A MAJOR, Opus 107, D 951

Composed: June, 1828
Manuscript: Deutsche Staatsbibliothek, East Berlin
First publication: Artaria & Company, 1828

Alfred Einstein called Schubert's *Rondo in A Major* "the apotheosis of all Schubert compositions for four hands."[117] This indicates the importance that at least one great scholar placed on the work. It is safe to say that it is the best of the three rondos. In the *Rondo in A Major* Schubert's innovations astonished and bewildered Schumann and his friends. There is a romantic, improvisatory feeling which stems from Schubert's decorative and free treatment of the themes. The rondo, which is dated June, 1828, was immediately sent to the publisher Artaria and Company, Vienna, who announced it to the public on December 11, 1828, as the "Grand Rondeau", Opus 107. Because Artaria accepted the composition so quickly after its completion, some believe that the work was commissioned by Domenico Artaria, the owner of the publishing firm.

If it were not for the fact that Artaria donated his Schubert manuscripts to the Deutsche Staatsbibliothek (East Berlin) the writers would question whether this manuscript is the final copy used by Artaria for publication. It would seem to be a mere link in the creative process rather than a fair (final) copy. There are several passages which Schubert crossed out and rewrote; there is evidence of much difficulty in accomplishing the modulation from C major to the return of the principal theme in A major. Beginning at measure 161 there are two pages of primo sketching which he later abandoned. The manuscript and the first edition differ; many ornaments are missing in the first and subsequent publications but are restored in the Henle edition.

The form of the *Rondo* is A B A C A B A, the C subject being a variant of the B theme. By this use of what are essentially developments of earlier material, the *Rondo* is thus made to resemble a sonata form.

There are two interpretive suggestions concerning Schubert's accents in the *Rondo*. The first concerns the accented weak beats or anacruses within the principal theme. These accents should lend emphasis, but not to the exclusion of the normal emphasis on the first beat of each measure. Secondly, Schubert clearly wrote accents (⟩) over the second quarter-note chord in the secondary theme (measure 70 and in analogous measures). Since literal interpretation of this mark would seem musically incongruous, the writers believe that Schubert used this means of indicating that he wanted the tension to extend from the first phrase to the second.

In the final year of Schubert's life he composed piano duets remarkable in quality and quantity: the *Fantasy in F minor*, the *Duo in A minor* ("*Lebensstürme*"), and the *Rondo in A Major*. We find new approaches to melody, dynamic range, and form. While Schubert's melodic writing remained essentially lyrical he developed an instrumental melodic style through embellishments, wider range, and short, repeated fragments. The opening themes of the *Fantasy* and the *Duo* are examples of this melodic style. Schubert's desire to widen the dynamic range is evidenced by his use of *fff* and *ppp*.

Nineteenth-century critics, some of whom took Beethoven and Mendelssohn as their models for judging form, said that Schubert's greatest weakness lay in his inability to use the sonata-allegro form successfully. By contrast and more recently, Schubert has come to be admired for having developed an individual use of the sonata-allegro form even while under the shadow of Beethoven. The Schubert scholar Maurice J. E. Brown aptly defined Schubert's musical objective in regard to form:

> He wished to feel intensely, and to express to the utmost of his powers, the present moment in his music: not for its significance as a link with what has gone and what is to come, but for its momentary effect as sound, as pleasure for the listener. This is not to say for one moment that he was indifferent to the structural

RONDO IN A MAJOR, Opus 107, D 951

Allegretto quasi Andantino

---

117 A. Einstein, *Schubert: A Musical Portrait*, 282.

necessities of sonata-form, in fact, the contrary has been urged where his purely transitional passages are concerned; but drive and cohesion... are not Schubert's first consideration.[118]

[Continued from Ex. 22, page 78 above.]

[Continued from Ex. 23, page 80, above.]

---

118 M. J. E. Brown, *Schubert: A Critical Biography,* 196-97.

CHAPTER VIII

General Performance Considerations

SCHUBERT'S OWN PERFORMANCE STYLE.

In formulating a performance style for Schubert's duets it is well to consider his own style and preferences. There are approximately forty historical documents which mention Schubert's piano playing as an accompanist, soloist, or duettist. From these writings we can glean a general idea of his pianistic accomplishments and his attitudes toward interpretation.

At the age of eight Schubert began to study piano with his brother Ignaz who relates:

> I was much astonished when, after only a few months, he informed me that he now had no further use for my teaching and would be quite able to get on by himself. And indeed he went so far in a short time that I myself had to acknowledge him as a master far surpassing me and no longer to be caught up with [by me].[119]

At the Schubert Museum in Vienna there are eight report cards from Schubert's student days at the Stadtkonvikt. On the first card (April 17, 1809) his piano grade was "*gut*" (good), but on all subsequent cards he was rated "*sehr gut*" (very good).

Sophie Müller, a leading actress and amateur pianist of Vienna, called Schubert one of "our most excellent pianoforte players."[120] Another description of Schubert's pianistic ability was written by Ferdinand Schubert in the *Neue Zeitschrift für Musik* (April 23–May 3, 1839):

> Although Schubert never represented himself as a (piano) virtuoso, any connoisseur who had the chance of hearing him in the private circles will nevertheless attest that he knew how to treat this instrument with *mastery* and in a quite *individualistic manner,* so that a great specialist in music, to whom he once played his last sonatas, exclaimed: "Schubert, I almost admire your playing even more than your compositions!"[121]

Documents concerning Schubert's personal preferences in interpretation are few. He once praised a performer for being "an extraordinarily fluent pianist" but was disappointed that she was "lacking in true and pure expression."[122] Schubert's friend and duet partner Joseph von Gahy said that to Schubert "clean, fluent playing"[123] was of the utmost importance. Perhaps the most revealing document concerning Schubert's pianistic style is a letter written by Schubert while visiting in Steyr on July 25, 1825:

> With the aid of a gallant pianoforte player I produced my four-hand Variations and Marches with notable success.... Several people assured me that the keys became singing voices under my hands, which, if true, pleases me greatly, since I cannot endure the *accursed chopping* [italics added] in which even distinguished pianoforte players indulge and which delights neither the ear nor the mind.[124]

SCHUBERT'S PIANO.

The writers have had the opportunity, on several occasions, to play Schubert's piano, which is now in the Schubert Museum, Vienna. Built by Konrad Graf

---

119 O. E. Deutsch, *The Schubert Reader,* 921.

120 *Ibid.,* 761.

121 *Ibid.,* 915.

122 *Ibid.,* 60.

123 O. E. Deutsch, *Schubert: Memoirs by His Friends,* 176.

124 O. E. Deutsch, *The Schubert Reader,* 435.

around 1810, the instrument has a wooden frame, a narrow range, and thin, low-tension strings which are struck by leather-covered hammers. It has a thin, clear, delicate sound which somewhat resembles that of a harpsichord. The action is very easy. Although the instrument is in need of tuning and repair, one can hear approximately the same sound which Schubert heard.

Considering the documents relating to Schubert's performance style and the kind of instrument on which he performed, the following general conclusions can be drawn.

Duettists should avoid thick sonorities, which were foreign to Schubert's instrument. In order to approximate the thin, transparent sound of the early nineteenth-century piano the inner voices, especially in the lower register, should be subdued. Balance must be determined by listening to all four hands—it cannot be learned individually. Schubert admired the feeling of one-ness in ensemble. He wrote concerning a performance in which he accompanied the renowned singer Johann Michael Vogl (1768-1840): "The manner in which Vogl sings and the way I accompany, as though we were one at such a moment, is something quite new and unheard of."[125]

In view of the limitations of the early piano, duettists should scale down their dynamic range except in the later works, during which time a more resonant piano was being anticipated.

> From 1800 piano makers throughout Europe were largely occupied in meeting the demand for a more powerful instrument, which would be suitable for larger concert halls and capable of standing up to the bigger orchestras that were becoming more common. They gradually increased the tension (and hence the size) of strings, and did their best to design frames that would be strong enough to support them.[126]

PHRASING AND SLURS.

Phrasing and slurs in Schubert's manuscripts are marked only occasionally; he obviously expected the publisher or performer to supply them. This lack of

consistency and detail in Schubert's manuscripts led musicians of the nineteenth century to think that he was careless in his writing. Actually, he was following the example of his predecessors, some of whom were even less exact in their phrase marks. The music historian Frederick Dorian writes: "The scarcity of phrasing marks is explained by the history of interpretation. Most of the great composers prior to the nineteenth century supervised their own performances and thus could enforce their wishes personally. In most cases, important instructions were given verbally by the composers to their singers and instrumentalists."[127] As late as 1834 phrases were not always clearly marked. Pierre Baillot states in *L'art du violon*:

> Slight separations [between phrases], such as rests of short duration, are not always indicated by the composer. The player must therefore provide them, when he sees that it is necessary, by letting the last note of the phrase die away. Indeed, in certain cases he must even let it end shortly before the completion of its normal duration.[128]

Schubert's slurs are evolved from string bow-markings (which indicate articulation rather than phrasing), and usually end before the bar line ♩♪♪♪ | ♩. This rather ambiguous symbol could be interpreted as either non-legato ♫♫ ♪] ♩ or legato ♫♫ |♩ |. One can generally say that if the slur connects only two notes, it implies emphasis on the first note and a semi-staccato on the second. If the slur connects a group of notes but ends before the bar, it is preferable to extend the phrase to include the note following the bar.

DYNAMICS AND ACCENTS.

Prior to 1824 Schubert's dynamic marks encompassed a range from *ppp* to *ff*; from 1824 on they were expanded to include *fff*. (He often placed his dynamic marks slightly early, i.e., ahead of the first notes to be affected.) Care must be taken in the extreme dynamic ranges: the *fff* passages should not result in "accursed chopping"; in the *ppp* passages the melodic line

---

125 *Ibid.*, 458.

126 H. Ferguson, *Style and Interpretation*, Vol. III, 7.

127 F. Dorian, *The History of Music in Performance* (New York, 1942), 161.

128 P. Baillot, *L'art du Violon*, cited by F. Dorian, *op. cit.*, 163.

Ex. 24. Schubert, *Rondo in A major,* D 951, m. 68-73.

Allegretto quasi Andantino

Ex. 25. Schubert, *Grand Sonata in B*^{b}, Opus 30, D 617, Andante con moto, m. 1-2.

Andante con moto

should remain clear, in a soloist-accompanist relationship, as it were.

Schubert was not consistent in his use of various types of accent marks: *fz, ffz, fp, sf,*

sfp. His accent marks and diminuendos were practically the same size and therefore difficult to distinguish, but the accent marks generally sloped upward

He usually used the abbreviation "decresc." rather than the symbol, until his later years. The first and subsequent editors often changed the accents which were on strong beats to diminuendos

Schubert frequently placed accents over notes that are not emphasized metrically. These accents may be interpreted as "compensatory"; they do not necessarily imply a louder sound than the metrically strong beat(s), rather, they remind the player to sustain intensity. In Ex. 24, above, one would normally expect a nuance and a clear distinction between the phrases since, at the semi-cadence, the harmonic tension is

lessened and the phrase line ends. Here, however, Schubert seems to want a long line, using the accent to prevent a relaxation on the last note of the measure.

In Ex. 25, Schubert placed an accent on the fourth beat in order to compensate for the short slurs. Had he not added the accent mark the line might have been played

This "lifting" of the fourth beat would have resulted in weakness, because the tension inherent in the major supertonic seventh (on the fourth beat) pulls toward a resolution to the dominant on the first beat of measure 2. In the main theme of Ex. 26 (next page), Schubert placed accents over the weak beats to prevent their being played as

The reason for slightly emphasizing the weaker beats is borne out by the importance of the off-beat in the variations which follow.

STACCATOS — DOTS AND STROKES.

Schubert was inconsistent in his use of dots ( ) and strokes ( ). Because of the inconsistency in his use of two different marks, early editors changed both symbols to the wedge (▼);

Ex. 26. Schubert, *Introduction and Variations...*, Opus 82, No. 2, D 603, m. 35-36; 51-52; 67-68.

Ex. 27. Schubert, *Fantasy in F minor*, D 940, m. 552-55.

Ex. 28. Schubert, *Fantasy in F minor*, D 940, m. 48-49.

later editors (except Henle and Bärenreiter) have chosen to use dots throughout, with rare exceptions. In the manuscripts of Schubert's last years he seems to have used the dot in semi-staccato or *leggiero* passages and the stroke for accents and combinations of accent and staccato. In Ex. 27, above, the music seems to demand that the strokes should be interpreted as accents without staccato because great sonority is required at this climactic point. In this same *Fantasy*, the strokes used in the B theme (Ex. 28) would be both ac-

cented and staccato in order to contrast with the lyrical principal theme.

PEDALING AND FINGERING.

Except for two pedal marks in the *Sonata in C*, Op. 140, D 812, Schubert has marked neither pedaling nor fingering. Since each player is generally confined to a narrow range of the piano, notes can usually be connected through legato fingering and with less pedal

Ex. 29. Schubert, *Marche caractéristique*, No. 1, D 886, m. 69-73.

Allegro vivace

than in solo playing. Since every piano and every hall has a different acoustical quality, the performer must adapt his pedaling to the situation at hand, keeping in mind Schubert's preference for "clean" playing.

TEMPO MODIFICATION.

Although Schubert admired "expressive" playing, a style that implies agogic freedom,[129] his manuscripts have Italian tempo indications generally at the beginning of major sections, rarely within sections. Ritards are infrequently indicated; only once does Schubert write accelerando—in measure 298 of the *Variations on a Theme from Hérold's "Marie"*. To find advice as to tempo and agogic freedom we may turn to Karl Czerny (1791-1857), a contemporary of Schubert who, in his *Complete Theoretical and Practical Piano Forte School* (commonly referred to as the *"Clavierschule"*), gives rules concerning ritardando and accelerando.

The Ritardando, according to the generally established Rule, is much more frequently employed than the Accelerando, because the former is less likely to disfigure the character of the piece, than the too frequent hurrying on in the speed of movement. We may ritard the time most advantageously

    a. In those passages which contain the return to the principal subject.
    b. In those passages which lead to some separate member of a melody.

    c. In those long and sustained notes which are to be struck with particular emphasis, and after which quicker notes are to follow.
    d. At the transition into another species of time, or into another movement, different in speed from that which preceded it.
    e. After a pause.
    f. At the Diminuendo of a preceding very lively passage; as also in brilliant passages, when there suddenly occurs a trait of melody to be played *piano* and with much delicacy.
    g. In embellishments, consisting of many quick notes, which we are unable to force into the degree of movement first chosen.
    h. Occasionally also, in the chief crescendo of a strongly marked section, leading to an important passage or to the close.
    i. In very humorous, capricious, and fantastic passages, in order to heighten the character so much the more.
    k. Lastly, almost always where the Composer has indicated an espressivo; as also
    l. At the end of very long shake which forms a pause or Cadenza, and which is marked diminuendo.[130]

Tempo alteration is appropriate in much of Schubert's music, but its degree and frequency are a personal matter. Some specific instances in which tempo alterations enhance Schubert's music are as follows:

---

129 *Agoge:* rate of speed, tempo. *Agogic:* relating to variations in tempo within a piece or movement.
130 C. Czerny, *Complete Theoretical and Practical Piano Forte School*, Vol. III (London, 1839), 33-34.

Ex. 30. Schubert, *Fantasy in F minor*, D 940 (Coda), m. 256-59.

Ex. 31. Schubert, *Grand March and Trio*, Op. 40, No. 5, D 819, m. 97-99.

1) Motivic repetitions should be played with agogic freedom to avoid monotony. (See Ex. 29.)

2) Cadenzas in Schubert's duets are not necessarily passages for technical display; they are *ad libitum* sections which lend a feeling of improvisation to the composition.

3) A variation of the original motive may be slightly broadened to emphasize alterations. (See Ex. 30.)

4) Slow sections should be played with agogic freedom in order to help the music breathe. The first mention of *rubato* came from the Italian singer Pietro Tosi who, in 1723, used the term to describe a *vocal* style. For Schubert, whose melodies were usually vocally conceived, the tension and relaxation within phrases is paramount; tempo modification is one of the features inherent in tension and relaxation.

Ex. 32. Schubert, "*Erstarrung*", D 911, m. 24.

Ich

Ex. 33. Schubert, "*Wasserfluth*", D 911, m. 1-4.

5) A wide dynamic range within a short span of time must sometimes be accommodated by tempo alteration. (See Ex. 31.) In this example the tempo must be held back on the fourth beat of measure 98 to allow the sound to diminish in preparation for the third-related pianissimo chord which follows.

Rubato is not usually advisable in sections with complicated rhythmic patterns, syncopation, *Siciliano* rhythms, et cetera. It is also inappropriate for marches, quick dances and contrapuntal works.

The metronome was perfected in 1816 by Johann Maelzel (1772-1838). Schubert, unlike Beethoven, did not make use of metronome marks in his four-hand manuscripts, nor were they added by his publishers. As a Romantic composer he may have felt that metronome marks were too restrictive, since tempos depend upon variable factors such as the quality of the instrument, the acoustical condition of the room, and the artistic temperament of the performer.

ORNAMENTS.

The five ornaments used in Schubert's duet literature are as follows:

1) the pralltriller ( ),

which usually comes before the beat, is short
using only three notes. In fast tempos it is easier to play only .

2) the trill *(tr)*, whose length is determined by the duration of the note, is generally played

Over a short note a trill may have only three notes, the first of which falls on the beat, as follows:

3) The turn (*Doppelschlag*)
which is written on the note is played on the beat,

Turns which are written *after* the note are played
or and

4) The appoggiaturas ( ) or ( )

used by Schubert are generally to be played short and quickly, coming before the main note.

5) Schubert used the arpeggio ( )

Ex. 34. Schubert, *Eight Variations on a French Song*, Opus 10, D 624, Var. 1, m. 1-2.

Allegretto

only in Variations II, III and IV of the *"Marie"* Variations. This sign indicates that the chord should be broken upward. It should be remembered that "Ornaments are delicate, instinctive things; if they are not ornamental they are worse than useless, and anxiety about the right way to play them must never be allowed to cloud a performer's sense of the underlying structure of the music they adorn."[131]

RHYTHM.

The question persists concerning the rhythmic figure:

in the music of Schubert. There are two approaches, each with musical advocates defending them. The first approach is to play in a strictly mathematical way, i.e. with the sixteenth-note falling after the last note of the triplet; the second way is to bring in the sixteenth-note early, exactly with the last note of the triplet.

As we have said, there are approximately forty documents which mention Schubert's own performances, but none are specific enough to include the problem just mentioned. One might expect to find some clue regarding Schubert's own interpretation of this rhythmic figure in the scores which he used for teaching the Esterházy daughters (his only piano students, as far as we know) - but these scores have long been destroyed or lost. Our only sources are the manuscripts themselves. These, unfortunately are of little help, since his script was hurriedly done and therefore inconsistent. This is understandable, since Schubert wrote over fifteen hundred works in a fifteen-year period; neatness and meticulous details cannot be expected.

There are a few examples which are cited by musicologists to substantiate their theory that should be played as

measure 24 in the right hand accompaniment to *"Erstarrung"* and measure 3 in the right hand accompaniment to *"Wasserfluth"*; see Exx. 32 and 33, preceding page. The manuscripts of these pieces from the song cycle *Winterreisse* presently exist in "rough copy" only; the "fair copy" (finished copy) which was used for the publication no longer exists. We must therefore rely on the first publisher, Tobias Haslinger, as our source. From among Schubert's compositions, one can give numerous examples in which the first publishers made deliberate changes from the manuscript, adding or deleting measures and/or sections, changing keys, adding titles, *et cetera*, not to mention the inadvertent omission of sharps, flats, naturals, rests, and mistakes in the notes themselves.

It was common practice until the 1850s for engravers to align the sixteenth note with the last note of a triplet (Ex. 34, above). By the same token, publishers often placed whole-notes in the middle of a measure:

expecting the performer to play it on the first beat.

The musicologist Franz Eibner says: "In works of Schubert with triplet accompaniment it is clear that the rhythm  is to be understood as

131 T. Dart, *The Interpretation of Music* (London, 1954), 102.

Ex. 35. Schubert, *Impromptu*, Op. 90, No. 1, D 899, m. 1-5.

Ex. 36. Schubert, *Variations on a French Song*, Op. 10, D 624, m. 9, 12

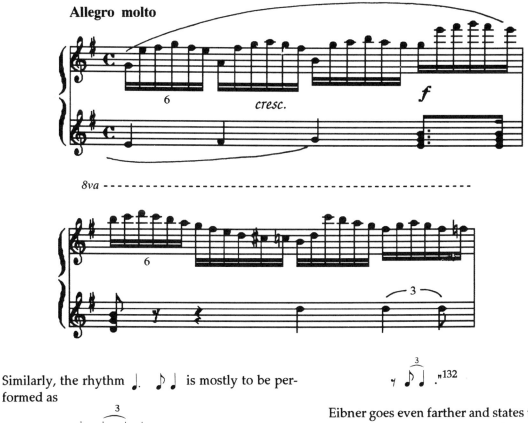

Similarly, the rhythm ♩. ♪ ♩ is mostly to be performed as

♩ ♩ ♪ ♩.

Occasionally ♪ ♫ stands for ♪ ♩ .[132]

Eibner goes even farther and states that the opening phrase of *Impromptu*, Opus 90, No. 1 should be played as shown in Ex. 35, following page. The music historian John Reed supports the same view; he writes,

---

132 F. Eibner, "The Dotted-quaver-and semiquaver Figure with Triplet Accompaniment in the Works of Schubert", *Music Review*, xxiii, 1962, 284.

"Conservative in all musical matters, Schubert, it seems, never imagined that his dotted notes might mislead performers, as they most certainly do today."[133]

On the contrary, however, Schubert was not conservative—neither in his life-style, nor in his music. Rather, he was an innovator. As for melody, he introduced a lyricism which influenced the entire nineteenth century. He was one of the earliest (Haydn being another) to have his secondary themes be an extension of his primary themes, influencing Robert Schumann *(Piano Concerto in A minor)*. As early as 1823 Schubert used a device which was later to be known as the *leitmotif* in his opera *Fierrabras*. His song cycle *Die schöne Müllerin* was the first of its genre. In his *Fantasy in F minor*, Opus 103 for piano duet he compressed a four-movement sonata into one movement, a device later used by Franz Liszt in his tone poems and in his *Sonata in B minor*. Harmonically, Schubert was ahead of his time, using chromatic shifts, modulating to third-related chords, and frequently alternating between major and minor. Since one of Schubert's favorite patterns was

which was a feeling of duplet "against" triplet, it seems inconceivable to the writers that he would not also have been drawn to the rhythm

How could Schubert have been ahead of his time with respect to melody, harmony, and form, but conservative with respect to his rhythm? In fact, the present writers maintain that Schubert was perfectly capable of writing both | and

where and when he wanted them, and did not confuse the two. For example, compare in the seventh variation of *Variations on a French Song*, Opus 10, D 624, measures 9 and 12 (last beats) (see Ex. 36, above).

The controversy began in the 1880s with Mandyczewski (one of the first editors of the *Gesamtausgabe*) and, no doubt, will continue.

* * * * * * *

The writers hope that these notes and suggestions will be helpful.

Performers should keep in mind that all interpretation is an attempt to fill the gaps left in musical notation. Musical logic is not universally valid, and it is not always amenable to verbal explanation.

May your pleasure in this extraordinary repertory be as great as ours has been!

---

133 J. Reed, *Schubert: The Final Years* (London, 1972), 139.

APPENDIX

A Critical Mosaic

COMPILED BY THOMAS P. LEWIS

This section, in addition to offering reflections on a number of the Schubert piano duets from a variety of perspectives, invites performers and listeners to enjoy a sort of "critics' roundtable", recalling some familiar and, perhaps, introducing some unfamiliar writers on this topic. The selections which follow may also be useful as a secondary reference, especially in preparing program notes for concert presentations. All works mentioned are included in the general index of titles found at the conclusion of the present volume.

A frequently-encountered theme is the special attractiveness which the Schubert duets hold for the players themselves, recommending these works not only for concert performance in differing situations, but also for private enjoyment and student attention and advancement.

Comments and analyses by:

Maurice J. E. Brown, 108, 120
Kathleen Dale, 95
Alfred Einstein, 94
Hans Gal, 94
Arthur Hutchings, 118
F. E. Kirby, 106

Cameron McGraw, 102
William S. Newman, 106
John Reed, 117
Franz Schubert, 93
Robert Schumann, 94
Douglas Townsend, 126

1. *A "NOTABLE SUCCESS"*

●FRANZ SCHUBERT, from Piero Weiss, ed., *Letters of Composers Through Six Centuries* (Chilton Book Company, 1967), 204.

Steyr, 25 July 1825

Dear Parents,
.... In Upper Austria I find my compositions everywhere, especially at the monasteries of Florian and Kremsmünster, where with the aid of a gallant pianoforte player I produced my four-handed Variations and marches with notable success....

Your
most faithful son
Franz

2. (THE COLORFUL) SCHUMANN ON SCHUBERT

●ROBERT SCHUMANN, from a Letter to Henriette Voigt, July 3, 1834; in Konrad Wolff, ed., *Robert Schumann: On Music and Musicians,* transl. Paul Rosenfeld (W.W. Norton & Company, 1969; orig. publ. Pantheon Books, 1946), 121-22.

Franz Schubert is the beautiful, pale youth around whose lips there always is a sign of approaching death. Indeed! In the *Divertissement* [*à la Hongroise,* op 54] there is an entire funeral procession—perhaps for a French marshall killed in battle—with its tall, veiled men, its catafalque and obsequies.

3. SCHUBERT THE NATIONALIST/ROMANTIC

●ALFRED EINSTEIN, from *Music in the Romantic Era* (W.W. Norton & Company, 1947), 57.

Even Schubert was... affected by the new [Romantic] enthusiasm for the national *as* national. When, alongside his lieder, he composes a series of Italian *canzonette,* they are—one might say—more Italian than those of Rossini himself, without being imitations of Rossini. To be sure, Beethoven also composed several vocal works with Italian texts and in Italian style, such as his scena "*Ah! perfido*", his terzetto "*Tremate, empi*" and several arias and canzonets; but he used Italian merely as one of the universal languages of music. With Schubert, Italian was already a fascinating, colorful costume. And this was true not merely of Italian. Schubert was more Viennese than his predecessors, than—for example—Mozart, who wrote "*Deutsche Tänze*" or "*Ländler*" that might have come from Salzburg or any other place south of the Danube. Schubert's "*Ländler*" turned into waltzes—a development that was something more than a mere change of name. Something more sensuous, flexible, luxurious pulses through them—a feature characteristic of the "City of Phæcians", as Beethoven called Vienna. And the fact that Schubert lived for a time on a Hungarian estate was not without its effect. How often did he give movements of his works a Hungarian tinge, even when his acknowledgement of it is not as clear as it is in his *Divertissement à l'hongroise, op 54,* for four hands: for example, in the Finale of his A-minor *Quartet,* in the Allegretto of his C-major *Fantasy for Violin and Piano,* op 159, and in the slow movement of his C-major *Symphony.* He utilized the minor mode, the particular harmonic resources, and the sharp rhythm of the Hungarian music dialect for his own, Schubertian melancholy; he was quite himself, even in Magyar costume. And he also knew how to wear French costume; among his works for piano four-hands are to be found no less than five "on French themes" (op 10; 63; 82, 1; and op 84, 1 and 2). Among his lieder, how different is his setting of an Ossianic poem from that of one of Hölty's neo-Classical odes, or one of Schiller's neo-Classical ballads! One of his earliest vocal works was a three-part romance, *Don Gayseros,* which displays pronounced Spanish coloring, although the youth of sixteen or seventeen who wrote it had never seen Spain.

4. SCHUBERT'S "DOMESTIC MUSIC"

●HANS GAL, from *Franz Schubert and the Essence of Melody* (Crescendo Publishing, 1977; orig. Victor Gollancz Ltd., 1974), 146-47.

Until the beginning of our century the humble pastime of playing piano duets stood paramount in all domestic musical activity. At that time no major orchestral work was printed without the simultaneous publication of an arrangement for piano duet. This applied to the symphonies of Brahms and Bruckner as well as to the symphonic poems of Richard Strauss, Mahler's first four symphonies and the orchestral works of Reger and Debussy; it was the most obvious method of introducing a new work to the public. Then came a rapid decline in the desire for domestic music — which, to be sure, coincided with the emergence of an orchestral style that made the reduction of the sound to the black and white of the piano more and more problematical.

With regard to original compositon for piano duet, just as with the *lied* and male-voice part-song, Schubert can claim pride of place as both founder and foremost representative. For this combination, which first appeared during the last quarter of the eighteenth century, there are three exquisite sonatas by Mozart, as well as some stimulating compositions by Beethoven and Weber which also preceded those of Schubert. But none of his forerunners explored as he did the possibilities of sound and technique offered by four hands on a keyboard, and no one before or after him wrote works in the grand manner for this medium. He clearly enjoyed playing piano duets, as did Brahms, who became his most distinguished successor in this field, though without rising to the same heights.

This is indeed domestic music in the truest sense, music addressed not to listeners but to players, and even today, when practically all types of music tend to find their way to the concert platform, the piano duet is rarely performed in public.[134] Nevertheless, Schubert's sonatas for piano solo, which are by no means lacking in technical brilliance, had to wait almost a hundred years before virtuosos began to take an interest in them.... One is astonished again and again at the length of time it took to recognise the greatness and nobility of music that appeals so directly to the hearts of players and listeners. Perhaps one day the same thing will happen with Schubert's piano duets, however little notice is taken of them today. That players love them above all else is, apart from the music itself, due not least to the comfort with which four hands can romp about freely on the keyboard, without ever getting in each other's way, or producing those thick couplings of sounds that are otherwise one of the perils of this kind of setting, particularly in indifferent, mechanical arrangements. And the pleasure of joint music-making as an end and aim was always a rich source of inspiration for Schubert. Our world would be the poorer without these treasures, which are available to all those who will just take the trouble to reach for them with four hands.

5. SCHUBERT SURVEY I

●KATHLEEN DALE, from Gerald Abraham, ed., *The Music of Schubert* (W.W. Norton & Company, Inc., 1947), 123-31.

Of all the great composers, Schubert left the largest number of works originally written for [piano duet]. Clementi, Mozart and Beethoven had each composed a few, but neither in numbers nor in range of style can their works be compared with Schubert's, which are designed in several different forms, and are of varying length, of remarkably diverse character and of unfailing interest to the players. This large collection of works doubtless owes its existence partly to Schubert's own love of concerted music-making and to the fact that he was able to count upon the collaboration of excellent pianists among his friends and pupils....

The [piano four-hand repertory] embraces about thirty works, some of which comprise two, four or even six separate items; the whole collection ranging in scale from a long sonata to the tiniest of *Ländler*; and in character, from the riotous splendour of a *Divertissement à la hongroise* to the solemnity of a *Funeral March for the Tsar*. The works may be sorted into their various kinds

---

134 Beginning in the 1970s, they have become increasingly popular as a medium for public performance. (DW/NA)

follows: overtures, dances, marches, variations, fantasies, rondos, miscellaneous works, and sonatas, in which order they will be surveyed [here]. As regards the disposition of the musical and technical interest between the two players, it may be said that in the simpler pieces, such as the dances and marches, secondo is almost entirely as accompanist, while primo luxuriates in the cream of the melodic and decorative passages. In the works of larger calibre and symphonic style, however, the players are treated more fairly as partners, and each is given an equal share of all harmonic or contrapuntal interest available.

Of the overtures, only two, the F minor, Op. 34, and the G minor (G.A. XXI, No. 6), were written originally as duets, the others being arranged by Schubert himself from their previous orchestral versions.[135] They are perhaps the only works among the duets which are of small interest. Conventional in style, they reflect the Rossini influence prevalent in Vienna at the time of their composition, and though charmingly tuneful, they are devoid of any typically Schubertian touch.

The dances on the other hand — two sets of *Polonaises* and a number of *Ländler* — display many of the composer's well-known characteristics, combined with a strongly "national" flavour which makes them delightfully stimulating to play. The trio of each *Polonaise* is, on the whole, of even greater attractiveness than the *Polonaise* itself, and yields many a treasure of harmonic and rhythmic subtlety. In the set of six, Op. 61, the trio of No. 4 is distinguished by its langorously nostalgic mood; that of No. 5 by an air of gaiety imparted to it by the yodel-like leaps of the melodic line; and that of No. 6 by the pianistic lay-out of the primo part, in which the combination of a scale in the right hand with an arpeggio in the left is particularly bewitching to the player. In the set of four, Op. 75, it is the trios, again, which provide the greatest delight. That of No. 3, in particular, compels admiration for the rhythmical cunning displayed in the joining of two phrases so that the listener is hardly aware where one ends and the other begins. The other dances belonging to this group are a few early *Ländler* and *Deutsche*, and a set of Four *Ländler* dated 1824, which are all of a type similar to [a number of] solo dances.

The marches form the most numerous category of the duets. From first to last, Schubert wrote seventeen, two of which are individual pieces of some length and distinction, and the remainder are grouped into sets of shorter items. Each march has a trio and a da capo repeat. The earliest are *Trois Marches Héroïques*, Op. 27, written probably in 1818. The first has a finely moving bass part, to which an interesting tenor part is added by primo's left hand; and the trio of the third opens with canonic imitations in the treble which recall wood-wind fragments in the slow movement of the "*Unfinished*" Symphony. Of the *Six Grandes Marches*, Op. 40 (1824?), some of the special points are secondo's pianistic accompaniment to the trio of No. 1; the rhythmic vitality of the second march; the felicitous division of the musical interest between the two players in the trio of No. 4, and the masterly shaping of the phrases of the trio of No. 6. But the high light of this set is the E flat minor march, No. 5 — the only andante among several allegros — whose furtive unison octave passages, and melodic line moving at times by progressions of descending thirds, give the duettists the feeling that they are playing a work by Brahms.

The next two sets are the well-known *Trois Marches militaries*, Op. 51 (before 1824), and *Deux Marches caractéristiques* (1826). Of this latter pair, both the marches recall the galloping fluency of Rossini, but the second is notable for some irregular accentuation, and for the appealingly Mozartian flavour of its trio.

The two most important works in the group, the *Grand Marche funèbre d'Alexandre I* (1825) and the *Grand Marche héroïque au sacre de Nicolas I* (1826), are both orchestral in conception, and though they may be made to sound tolerably effective on the piano, they can hardly be adequately interpreted through this medium. In the trio of the first, for instance, secondo is called upon to perform a series of quickly repeated and tremolando pedal-points which simply cry

---

135 Mandyczewski in his critical notes to the *Gesamtausgabe* thinks that the G minor Overture, too, is an arrangement of an orchestral composition of which the score has disappeared.

out for instruments of percussion. The second, the longest of all the marches, has two trios, the first of which, with its reiterated metrical scheme and the harmonic progression of pulsating bass chords bears a likeness to the minore of Grieg's *Symphonic Dance*, No. 1. Figures from this trio re-appear in the coda and lend unity to the work as a whole. Schubert wrote only one more march: a tiny *Kindermarsch* in 1827, for the youthful Faust Pachler, the son of his friends in Graz. This trifle is unimportant musically, but is a charming reminder that Schubert, so near the end of his life, and so busy with the composition of large works, could yet make time to write a piece for a child.

Of the five sets of variations, that in E minor, Op. 10, upon an old French song, "*Reposez vous, bon chevalier*", written in 1818, shows a distinct advance in style upon the early sets for piano solo. A wider range of key is employed for the individual variations; one is in C major, another in C sharp minor, and some unexpected modulations heighten the interest. Particularly effective points occur at the opening of the third variation, where primo starts off, solo, with the theme in C major, only to be quickly spirited away with secondo's connivance into E flat major. In the long finale, tempo di marcia, the first eight bars of the theme are at one point divided between three keys (bars 58 *et seq.*): four bars in A flat major, two in A flat minor, and the last two in E major, during which tonal adventure, secondo keeps up a uniform figure of accompaniment with complete unconcern. Schubert dedicated this work to Beethoven, who is said to have been pleased with it and to have played it with his nephew Karl.

The eight *Variations upon an Original Theme in A flat*, Op. 35, were written about six years later and are serene and somewhat restrained in character, though less so that those of the solo set in A minor. The variations, with one exception, remain in A flat, only the fifth being in the minor mode. The seventh, più lento — which stands quietly between its decorative predecessor, maestoso, and the more elaborate finale, allegro — presents a great contrast to the others, not only by its infinitely more simple texture consisting mainly of four- or five-part harmony, but by its extended tonal range. Bearing the signature of four flats and ostensibly in F minor, it opens with the chord of C minor; but an unexpected G flat causes the key-centre to shift down to B flat, whence a sequence takes it through A flat to the desired key of F minor, the effect of the last modulation being heightened by the melody note C, sustained in the upper part:

Ex. 37. Schubert, *Variations*, Op. 35, D 813

Throughout the whole variation the tonality constantly shifts: new and unexpected harmonic light is shed upon the theme; independent inner voices and prepared and unprepared discords add a pungent flavour to the already fugitive key-scheme. It comes to rest only when it reaches the widely spread chord of the dominant of A flat, there to pause while primo executes a pianissimo cadenza leading into the lively finale.

The *Andantino varié*, on an original theme in B minor, Op. 84, No. 1, written round about 1825, is shorter and simpler than the preceding work, comprising only four variations, of which the first three are straightforward ornamental versions of the theme, and the last a double variation and coda. The theme itself is of great charm. Written in   ₵ ,   , it is punctuated by several accented minim chords occuring on the less strong beats, and the melodic line, moving almost entirely by step, has a quietly purposeful character:

Ex. 38. Schubert, *Andantino varié*, Opus 84, No. 1, D 823

The two remaining sets, which, though bearing the same opus number, 82, belong to the years 1827 and probably 1818, are written respectively upon an air in C ("*Was einst vor Jahren*") from Hérold's opera *Marie*, and an original theme in B flat. They are of small significance musically, but they offer many pages of pianistic enjoyment to the players. The first set contains charmingly graceful variations in A flat major and A minor, and the second set is notable as being the only one of all Schubert's piano works in variation form in which a long introduction precedes the first statement of the theme.

Among the *Fantasies*, only the F minor, Op. 103, composed in 1828, is of permanent value. The three others were all written in Schubert's boyhood and are of interest only as curiosities. Like some of his earlier songs, they begin in one key and end in another. The first is of immense length, and has twenty-four different tempo-indications in its thirty-six pages. The fugal finale of the third is the only feature which points forward to the great F minor Fantasy of 1828. This extremely beautiful work is composed, like the *Wanderer* Fantasy, in four sections of contrasted character, but differs from it in lacking a definite theme to act as motto to the whole work and to bind the separate sections closely together. The two middle sections—one a fascinating movement of rondo type—have little in common with the first and last. The haunting opening theme of the first, however, appears several times during the course of the work and again in the coda, giving a sense of cohesion, and another important figure from the first section is used as a counter-subject in the final fugue. The *Fantasy* is the one of the most satisfying of all Schubert's duets. Intensely poetic in its musical content and pianoforte style, it is as enchanting to players as it is delightful to listeners.

Schubert's three rondos were written at long intervals between 1818 and 1828. The second, a *Rondo brillante* on French themes, Op. 84, No. 2, written about 1825, sorely needs orchestral colour to provide the indispensable sheen requisite to its somewhat superficial glories. The other two, on the contrary, are as pianistic as anything Schubert ever wrote for duet. The first, entitled *Notre amitié est invariable*, Op. 138, a movement in D in older rondo form, flows gently throughout, while the players occasionally take it in turn to present the graceful theme, as though nothing in the world could ruffle their amity, the invariability of which is emphasised symbolically in the coda by the interlinking of their arms throughout the last fifteen bars of the piece. This passage is one of the very few in the whole of Schubert's four-hand works in which he has recourse to a device so effective in giving due expression to a middle part. The third of these pieces, the *Grand Rondeau* in A, Op. 107 (1828), is a longer movement in modern rondo form. It is of such strongly lyrical nature that it seems to sum up in itself the characteristics of Schubert's more idyllic songs. The second subject, indeed, contains their very quintessence:

Ex. 39. Schubert, *Rondo in A Major*, Opus 107, D 951

So like is it to so many of them that it is difficult to name the one it most resembles; though "*Im Frühling*" may perhaps be considered a very near relative of this placid, five-bar melody, and "*Die Forelle*" a more distant connection of its rising semiquaver bass.

Of the miscellaneous works, two, which stand poles apart from each other, have each a distinctive style: the rhapsodic *Divertissement à la hongroise*, Op. 54, and the very dry little *Fugue*, Op. 152. The three other pieces are all movements in sonata form, though their titles do not indicate their content.

The *Divertissement* owes its Hungarian style and colouring to the fact that it was composed during one of Schubert's summer holidays with the Esterházy family at Zseliz. The nostalgic opening theme is a Hungarian folk-tune, which he heard sung by one of the servants on the estate, and which he immediately seized upon as the basis of the work into whose pages he introduced a Hungarian march and trio, and several episodes made from national dances; the whole interlaced with cadenza-like passages evoking the confused metallic resonance of the cimbalom:

Ex. 40. Schubert, *Divertissement à la hongroise*, Opus 54, D 818

It is the longest and most picturesque of the single-movement duets, its lively and varied metrical figures and resplendent piano-writing making it highly effective and enjoyable to play. One of the episodes, the allegretto, was written by Schubert as a piano solo before he utilised it in the compositon of the duet. This original version has been discovered and published only in recent years and is not yet as widely known as the transcription of the whole *Divertissement* made by Liszt in 1846. A greater contrast to this colourful work can hardly be imagined than the little *Fugue* in E minor, originally "for organ or piano" and dated June 1828, which is thought to have been written merely as an exercise in counterpoint. It lacks every kind of pianistic embellishment, but the playing of it is rewarding, since it makes possible a stimulating contrapuntal contest between the two partners.

Among the pieces in sonata form is a *Divertissement en forme d'une marche brillante et raisonnée*, Op. 63, which is generally regarded as the first movement of a complete sonata whose other movements, the *Andantino varié* in B minor and the *Rondo brillant*, Op. 84, Nos. 1 and 2 already mentioned, were separated from it by a timid publisher who thought the pieces would enjoy more success if printed singly. The other pieces are an undated *Allegro moderato* in C bracked with a short *Andante* in A minor, and a very much longer *Allegro* in A minor, Op. 144, which was published after Schubert's death, under the title *Lebensstürme*. None of these works is of striking musical interest,[136] and each suffers by being isolated from other movements which might lend it support and offer it contrast. They do, however, serve to throw into brighter light the complete and undivided *Sonata* in B flat, and to prepare the way for the greatest of all Schubert's duets, the *Grand Duo* of 1824.

The B flat *Sonata*, Op. 30, written at Zseliz in 1818, but showing few traces of Hungarian influence, exhibits several interesting features in addition to its intrinsic charm. One is its opening three-bar flourish: the only example of its kind in any Schubert sonata, solo or duet. Another is the presentation of the second subject in an unusual key (D flat in the exposition and G flat in the recapitulation) before it appears in the expected tonality, and yet another is the translation of the opening minor section of the slow movement into the tonic major on its reappearance after the episode — this last device being a favourite of the composer....

The *Grand Duo* in C, Op. 140, also written at Zseliz, in 1824, holds an unusual place among all Schubert's works. Irrefutably symphonic in conception and orchestral in style, it exists only in an autograph version for four hands.[137] In playing it, duettists enjoy the unique experience of interpreting an apparently original work which at the same time sounds like a transcription: a pianoforte arrangement, that is to say, of an orchestral work whose hypothetical existence has been vouched for by experts equipped to make such a bold surmise.[138] The effectiveness of the orchestral version made by Joachim lends support to the theory that Schubert intended the work as a symphony; but unless the original score should ever be discovered, duettists may meanwhile be allowed to regard the *Duo* as a special treasure of their own.[139] Considered from the essentially pianistic aspect, the work is innocent of nearly all the enchanting devices which

---

136 The present writers consider the *Lebensstürme* to be one of the greatest of Schubert's piano works. (DW/NA)

137 It was published in 1838 by Diabelli & Co., Vienna. (DW/NA)

138 More recent studies prove that it is definitely an original duet. (DW/NA)

139 In fact, attempts to identify the *Grand Duo* as a misplaced (or unfinished) "symphony" have been pretty much discredited. See the authors' text, page 45 above, and other remarks on this subject throughout the present *Appendix*. (TL)

delight the players in most of the other Schubert duets. For this very reason, however, the attention of the performers may be the more closely concentrated upon the music itself, whose sublimity far outweighs every consideration of pianistic suitability. The work is more evenly divided between the partners than any other of Schubert's duets. If secondo has occasionally felt that he has not received quite his fair share of the musical interest, he finds his part in the *Grand Duo* to be more than the equal of primo's: indeed, in the first three movements it is he who is entrusted with the presentation of new themes before primo is allowed to share them.

The first movement, in C, in very concise sonata-form, is of great dignity. The principal and second subjects have features in common: a similar opening metrical scheme and a certain amount of step-wise motion. The second subject, first presented by secondo in A flat in the exposition, and in C minor in the recapitulation, is distinguished by its nine-bar length. The movement is not characterised by thematic contrast, but by the continual working of fragments of the subjects, separately or together, and by their unexpected excursions to distant keys. The andante, in A flat, 3/4, opens with a long melody, so ineffably serene in effect that it is difficult to realise that its twenty-five bars are composed of at least eight individual one-bar sections of different metrical patterns, which recur in different order and at different pitches to form one unbroken whole; and that when the melody reappears in the recapitulation, its segments are even further re-arranged. However, the beauty of the movement does not rest on the melodic line alone, but also upon the exquisite part-writing which accompanies it. The quicker notes of the second subject — so like a figure in the larghetto of Beethoven's *Second Symphony* (bar 82) — introduce a touch of sprightliness; but the prevailing sense of tranquillity is so strong that when the players reach the last bar, they may feel they have completed a timeless wandering through the Elysian fields. In structure, the scherzo, in C, is very highly organized. After a four-bar introduction containing a thematic figure which is concealed beneath an upper dominant pedal, the curiously angular principal subject is presented by secondo, who retains it as his personal property almost throughout. The middle section is entirely devoted to a discussion of the introductory theme by both partners, after which secondo restates his main subject, this time in G before it returns slightly extended, to the tonic for the coda: a lively canonic disputation of the introductory theme. The trio in F minor, in short, modified ternary form, is as sinuous as the scherzo is serrated. Written in 3/4 time, its melody and bass proceed entirely in double-octave crotchets on the third beats, tied over to minims on the first beats. There is never a variation in the lulling trochaic metre and never a beat's silence the whole way through these seventy pianissimo bars, and the return to the bustling trio is like a transition from night to day.

A double-octave E prefaces the finale, allegro vivace in C, 2/4, after which peremptory summons to attention, the movement plunges into its unflagging course with a lively subject which begins in the relative minor (A), and only gradually works its way into the tonic. This irregular procedure is counter-balanced in the recapitulation, where the subject appears alternatively in the tonic minor and its relative major (E flat), and gives rise to further modulations before the tonality is readjusted. Even then, the normal key basis does not remain secure till the end of the movement, but shifts perilously to C sharp minor and is held in suspense through a mysterious, pianissimo più lento section while little figures from the principal subject grope their way back to C major for the last, energetic summing up of the whole argument. After playing the *Grand Duo*, the most ardent of duettists will concede that only a full orchestra can do justice to this magnificent sonata; but they will nevertheless have rejoiced in the opportunity of taking part in the performance of a Schubert work of symphonic proportions, apparently designed expressly for them.[140]

---

140 A curious instance of damning (the piano duet medium) with faint praise, perhaps. Again, see above. (It may also be remarked that, possibly, it makes as little sense to judge the piano duets as under-orchestrated orchestral works as it does to consider them over-orchestrated solo pieces. The fact remains, certain works were composed for and exist in the particular medium in which they appear.) (TL)

6. SCHUBERT SURVEY II (PERFORMANCE NOTES)

•CAMERON MCGRAW, from *Piano Duet Repertoire: Music Originally Written for One Piano, Four Hands* (Indiana University Press, 1981), 254-59.

Allegros:

Allegro moderato (C) and *Andante* (a), also called *Sonatine*, D 968 (1828, or possibly as early as 1812). The authenticity of these two minor works has been questioned. However, they are ingratiating and quite easy to play; the structure of both is simple; and the themes are melodious. (Lower intermediate-intermediate)

Allegro (a) ("*Lebensstürme*"), Op. post. 144 D 947 (1828). Considered by some to be part of a larger composition, this extended single-movement piece in sonata form is one of Schubert's most dramatic and exciting works, containing sharp contrasts of mood, tender lyricism, and fiery passion. The bold main theme is orchestral in character. The second subject, subdued and gently moving, is introduced and soon embellished with delicate rising and falling scale passages, triple pianissimo. The dramatic and concisely organized development section leads into a return of the two themes and to a brief, fervent coda. (Advanced)

Dances:

Deutscher Tanz with two trios and coda (G), and *Two Ländler* (E), D 618 (1818). The first trio (G) of the *Deutscher Tanz* is identical with that of No. 7 of the *Seventeen Ländler* (also known as *Deutsche Tänze*) for piano solo, D 366. The second of the *Two Ländler* was originally intended as a trio to the first. The manuscript of these two fresh, charming dances was first discovered by Brahms in the library of his friend Julius Stockhausen. Unpublished until 1934.[141] (Lower-intermediate-intermediate)

Zwei deutsche Tänze (E♭, C), Op. 33, D 783a (1824). Delightful, short, melodious dances also occurring in a version for two hands. (Lower intermediate/intermediate)

Vier Ländler (E♭, A♭, c, C), D 814 (1824). Fresh and tuneful, these four short pieces are Schubert's easist four-hand works. (Upper elementary-lower intermediate)

Eleven Ländler, D 366, arr. for piano four-hands by Johannes Brahms.

Divertissements:

Divertissement à la hongroise (g), Op. 54, D 818 (1824). Written after the composer had spent a vacation at the Esterházy estate in Zseliz, where he was first introduced to Hungarian music. Extended work in three sections: Andante; a short Marcia; and Allegretto. The music has a strong Hungarian flavor, modal at times, with pronounced Magyar rhythms, florid cadenzas, and imitations of cimbalom tremolos. According to one source the work also contains an actual Hungarian folk melody Schubert is said to have overheard a servant singing as she worked in the Esterházy kitchen.[142]

Divertissement (à la française) (e), Op. 63 and Op. 84/1 and 2, D 823/1,2 and 3 (ca. 1825). There seems to be no question that this brilliant, large-scale work, built on three marchlike themes, was conceived and written as one three-movement composition. However, it was divided by the publisher, apparently without Schubert's consent, and the movements were issued singly with different titles and opus numbers. 1. *Divertissement en forme d'une marche brillante et raisonnée*, Op. 63. The dazzling, technically demanding opening movement is in sonata form with a strong, assertive main theme and a lyrical second theme. Energetic development with brilliant passage work; exciting climaxes. 2. *Andantino varié*, Op. 84/1. The beguiling, tranquil,

---

141 In fact 1909; see our text. (DW/NA)
142 Advanced level. (NA)

jewel-like middle movement maintains its dreamy quality throughout the three exquisite variations. Contains some of the most delicate writing in Schubert's four-hand works. 3. *Rondeau brillant sur des motifs originaux français*, Op. 84/2, though somewhat less inspired than the other movements, is melodious and well written. A simple rhythmical pattern, introduced as part of the first theme, develops into a repeated dactylic figure that pushes its way on with relentless drive to the end of the piece. (Intermediate-lower advanced)[143]

Fantasies:
Fantasia (G), D 1 (1810). Rambling youthful work; long, repetitious, and lacking in formal organization but offering occasional glimpses of the more mature Schubert, especially in the Allegretto section. (Intermediate)
Fantasia (g), D 9 (1811). Discursive and naive, but somewhat shorter and more compact than the preceding *Fantasia*. Demonstrates greater control of the thematic and formal development. (Intermediate-upper intermediate)
Fantasia (c), D 48 (1813). Early work; impressive for its use of chromaticism and counterpoint, although there are occasional crudities in writing and in the sequence of sections. It appeared in two versions, first as *Grosse Sonate* and later as *Fantasia* with a concluding fugue. (Intermediate-upper intermediate)
Fantasia (f), Op. 103, D 940 (1828). Schubert's best-known four-hand work and one of the great masterpieces of the medium. Represents the composer at the height of his creative powers in its harmonic richness and orchestral color, its haunting melodies and rhythmic vitality, and especially in its structural inventiveness and cohesion. In formal design and organization the work reflects the influence of Mozart, notably the two *Fantasies*, K 603 (f) for organ or piano four-hands and K 475 (c) for solo piano. The fantasy begins with one of Schubert's most sublime and radiant melodies; it is developed and expanded and soon progresses into a dotted-note Largo section in French overture style, which in turn gives way to a brilliant Allegro vivace scherzo and trio. A return of the first theme leads into a fugal development of the closing theme of the first section. A fiery, sonorous coda follows, and a final quiet reiteration of the first theme concludes the work. (Upper intermediate-advanced)[144]

Fugue:
Fugue (e), for organ or piano duet, Op. post. 152, D 952 (1828). Originally written for organ,[145] this fugue was composed as the result of a lighthearted competition between Schubert and his friend Franz Lachner to celebrate their visit to a Cistercian abbey during a summer walking tour. Following traditional contrapuntal practice, Schubert wrote the four-voice fugue on four staves instead of two, in order to extend the range of the individual voices. Under the mistaken assumption that the work was intended as a piano duet, the *Fugue* has traditionally been included in collections of the composer's complete four-hand works. As an academic exercise the *Fugue* is irreproachably correct, but its principal interest lies in its unexpected chromaticisms. (Intermediate)

Marches:
Three marches héroïques (b, C, D), Op. 27, D 602 (1818). Spirited, melodious works. The first march is the most interesting; short and compact. The second and third have harmonic and rhythmic variety, though they tend to be somewhat spun-out. (Intermediate-upper intermediate)

---

143 In our opinion, advanced level. (DW/NA)
144 Advanced level, in our opinion. (DW/NA)
145 Opinions vary; see page 80, above. (DW/NA)

Three marches militaires (D, G, E♭), Op. 51, D 733 (ca. 1822). Begins with the familiar *Marche militaire* (D). Charming, lightweight marches in popular style. They have a bandlike quality but are nonetheless very Schubertian in the variety and richness of their melodic and harmonic development. (Intermediate-upper intermediate)

Six grandes marches and trios (E♭, g, d, D, e♭, E), Op. 40, D 819 (1824). Extraordinarily fine series; abundance of dynamic and harmonic shifts and ever-present lyricism. Mood ranges from brilliant and exciting in the opening march; through the Hungarian style of the third; the slow, introspective dirgelike solemnity of the fifth; to the exuberant final work of the group with its enchanting trio. (Upper intermediate-lower advanced)

Grande marche funèbre à l'occasion de la mort de sa majesté Alexandre I, empereur de toutes les Russies (c), Op. 55, D 859 (1825). It is not known what prompted Schubert to commemorate the death of Czar Alexander I of Russia in the present work, or the coronation of Czar Nicholas I in the following one. Possibly he was hoping for some modest financial remuneration from the Russian court. In any case he honored both historical events with stirring, imaginative marches, written in his most refined style. The first is a solemn funeral march with dotted rhythms and a trio featuring drum-roll figures in the Secondo part.

Grande marche héroïque composée à l'occasion du sacre de sa majesté Nicolas I, empereur de toutes les Russies (a), Op. 66, D 885 (1826). Similar in character to D 859, but longer and with a much more complex and advanced formal structure. The opening festive Maestoso is followed by a contrasting Trio (I), a well-developed Allegro giusto section, and a second Trio (II). The return of the full Allegro giusto gives way to the coda, with detailed references to Trio I and to the beginning Maestoso. A remarkable work, abounding in melodic variety; approaches the *Fantasia* (f), D 940, in the grand scale of its architectural design. (Upper intermediate-lower advanced)

Two marches caractéristiques (C, C), Op. post. 121, D 886 (1826). Brilliantly exciting, energetic marches in 6/8 time; similar in their joyous sparkle and dynamic drive. (Upper intermediate-lower advanced)[146]

Children's march (Kindermarsch) (G), D 928. Schubert's only essay into writing for children, this is one of his easiest and, at the same time, most perfunctory works. It was written for the birthday of a friend's young son.[147] (Upper elementary-lower intermediate)

Overtures:

With the exception of *Overture* (F), D 675, and possibly *Overture* (g), D 668, the Overtures below are four-hand arrangements made by the composer from his original orchestral versions; they are especially noteworthy for the sensitivity and creative skill Schubert used in transferring his own symphonic works to small, chamber-music proportions.

Overture "im italienische Stile" (D), D 592 (1817), arr. from D 590. (Upper intermediate)

Overture "im italienische Stile" (C), D 597 (1817), arr. from D 591. (Upper intermediate)

Overture (g), D 668 (1819). Because of its orchestral character and layout, this is most likely a four-hand sketch of a lost or never-completed symphonic work. It is nonetheless charming, melodious, and effective in its duet version. (Upper intermediate)

Overture (F), Op. 34, D 675 (1819). Originally written for four hands. Long, diffuse, undistinguished work with engaging moments, but fails to generate very much musical interest. (Upper intermediate)

Overture to "Alfonso und Estrella", Op. 69, D 773 (1822), arr. for four hands in 1823. (Upper intermediate)

Overture to "Fierrabras", D 798 (ca. 1824). (Upper intermediate)

---

146 Advanced level, in our opinion. (DW/NA)

147 We believe it was written for mother and son to play for his *father's* birthday. (DW/NA)

Polonaises:

Four polonaises (d, B^b, E, F), Op. 75, D 599 (1818).

Six polonaises (d. F. B^b, D, A, E), Op. 61, D 824 (1825). Both sets of these delightful short pieces, similar in form to the marches, are fresh and rich in inventiveness, containing some of Schubert's most lyrical and engaging music; several of the trios are especially felicitous in their grace and delicacy. (Intermediate-upper intermediate)

Polonaise (B^b), D 618A, completed for practical use by Fr. Reinhard van Hoorickx, Provisory Edition (pro manuscripto), n.d. Competent reconstruction in Schubertian style from a manuscript in the Houghton Library of Harvard University; a curiosity. (Intermediate-upper intermediate)

Rondos:

Rondo (D) ("*Notre amitié est invariable*"), Op. post. 138, D 608 (1818). A work in the composer's lighter vein, this gem charmingly combines a lilting melody in the nature of a polonaise, elusive harmonic shifts, florid passages, and frequent contrasts in instrumental color. The crossed hands at the end provide an amusing diversion, perhaps a whimsical commentary on the sub-title. (Upper intermediate-lower advanced)

Rondo (Grand rondeau) (A), Op. 107, D 951 (1828). One of the most direct and accessible of Schubert's four-hand pieces. This extended work is instantly appealing with its haunting lyrical melodies, harmonic subtlety, and effective writing for both parts. (Upper intermediate-advanced)[148]

Sonatas:

Sonata (Grande sonate) (B^b), Op. 30, D 617 (1818). An early work, this three-movement sonata is set in a broad structural framework and shows a mastery of form and skill in the manipulation of thematic materials. It is full of melodic warmth, orchestral color and harmonic variety. The opening movement, Allegro moderato, is prefaced by a short cadenza; the graceful first theme and its companion second theme in triplets are richly developed in melodious passages with unexpected modulations. The lyrical Andante con moto second movement is one of the composer's most beautiful creations. The finale is a flowing Allegretto. (Upper intermediate-lower advanced)

Sonata (Grand duo) (C), Op. post. 140, D 812 (1824). This monumental four-movement work is filled with soaring lyricism and emotional intensity; at times it is brilliant, at others delicate and tender. Although it is symphonic in scope and frequently emphasizes orchestral textures, it remains thoroughly pianistic in feeling and setting. The extraordinary structure of the sonata and the demands it makes on the performers often seem to exceed the expressive and technical powers of the piano, an impression that suggests the work may be an arrangement of a projected or lost symphony. Robert Schumann was the first to voice this opinion and was supported by a number of critics; more recently, however, the theory has been disputed. Joseph Müller-Blattau, the German musicologist, offered a reasonable compromise in "*Zur Geschichte und Stilistik des vierhändigen Klaviersatzes*", *Jahrbuch der Musikbibliothek Peters für 1940*, XLVII (Leipzig, 1941). He describes the works as the "first four-hand symphony," pointing to its specific pianistic effects, which are used in conjunction with other features more characteristic of symphonic style. The first movement of the *Sonata*, Allegro moderato, opens simply with a gentle theme in octaves; passage work in triplets and orchestral-sounding bass tremolos lead into the songlike second theme introduced in the Secondo. Free modulation and thematic imitation are effectively used throughout the movement. The tranquil and graceful Andante follows, with moments of unusual harmonic color and suggestions of Beethoven second movements. The

---

148 The author has overlooked *Rondeau brillant*, Op. 84/2. (DW/NA)

brilliant Scherzo, a driving Allegro vivace with some dramatic biting dissonances, contrasts with the velvet quality of the enigmatic and unearthly Trio. The work concludes with an energetic Finale, exciting and forceful. One of the towering achievements of Schubert's creative life, the *Sonata* is a nobly inspired and prodigious masterpiece, and one of the most challenging works of the four-hand repertoire. (Advanced)

Variations:

Introduction and variations on an original theme (B^b), Op. post. 82/2, D 603 (1818). This amiable, flowing set of four variations is an early work that alternates between tranquil and brilliant passages, and concludes with a jovial Vivace finale filled with echoes of *Ländler* and German dances. Nottebohm placed this work among Schubert's "spurious and doubtful" compositions when it first appeared in 1860, but subsequent scholarship has confirmed its authenticity. (Upper intermediate-lower advanced)

Eight variations on a French song (e), Op. 10, D 624 (1818). Schubert's first published duet (1822). This set of genial variations was dedicated to Beethoven, who criticized the score and encouraged the young composer. The variations are set in artful Schubertian style, and while not as fully developed as later works, they are alive, interesting, and full of melodic and harmonic invention. (Upper intermediate-lower advanced)

Eight variations on an original theme (A^b), Op. 35, D 813 (1825). The longest and most diversified of the composer's works in this form. Here Schubert is particularly inspired and imaginative as he subjects his theme—broad, stately, and eloquent—to the most ingenious and versatile kind of development, submerging it in florid passages, refining it into a solemn and plaintive chorale, or permitting it to burst into brilliant flashes of color and rhythmic excitement. It is a work rich in variety and invention. (Upper intermediate-lower advanced)

Eight variations on a theme from Hérold's opera "Marie" (C), Op. 82/1, D 908 (1827). Difficult set of variations written in the [penultimate] year of the composer's life and based on a theme from a currently successful French opera. Although the work is not as absorbing or ingratiating as the other sets of variations, the writing is sure-handed and effective throughout. (Upper intermediate-advanced)

7. DUET SONATAS

●WILLIAM S. NEWMAN, from *The Sonata Since Beethoven* (W. W. Norton & Company, Inc., 1972; orig. publ. 1969 by the University of North Carolina Press), 218-21.

The best of [Schubert's sonatas] for piano duet rank by general consent among the best in piano duet literature.... [The sonata in c minor, D 48 (1813)] is an early work, whose five free sections, culminating in a scholastic, four-voice fugue, make the title *"Fantasia"* in the second version more appropriate than *"Grand Sonate"* in the first version....

[The sonata in C/a, D 968] may be one of Schubert's earliest piano duets, related curiously to a lost Mass by him or one by his brother Ferdinand that utilizes the materials. [The sonata in B^b, Opus 30, D 617 (1818)] was the one ensemble sonata published in Schubert's lifetime [by Sauer & Leidesdorf, in 1823]. But no mention of it can be found until Schumann's, in 1834, as one of Schubert's least original works, with only occasional flashes, although a masterpiece under any other composer's name.[149] Finally, [the sonata in C, Opus 140, D 812 (1824)] is the so-called "Grand Duo" [which occasioned one of his most important and ardent champions,

---

149 It got higher praise in *The Musical Times* XIII (1868) 318, and, more recently, in A. Einstein, *Schubert: A Musical Portrait* (1951), 152, and M. J.E. Brown, *Schubert: A Critical Biography* (1958), 88.

Schumann, to describe Schubert as Beethoven's feminine counterpart, in his 1838 review of this work. Schumann also viewed the piece] as a potential symphony.[150] Not only its idiom but its elaborate treatment of ideas suggests symphonic thinking. It is, in fact, 145 measures longer than the longest solo sonata, 52 longer than the Quintet in C, but 1,366 shorter than the "Great Symphony" in C. And both in quality and spirit, however unsatisfying may be its duet idiom, it would be placed here on a par with those latter two masterpieces in C. Perhaps, though not a quartet, [the *Grand Duo*] was one of the consequences of a statement Schubert wrote three months earlier, "I want to write another quartet, in fact intend to pave my way towards a grand symphony in that manner." The finale of [the *Grand Duo*], by the way, is another that recalls that in Beethoven's Quartet Op. 130. Since Schubert's finale is the earlier of these two and no known biographical circumstances indicate that Beethoven could have known it, one begins to suspect that its ideas and style were then "in the air".

8. SCHUBERT FANTASIAS

●F. E. KIRBY, from *A Short History of Keyboard Music* (The Free Press, 1966), 245-48.

In the keyboard music of Schubert... there is established a broad division of compositions into two main classes, the one representative of the old large form of keyboard music [e.g. Sonata] handed down from the work of Haydn, Mozart, and Beethoven and the other the new, small, essentially lyrical character piece that was to become of prime significance for Romantic music....

Unlike Beethoven but somewhat like Mozart, Schubert wrote a number of pieces for piano duet. Most of these are clearly domestic, small, easy, and pleasing works for entertainment at home. Among these can be mentioned various kinds of dances, especially the *Ländler* and *Deutsche Tänze* or marches (among them the famous *Marches militaries, Op. 51*, D 733, of around 1822 and published in 1826) or the two three-movement *Divertissements*, one *Hungarian* in g (D 818), the other *French* in e (D 823), as well as several overtures... But there are also large compositions for the duet medium: variations, sonatas, and fantasias....

[We find the first two of Schubert's four piano-duet fantasias] among his earliest compositions: the three-movement *Fantasia in G* (D 1), his first known composition, and the four-movement *Fantasia in g* (D 9); both works seem very much like sonatas. But the next work, a *Fantasia in c* (D 48) also known as the *Grande Sonate*, reveals a relationship to Mozart's large quasi-Baroque piano fantasias with its toccata-like passages and concluding fugue with chromatic subject. (The fugue does not appear in the first version.) The [fourth] and last of Schubert's fantasias for piano duet is one of his largest and most characteristic works: the *Fantasia in f* (Op. 103, D 940) composed in 1828 and published in 1829, in movements played without pause and with the cantabile principal theme of the first movement reappearing immediately before the finale.

---

150 Schumann's review runs, in part: "To [any-]one with a measure of feeling and training, Beethoven and Schubert will be [both] related and differentiated on the[ir] very first pages. Schubert is a maidenly character [when] held up alongside the other, much more garrulous, delicate, and spacious; alongside the other, [he is] a child who sports recklessly among the giants. Thus do these symphonic movements relate to those of Beethoven, and [yet?] in their intimacy [they] certainly could not be thought of as [being] other than by Schubert. To be sure, he too introduces his vigorous passages, he too calls up large forces; nevertheless, he keeps relating as woman to man, entreating and persuading where the other commands. But all this [applies] only in contrast to Beethoven; alongside others he is still man enough—in fact, the most daring and freethinking of the newer musicians."—Obviously a provocative description, by today's standards; quoted in Newman, 193. (TL)

9. FANTASIA IN F MINOR, *OPUS 103, D 940 (1828) (1)*

●MAURICE J. E. BROWN, from *Essays on Schubert* (St. Martin's Press, 1966), 85-100.

A remarkable fact emerges when we glance over the list of [Schubert's] mature piano duets; it is that every single one was published commercially. By that is meant that none of them remained to be published by the editors of the *Gesamtausgabe* as a duty to be done in fulfilling the obligations of a complete edition. There is an exception, the *Overture in G minor*, composed in October 1819, but since it did not come to light until 1896 it was never available to nineteenth-century publishers. There are twenty major piano duets; fourteen were published in Schubert's lifetime, and the remaining six appeared from various publishing houses by 1840, only twelve years after his death. Each of Schubert's duets, then, carries an opus number, however irrelevant it may be. (Even the last duet of all, the short and unimportant *Fugue in E minor* of June 1828, appeared in 1844 as Op. 152). This full publication is an indication of the immense popularity of the piano duet in the last century, and it throws into greater relief the almost complete disregard of the medium today. In these times of broadcasting and gramophone records the piano duet has lost its main purpose:[151] it is now no longer the only effective way of performing in the home works originally written for orchestra or large chamber-music combinations. With the disappearance from the musical scene of such arrangements, much original work for piano duet, including Schubert's, has been silenced too.

The music of the Schubert duets was cast in forms that are varied but conventional. There are marches, polonaises, divertissements, fantasias, variations, rondos, and sonatas. The two years 1818 and 1824, the summers of which he passed as music master of the two daughters of Count Johann Esterházy, each produced a group of piano duets. The two groups have a noticeable similarity of content—each contains a sonata, a series of marches, a set of variations, a set of polonaises. The second group, from 1824, includes such primary masterpieces as the *Variations on an Original Theme, in A flat*, Op. 35 (D 813) and the *Sonata in C major* (the "Grand Duo"), Op. 140 (D 812). Nevertheless, it yields first place to the final group, which he composed in 1828, the *Fantasia in F minor*, Op. 103 (D 940), the Allegro in A minor (known as *Lebensstürme*), Op. 144 (D 947), and the *Rondo in A major*, Op. 107 (D 951). In these three compositions the expression is, of course, more mature and the style more graceful than in the earlier works, but the musical material itself is so much finer. In the short, significant phrase or in the sustained melody Schubert's devising is superb. One can only wonder at these themes; analysis or explanation adds almost nothing. His use of the material, however, is worthy of both analysis and investigation, for the discoveries add to our knowledge of his wide-ranging powers and of his gifts for musical edifice. I have suggested elsewhere that the music he composed in 1828 shows new powers of intellectual development and that the *Winterreise* songs first tapped these depths of his musical being. The three piano duets of 1828 are not surpassed, even by their companion masterpieces of that year, in the revelation of those methods of development, and the compositions of 1824, for all their endearing qualities, contain nothing so magnificent in the treatment of theme and pianoforte figuration as we find in the last three duets.

The *Fantasia in F minor* was first sketched in outline in January 1828 while Schubert was living in the home of his friend Schober. The manuscript containing these sketches was discarded, but not destroyed, by the composer as soon as his final version was finished. For a reason that can be discussed later he kept the first and bulkiest part of the sketches and took it with him

---

151 The present writers - naturally - challenge this view. (DW/NA)

when he left Schober's home in August 1828 to live with his brother Ferdinand. The remainder, a few leaves containing notes for the last section, remained with Schober, and passed from him to his niece Isabella Raab. Either from Schubert's section, or from Schober's, a connecting leaf or two was lost, but the rest survived.[152]

The final version must have been completed from this preliminary draft in February 1828, for Schubert offered the work to the music publishers B. Schott's Sons of Mainz, on 21 February 1828, but the fair copy he made was not ready until April.[153]

A little later, on 9 May 1828, Schubert and his friend Lachner visited Bauernfeld and played the fantasia to him from manuscript. Bauernfeld, in his diary entry for that day, recorded: "Today Schubert (with Lachner) played his new, wonderful four-handed *Fantasia* to me..." and years later, in 1881, Lachner himself wrote some reminiscences of Schubert in which he recalled the performance of—in his own words—"Schubert's glorious Fantasia in F minor, Op. 103, for pianoforte duet...." These adjectives show the depth of the impression made on the two friends, and they are welcome comments for the fantasia tends to be undervalued among Schubert's piano duets. It is good to know that even in his own day friends were not lacking to appreciate its value.

B. Schott's Sons did not accept the work offered to them; it was published posthumously by Diabelli & Co. of Vienna, in March 1929, and called Op. 103 (this was Schubert's own designation). The composer dedicated the work to his former pupil Countess Karoline Esterházy, the woman with whom he was said to be in love. Some biographers of Schubert, wishing to call the legend of the love affair into question, and indeed it has no serious foundation, have suggested that the dedication of Op. 103 to Karoline derives from the publisher, not from Schubert himself. But the composer, in the letter to Schott's Sons already mentioned, specifies the F minor *Fantasia* as "dedicated to Countess Karoline Esterházy", which is conclusive.

The unassuming way in which the fantasia opens brings to one's mind a general thought about the big masterpieces of Schubert: how rarely they start with the bold flourish, or with the theme proclaimed emphatically by the full instrumental array! Rather do they steal on the ear, persuasive and appealing. One is reminded of the quiet, conversational scene with which Shakespeare will open one of his great tragedies. We recall, for instance, Schubert's two mature symphonies: the cellos and basses in the "Unfinished", the *pianissimo* horns in the great C major; or the soft, unaccompanied bass that ushers in the first movement of the A minor *String Quartet*. The powerful opening of the D minor *String Quartet* and that of the "*Wanderer*" *Fantasia* in C are the exceptions rather than the rule. The scale upon which he will work during the course of the F minor *Fantasia* is not revealed by the surprisingly modest gesture at the start; it begins with two bars of simple, broken chords in F minor. Above their persistent, soft accompaniment the wonderful theme of the fantasia floats:

Ex. 41. Schubert, *Fantasia in F minor*, Opus 103, D 940

---

152 The larger part, ten leaves, is now in the Louis Koch collection: Rudolf Floersheim, Muzzano-Lugano [now at the Pierpont Morgan Library, New York City (DW/NA)]. It extends to the close of the Allegro vivace movement. The last part, two leaves, consisting of sixty-six bars, belongs to Dr. Max Josef Mannheim, London.

153 The fair copy, dated April 1828, is in the Vienna City Library.

In the subsequent treatment of this theme, Schubert shows what I have called his powers of linear development. The theme is not used as the basis of a structural mass, there is no evolution of a pattern based on imitation, nor is there any scheme of key-contrasts exploiting the theme or part of it. Instead, by unexpected and detailed changes in its structure, he evolves a long, flexible, and varied melody. When this turns into the major key, the introduction of B natural (bar 2 of Ex. 42) leads to a sudden upsurge in the melody, delightful in itself, and which at once suggests further delights in the course of its linear development:

Ex. 42.

However gently Schubert may open a movement, once he has ingratiated it with the listener, he usually proceeds to vigorous—even explosive—figures which generate energetic and ornate episodes. Quite often these give the impression that the quiet theme at the start is merely a prelude, to be dropped as soon as it has served its purpose. This is rarely the case. It is one of the features of Schubert's constructions that, however modest-seeming his opening theme may be, it is, for all that, his *main* idea. The theme of the F minor *Fantasia*, after its appearance in the major form quoted in Ex. 42, leads to a lively, *staccato* figure in the bass, taken up directly after, and decorated, by the Primo part:

Ex. 43.   Secondo *(8ves)*

Had Schubert been planning a "first" movement in this section of his Fantasia, we could be reasonably sure that the development section would have concerned itself with the theme at the start of the work, and not with the more obvious, *staccato* figures of Ex. 43. As it is, one might now try to see what form he has actually planned for the fantasia, what is its underlying, basic structure, if so rigid an analysis can be applied to a form that, as its very title implies, may be formless if the composer chooses so. In fact, Schubert is attempting in this work in F minor to pursue the same kind of constructiona l efforts that he made in the *Fantasia in C major* for violin and piano, Op. 159, of the previous month, December 1827. In both works he tries to loosen the conventional structure of the four-movement sonata: to loosen it: he will not entirely break with convention and avoid it altogether. The "first" movement, i.e., the true "sonata" movement, is dispensed with. In the C major *Fantasia*, for violin and piano, episodes from one section recur in subsequent sections in an attempt to fuse them together and give them a greater unity. In the F minor duet *Fantasia* the material of the opening section reappears at the end of the work and is there given an extended treatment, is developed, as it were, to form the Finale; a formal unity is obtained in a different way.

There is little development, in the accepted sense, of this material in the opening section itself. Apart from the melodic changes of the lyrical theme, the Allegro molto moderato consists of a series of alternations of his two contrasted ideas, the lyrical and the dramatic. The section ends with an F major version of the *staccato* theme in Ex.43, so subdued and smooth that it is almost as if Schubert were trying to amalgamate the two ideas into one:

Ex. 44.

The resemblance between the two phrases marked "A" in Ex. 41 and Ex. 44 is apparent, and links one with the other. The next two "movements" of the fantasia are a Largo and an Allegro vivace, corresponding to the slow movement and the scherzo of orthodox sonata construction. The first is short, little more than an interlude, but the second is a long, vividly written movement, containing some of Schubert's finest scherzo writing and forming the real, solid heart of the fantasia.

The Largo is in the remote key of F sharp minor. An earlier, parallel case can be found in another of his fantasias, the "Wanderer"; the key of this work is C major, the slow movement is in C sharp minor. The choice of key in each case provides a further instance of Schubert's relish for the "Neapolitan" shift to keys a semitone away from the prevalent key. The transition in the F minor *Fantasia* between F major at the close of the first section and F sharp minor for the start of the Largo is abrupt, almost gauche:

Ex. 45.

It emphasizes, as nothing else does, that when Schubert dispensed with sonata-form, he dropped with it his careful and, in most cases, inspired transitional work from episode to episode. There are similar perfunctory moves between one section and the next to be found in the *impromptus* and *moments musicaux*: the sections are simply pasted together, as it were, by a few chords. Having reached F sharp minor, Schubert indulges in *fortissimo, ben marcato* chords and plentifully double-dotted — or triple-dotted — phrases where, as it has been said, he tends to mistake violence for power. But the outburst over, there comes suddenly one of those surprising interludes, soft and melodious, which he delights to add to his fiery expostulations. And the snatch of melody is one of his golden inspirations, all the more precious because it comes but once and is gone:

Ex. 46.

This snatch of melody is full of the romantic sentiment to become so familiar during the middle years of the nineteenth century — one of the earliest manifestations of it. It is a striking example of the way in which genius, almost unwittingly, glimpses those intangible moves of the spirit of music, and first gives a tendency form and substance. Nearly contemporary with Schubert's melody, there is another, similar foreshadowing of coming events, and this, too, is a work of young genius; two years later, in Warsaw, Chopin penned his *Étude in E major*, Opus 10, No. 3, and although his melody has nothing physically in common with that of Schubert's quoted above, both are unmistakably full of the spirit of the future — romantic themes akin to those we find in Liszt, Berlioz, and Verdi. More particularly, Schubert's melody has an affinity with the short, Wagnerian leitmotiv, those in the *Ring,* for instance. It could easily come from the Brünnhilde music of *Siegfried* or *Götterdämmerung.* Perhaps it is that fall of a seventh at "B" in the quotation above, suggesting the melody associated in *Götterdämmerung* with "Redemption":

Ex. 47.

A short passage based on the *marcato* phrases concludes the Largo and leads to the third section of the work, a Scherzo in style, although not so called by the composer. The movement, an Allegro vivace in the same key of F sharp minor, is the longest section in the fantasia. It presents in rich array all the elements of the Schubert Scherzo and adds to them a polyphonic texture that is new and invigorating. The construction of the movement is conventional, with no deviation at all from the ground plan of the movement — that of a rondo. The first theme is quoted below, for several points of note arise in considering it. Only the outline is given:

Ex. 48.

The swinging gait of this theme, so typical of Schubert's on-striding rhythms, is maintained without relaxation throughout the section. The octave jump, the grace-notes, the small figurative elements in bars 9 and 10, and the broken chords a semitone apart in bars 13 and 14, all these are the ingredients of the Schubert Scherzo theme: they are rarely all present together as in this one, and all contribute to the general architectural mass of the movement. He seemed to be particularly fond, during the last three years of his life, of one of these features: the juxtaposition of chord arpeggios a semitone apart (bars 13 and 14). How the feature permeates the whole of the *String Quartet* in G of 1826! And the last four sonatas contain many passages based on the idea. It is, one feels, yet another embodiment of his addiction to the "Neapolitan"-sixth chord and the possibilities of harmonic colour implicit in the progression. Before we leave consideration of the Scherzo theme there are deeper implications to notice. The first is the harmonic basis. Without being in any way extravagant, it has a quiet originality and the characteristic discovery of what I have called elsewhere the unimplied harmony of the note progressions. By that phrase I mean that the obvious harmonization of the melody is not so much deliberately avoided, as that an unusual, but perfectly convincing, scheme is found to support the notes of the melody, which is not necessarily implied by them. Once our ears have associated the melody with Schubert's harmony, however, the substitution of the more conventional chords would sound extremely insipid. The result is that listeners tend to imagine that Schubert's harmonic schemes—here and in hosts of other places—are the obvious ones, and his quiet and unobtrusive originality in this way is overlooked. But is it obvious that the first four bars should be harmonized thus?

Ex. 49.

The E natural instead of E sharp in the second bar, the plagal cadence in A major instead of in F sharp minor in bars 3 and 4, are surely both a little unexpected? But how much less vivid the passage would be if we restored the "proper" harmonies! The second point of interest in this theme is the way in which Primo and Secondo exchange parts at the close of the passage—a small example of invertible counterpoint. This device awakens in Schubert an impulse towards canonic structure, and much of the splendid surge forwards of the Scherzo springs from this treatment. The next idea is a pure canon and is worked with tremendous verve in the short development of the movement. We are reminded of the Scherzo in the Pianoforte Trio in E flat, Opus 100 (composed only a month or two before the present one), but that Scherzo is a purely melodic canon; in the fantasia, harmonies, contrapuntal figures, the very musical thought, all spring from the primary "canonic" impulse. In one passage Schubert unifies his two ideas: for a moment the conflict is resolved, and, with a little adjustment, the two themes go together in a perfect contrapuntal fit. The adjustment gives a chance to hear how vital his initial harmonization was, since it is necessary for him to alter the E natural, for once, into E sharp to justify the counterpoint.

The central Trio episode, *con delicatezza*, in D major, continues the basic impulse. Light arpeggios, at a bar's distance, rise and fall between the players, and sparkle in various key-colors, F sharp major, C major, B flat major. This interlude finished, the music of the Scherzo is recapitulated. Another scissors-and-paste join occurs between the concluding bars of the Scherzo and the Finale, designed to pass as quickly as possible from F sharp minor to F minor for the introduction of the themes from the opening Allego molto moderato.

There is always the possiblity—one almost writes the word "danger"—that the emotional overtones that are inherent in music may serve a composer in a merely mechanical way. A shift into soft, minor harmonies, whatever the quality of the music, conveys to the listener the sense of deepened, even saddened, emotion. The association of various sentiments with various musical devices has been so closely welded by all composers, great and small, over the centuries, that our response, as listeners, is as closely welded to them. Nor need these emotions be so obvious as those associated with the quick march on the one hand, or the mournful elegy on the other; much subtler emotional responses are evoked by the chances and changes of music. It has been said of Schubert that his major to minor, or minor to major, changes are sometimes so mechanical as to be suspect.[154] This may be so in some of his lesser songs, for example. But the wonder of his craft in the greater songs and instrumental pieces is that these transitions of his, from one musical emotion to another, do always seem inspired by genuine feeling. They have the unmistakable ring of sincerity. And so when the exhilarated mood of the Scherzo passes— by a somewhat mechanical bridge-passage, as has been admitted—to the sensitive, tender melody of the opening bars, the listener is subjected to a change of emotion that, one can be certain, was first experienced by the composer himself. The result is that when the short recapitulation of the initial melody is past Schubert can rise easily to a no less sincere, but nobly exalted, mood in which the music deals sublimely with the theme first announced in Ex. 43. It serves as a kind of *cantus firmus* to an elaborate web of counterpoint: the four hands of the players become four voices (using the term in its sense of parts in a polyphonic work). The various ideas, chromatic and highly individual, pass between the players and appear at all points of the keyboard. There is no doubt that Schubert was, in this impressive page, deliberately exercising his contrapuntal powers, making them the prime sources and not using them as a decorative, subsidiary background. The piano duets and the church music of 1828 all reveal this tendency towards conscious contrapuntal textures, and the composer's motives in displaying them were probably not unmixed. All the usual academic devices appear in the closing section of the fantasia, and the climax is prepared for by a "pedal point" on the dominant, a long, rolling bass octave on C. The *fortissimo* chords at the climax suddenly break off; there are two bars of silence, and the soft, opening theme appears again; it concludes suddenly and the work ends with the most remarkable cadence in the whole of Schubert's work:

Ex. 50.

154 Plunket Greene in *Music and Letters*, October 1928, 317.

In conclusion, we might glance at the sketches for the fantasia, not only to trace Schubert's creative working on them, but also to see, possibly, why he kept those first ten leaves after he had finished the final version for the publisher. The whole of the opening section is sketched through and, in essentials of construction, is almost unchanged in the finished work; but the indications are almost entirely melodic, that is, the whole of the music springs, as it were, from a melodic conception. The appearance of these pages is of an unaccompanied melody, chiefly in the right hand of the Primo part; the other three staves are blank. The original form of Schubert's main theme was as follows:

Although this was strengthened for the final version, the faltering effect at the close of the phrases is not unattractive. The melody appears thus throughout Schubert's sketch.

The slow movement is complete in the sketch. It was marked originally Andante molto, then Andante. The decision to have an even slower tempo, Largo, is, it will surely be agreed, a wise one.[155] The Scherzo is also practically complete in the sketch. It is here that the most interesting point of the manuscript is to be found. Schubert's first idea was to write a march as a Trio to the Scherzo. He has composed a continuous, though fragmentary, movement in common time, D major, marked Tempo di marcia. It is heralded by a sustained note on C sharp. The theme is an undistinguished motif based on heavily dotted chords, deficient in melodic interest, though rhythmically alive:

Ex. 52.

As with other markedly rhythmic marches of Schubert's, this one also repeats its basic rhythm to the point of monotony. Unlike the present Trio, which replaced it, the march was to have made a second appearance after the recapitulation of the Scherzo. This would have lengthened the work to almost impossible proportions, and no one will quarrel with his decision to dispense with the protracted march in favour of the delicate and more homogeneous episode, in the same key of D major, which now serves as the Trio. That he decided to cut out the Tempo di marcia section, while still engaged on the sketches, is clear from the fact that ideas for the final D major "Trio" make their appearance in the unfilled staves beneath the chords of the march theme.

But that he had got down on paper so substantial an amount of the march was doubtless the reason why he kept his sketches, intending to return to the half-finished draft and complete it later on, as a separate work, if the occasion arose. The only idea in the sketched march that he used was the sustained C sharp; this, becoming enharmonically a D flat, still serves as the link between the Scherzo, in F sharp minor, and the closing section in F minor.

The sketches for the transition between the two sections have been lost. The final two leaves of the sketch (four pages) resume at approximately the twelfth bar of the finale. Judging from these pages, Schubert did not find the devising of his contrapuntal finale an easy task: passages apparently complete were rejected, and another, of twelve bars, fully scored, is cancelled and recommenced at once. The final version, in every case, amplifies the first conception; unisons are made into octaves, chords more fully filled in. The remarkable coda... belongs to his final work on the fantasia; in the sketch it is a plain, full close in F minor. As always, when one compares for the first time Schubert's unfamiliar sketches and the final version, with which one has always been familiar, one is struck by the enormous amount of work that went into the preliminary drafts for the fantasia. He does not jot down short ideas of melody, rhythm, transitional episode, and so forth and develop them individually on paper, nor does he record subsequent piano improvisation on them. The movement, still hazy in details, is there in his mind: the paper is the instrument on which he records, corrects, improvises, if so inspired, or amplifies. He is said to have composed while standing at a high desk; this implies work away from the piano, and the implication would seem to be borne out by his sketches. He composes right through, so to speak, and it is fascinating to see the strokes of poetic genius born on paper as he composed. It is fascinating, too, to examine the wealth of accompanimental detail used to support the melodic line that he has drawn so continuously and without deviation for page after page and to note his tendency to deepen the emotion whenever, momentarily, his melody darkens. This tendency to deepen emotion goes hand in hand with the tendency mentioned above to amplify and adorn the technical embodiment of that emotion. With some composers and poets the creative method is to select from profusion, to compress and refine; with Schubert the opposite is almost without exception the case. He amplifies his original ideas, he extends their emotional range and enriches their harmonies and accompaniments. But this is not the same thing as repetition of musical ideas; his sketches give no support to the criticism that he repeats himself, if by that is meant a mechanical repetition designed merely to lengthen a section or to hide an impoverished invention. Among the numerous sketches for his mature work, those for the F minor *Fantasia* stand almost alone in value, in interest, and in the light they shed on his methods of work. Only the sketch for the slow movement of the *Pianoforte Trio* in E flat, Op. 100, surpasses them in importance.

10. FANTASY IN F MINOR, *OPUS 103, D 940 (2)*

●JOHN REED, from *Schubert: The Final Years* (St. Martin's Press, 1972), 177-79.

Our knowledge of the attachment between Schubert and the young Countess Karoline rests mainly on the testimony of Bauernfeld, but it seems to have been accepted as a fact by his friends. When in the 1860s Schwind came to conceive the idea of painting a picture which would be both a documentary record and a reincarnation of the spirit of the Schubertiad, he incorporated Karoline's portrait, which hangs on the back wall of Spaun's room in his famous *Schubert Abend bei Josef von Spaun;* and he would hardly have done that if he had not felt that Karoline had a right to be there, that she in some way represented the idealistic side of Schubert's nature. One does not need to sentimentalise the situation to believe that Schubert's feeling for his young pupil played an important part in his life. The phenomenon is common enough, and an attachment of this kind, hopeless in a practical sense but capable of engaging strong feelings of affection and respect, would appeal to a nature like Schubert's.[156] At all events, Karoline's association with the piano duet *Fantasia in F minor* is proved, not simply by the dedication, but by the music itself, the Hungarian flavour of which looks back to the *Divertissement à la Hongroise*. Spaun actually links these two works as both resulting from the visit to Zseliz in 1824, and in the sense that they stem from common sources he may be right. What is quite certain, however, is that the *F minor Fantasia* took shape in January 1828, and not before. If one wants to believe that Schubert's association with the young Countess was renewed about this time, it is not difficult to think of plausible explanations. On 1st December 1827 Karoline's sister Marie (Schubert's other, but not so favourite pupil) married Count Breunner Enkevoerth, an occasion which may well have brought their music teacher back into the family circle again. Whether this, or some similar social occasion, brought them together we do not know; but that they were still in touch is clearly shown, not merely by the dedication of the *Fantasia*, but by the fact that Schubert gave Karoline the manuscript of the E flat trio, just completed. It remained with her through what seems to have been a not very happy lifetime.

The *Fantasia* is Schubert's finest work for piano duet, and arguably his finest keyboard composition. A single movement from a sonata—the *andante sostenuto* from the very last for instance—may move us as deeply; the *Impromptus* and the *Moments Musicaux* may seem more beautifully idiosyncratic; but the *Fantasia's* unity of form and content is unique. It sustains its initial impetus over what is in effect a four movement work with cumulative effect. The familiar Schubertian devices, minor/major shifts, canonic imitation, work here with fresh and unsurpassed effect. The scherzo in F sharp minor, in a sense the centre of gravity of the work (though what distinguishes the piece is that each section plays its part in the whole) is a miracle of grace and lightness. The fugal finale is unique, Apollonian in its concern simply with "the notes in their relations", yet providing a logical and satisfying conclusion to the musical argument, achieving an effect analogous (was that what Schubert intended?) with the fugal episodes in the finale of Beethoven's Opus 110. What a step forward this is from the bravura gestures which serve the *"Wanderer"* Fantasy for finale. It is not, perhaps, quite true to say that reservations about the work do not exist. It is possible to feel that the Rossini-inspired tune in the second (Largo) section is out of place (equally possible to believe that Schubert here brought off an effective stylistic marriage); it is possible to think that Schubert's fugal finale is a little short-winded, which, if true, would not be surprising. It is not possible, however, to deny that in the *Fantasia* he broke new ground, and produced a work which in its structural organisation, economy of form, and emotional depth represents his art at its peak.

---

156 One of Schubert's favourite heroes, [Goethe's] Wilhelm Meister, also fell in love with a countess.

11. *SCHUBERT SURVEY III*

●ARTHUR HUTCHINGS, from *Schubert* (J. M. Dent & Sons Ltd, 1973), 150-53. A volume in "The Master Musicians" Series.

When we turn to Schubert's four-handed essays we... find the grandest conceptions, such as the *Grand Duo* [D 812], to be highly orchestral, but without the feeling imparted by the two-handed sonatas that inner parts are missing. We have instead the illusion that we are playing duet arrangements of symphonic scores:

Ex. 53.

The *Grand Duo,* fired by a complete Schubertian orchestral conception, includes not only a scherzo worthy of its first two movements, but a finale whose first held note shows us that Schubert had forgotten that he was writing for the keyboard:

Ex. 54.

It is therefore a splendid final movement to a splendid work. Its first tune reminds us of the finale to the B flat *Trio.* (Was it in the back of Brahms's mind when he wrote the corresponding movement of his F minor *Quintet?*) The tune, like the triplets in the C major *Symphony* or the saucy march tune in the *Octet,* prepares the ground excellently for a heavy chordal second subject, but only Schubert, and he in his more inspired moments, could have worked these materials into so magnificent a coda. The *Grand Duo* has been fully discussed in Tovey's *Essays in Musical Analysis* (vol. i) as a symphony orchestrated by Joachim, whose scoring is somewhat Lisztian and therefore too much of its age to be wholly acceptable to some ears. Elsewhere I have quoted the [largely discredited] theory mentioned by Tovey that the work may be the lost Gastein Symphony; a rival candidate for that honor is the C major *"Reliquie"* Sonata written in the same year, whose two movements would have quite as good a claim but for the story that the lost symphony had all four movements complete in detail.

   Almost contemporary with the *Grand Duo* is the *Divertissement à la hongroise, Op. 54,* once the most popular of Schubert duets, probably on account of its local colour—the alternation of melancholy *cantabile,* quick vigorous march themes and Hungarian syncopated dance rhythms. Schubert is said to have been induced to write it after hearing a girl singing local folk music while on his walks near Castle Zseliz in the company of Baron von Schönstein. Two other four-handed pieces on a magnificent scale and written in the last year of his life are the *Allegro* in A minor, Op. 144, entitled *Lebensstürme,* and the *Fantasia* in F minor associated with Countess

Caroline Esterházy to whom it was dedicated, some say with hidden love, though concealment, worm i' the bud or no, never seems to have done much damage to Schubert's complexion.

No composer has left such a wealth of music for piano duet, but I think too much is made of the theory that a great deal of the pile represents Schubert's failure to secure performances of major orchestral works. No doubt he suffered keen disappointment from his operatic misadventures, but few composers of thirty can have had a very much better orchestral innings, and had he lived another ten years he might well have heard both the B minor and C major *Symphonies* — the former finished, perhaps. Moreover, very little of the duet music emulates the pathos and symphonic dimension of the *Grand Duo*. Four-handed writing is essentially a sociable branch of music, and what musician does not recall the four-handed orgies of his bachelor Schubertiads? If he is lucky enough to be married to the right wife, how he must still enjoy the encroachments over the half-way line of a stool made for one, the side-kicks for control of the pedal when phrasing is at variance and the vicious straying of the female little finger-nail! Schubert was a most sociable creature; his best work was done for his circle of friends and for the good ladies and gentlemen on the edge of that circle who gave invitations and held Schubertiads, so that the friends could forgather in larger rooms than those of their lodgings. These more prosperous citizens, the Paumgartners at Steyr, the Pachlers at Graz, the Spauns at Linz, Sophie Müller, the Fröhlich sisters, the Witteczeks, Bruchmanns, Sonnleithners and Hönigs in Vienna — these people were to him what the van Swietens, Lobkowitzes, Rasumovskys, Lichnowskys and other aristocrats of a type fast disappearing had been to the former generation of musicians with their old-time "academies" and *salons*.

For these middle classes and for the more intimate circle — Schwind, Kupelweiser, Bauernfeld and Co. — the piano duets were written, rather than for awe-struck posterity. Thus, beneath the title of the *Rondo in D major*, Opus 138, Schubert writes "*Notre amitié est invariable*,"[157] while on a sheet of the *Children's March in G*, for little Faust Pachler to present on his father's birthday, he writes an affectionate letter to Frau Marie Pachler while Jenger adds a longer one to Faust from "Schwammerl and me". There is not space to review all the duets in detail, but they contain some of his best light music, and good light music for the piano is not plentiful in substantial lengths. How enjoyable at gatherings of musical folk are works like the *Grand Rondo in A major, Op. 107*, the D major *Rondo* mentioned above or some of the four-handed overtures! One recalls with pleasure the choice of the first-named of these pieces by two members of a summer-school held at Oxford; what Falstaff would have called a "yarked up" concert was proposed one evening in a dining-hall. The college music library was examined, and one felt that the chosen *Rondo* was to us and to Schubert's bourgeois friends what serenades and divertimenti had been to a more formal age. This is the same pleasing kind of music as the *Octet*.

There can be no need to recommend Schubert's duets to undergraduates and music students whose leisure hours offer just the atmosphere for a Schubertiad; yet one wishes that some of the duets, important or light, could be included in such concerts as those held during lunch hours in some of our big cities. If great virtuosi cannot unbend to "glass chandelier" music, let us exalt more humble players, one of whom, however, draws a line at the more clangy sets of variations. Schubert is *not* interesting as a writer of variations, though the duet volumes show sets which, by their dates, represent all stages of his musical growth, and a very slender growth it would appear if judged by variations alone.[158] The polonaises, too, are pretty pedestrian, but nearly all the marches are attractive, especially the *Characteristic Marches, Op. 121*. Why do we hear only the one in D major of the three *Military Marches*? These pieces in general make us wonder whether the friends had a special liking for marches or whether Schubert thought there

---

157 Most likely given by the first publisher. (DW/NA)

158 In our view Schubert himself would have challenged this. Had he not considered it one of his best efforts, he would not have dedicated his *Variations on a French Song* to Beethoven, whom he revered. (NA)

was an opportunity to score them for military band. Do we not hear the whiff and dub of a parade occasion in the second of the six-eight *Characteristic Marches?*

Ex. 55.

12. *SCHUBERT SURVEY IV*

●MAURICE J.E. BROWN, from *Schubert: A Critical Biography* (Da Capo Press, 1977; orig. publ. 1958 by The Macmillan Press Ltd., London), 80-81, 86-89, 160-61, 186-88, 286-87, 301.

[1. 1818-1819]

[The] *Rondo* in D major for pianoforte duet [was] the first original work in this medium since his juvenile efforts of 1810-1813. [Schubert's] manuscript bears the simple indication "*Rondo* for 4 hands, 1818" (there is no month).[159] Diabelli published an arrangement of the work in 1835 as Op. 138, calling it "*Notre amitié est invariable*". Until 1897, when the autograph was discovered, Op. 138 was taken to be an entirely original work of Schubert's. Diabelli had given the manuscript, together with a number of other Schubert and Beethoven MSS., to his son-in-law, Josef Greipel, who became *Kapellmeister* of the Peterskirche, Vienna, in 1847. Greipel remained in this position for fifty years, and as an old man with failing powers had no realisation of the value of his autograph possessions. These were all purchased at his death by the National-bibliothek, Vienna, but even then they remained obscure, and unexamined. Accordingly biog-raphers and cataloguers, right down to the Deutsch Catalogue of 1951, have given the *Rondo* of 1818 as a complete Schubert work. O.E. Deutsch does label the MS. as a "sketch", but even that is an inexact description. It is an incomplete fair copy, probably intended to be a playing copy for Schubert and a partner; although possibly not quite good enough for a publisher's engraver, it is certainly no first, rough draft. Schubert's *Rondo* is in the form A B A: *codetta*: A C A: *coda*. The "C" section is not quite finished, but a few empty leaves in the manuscript show that Schubert intended to finish it. Diabelli's hack simply cut away the " A C" portion and published the rest. The excised part was published as a supplement to an article on the *Rondo* by Leopold Nowak.[160] The fictitious title has been explained as an indication that the *Rondo* was Schubert's offering to his new friend, the pianist Josef von Gahy. He had recently been in-troduced to Gahy, who was a friend and colleague of Spaun, and he delighted to play pianoforte duets with this new friend. At the close of the *Rondo* the players' hands cross, and this is sup-posed to be Schubert's gesture of friendship. Unfortunately, an examination of the manuscript shows that the hand-crossing is due to the rearrangement by Diabelli; there is no justification for it in the original, and it could not have been a gesture of Schubert's at all. But one of his scribbled notes about the work has a certain interest in this connection. He sent Spaun a rough copy of his song "*Lob der Tränen*" and on the bottom margin he has pencilled the words: "Spaun! don't forget Gahy and the Rondeau".[161] He was referring to this duet and perhaps Spaun was going to hear its first performance by the composer and his friend Gahy. The work is quite

159 The ms. clearly says "January". (DW/NA)

160 *Oesterreichische Musikzeitschrift*, Vienna, November 1953.

161 The song manuscript is in the Vienna Stadtbibliothek.

attractive; Ludwig Scheibler wrote of it as a "Polonaise alla Rondo" which is a more congenial title than Diabelli's. It heralds a series of pianoforte duets that year. They were the result of a new position which the composer took up in the following July, [namely his] appointment, as music master, to the establishment of Count Johann Karl Esterházy....

If we associate the years 1815 and 1816 with the composition of songs, and 1817 with sonatas, then 1818 and 1819 could be called the Pianoforte Duet years. A number of works for this medium were written, the first fruits of a rich production of pianoforte duets composed during the next six years or so. It was a sociable medium one might say — and a substitute one. Schubert could play the duets with Gahy, or another friend, Franz Lachner, a Bavarian musician who came to Vienna in the autumn of 1822, or Johann Baptist Jenger, for the mutual pleasure of himself and his partner, or for the enjoyment of a circle of friends; a substitute medium, because it so conveniently adapts itself to orchestral arrangements. Nearly all of Schubert's overtures and symphonies were arranged by himself or his friends for pianoforte duet, and he, like all other musicians, came to know intimately the symphonies of his predecessors, great and small, in a similar fashion. Some critics and other writers have even tried to enlarge the process and they hold that Schubert's original pianoforte duets are orchestral works in disguise; a view with no evidence to support it and which can only be taken seriously because of the hold it has gained amongst music-lovers in general.

A few of the pianoforte duets are known to have originated at Zseliz, and it is obvious why they did so. They formed teaching material for Marie and Karoline Esterházy. The first is a set of *Eight variations on a French Air in E minor.* The "Air" was a song *"Le bon Chevalier (Der treue Reiter)"*, supposedly by Queen Hortense of Holland. It is a setting of words beginning

> *Reposez-vous, bon Chevalier!*
> *Laissez-là votre armure...*

and in substance very like Sir Walter Scott's poem "Soldier rest! thy warfare's o'er", which Schubert set at a later date. The variations are the finest of the early sets, with some notable modulations and vigorous writing in the final two or three. They were published in April 1822 as his Op. 10, dedicated to Beethoven by his "admirer and worshipper, Franz Schubert". Another less famous, and less worthy, set of variations for pianoforte duet, which are almost certainly of that period, although possibly a little earlier than 1818, are those in B flat, published posthumously as part of his Op. 82. It is again in the last variation and the finale of the set that the individual Schubert is to be found. The *Rondo* in D major has been mentioned; its musical style and piquant rhythms are very like those in the *Four Polonaises* for pianoforte duet, published as the composer's Op. 75. Only of very recent years has it been possible to date these *Polonaises*, and to realise that they were written at Zseliz; a manuscript sketch for nos. 2 and 4, and the Trio of no. 3, turned up in the posthumous papers of the violinist Otto Dresdel, a friend of the composer Robert Franz. The sketch bore the date "July 1818". The *Polonaises* are charming dances, full of varied melodies and poetic fancies; their marked rhythms *alla polacca* give them strength and drive, and the graceful, fluid piano writing recalls Chopin. Why are they so neglected? In the sketch mentioned there is a fragmentary tune marked by Schubert "Des" (= D flat). It runs as follows:

Ex. 56.

It evolved into the "Trio" section of the third *Polonaise*, where it appears in this form:

Ex. 57.

But it also generated a second melody, more familiar to the reader, probably, than the *Polonaise* tune:

Ex. 58.

This is from the "Trio" of the sixth piece in the *Moments Musicaux*, Op. 94, the Allegretto in A flat. It means that the date of composition of the Allegretto is round about 1818 and it is, therefore, the earliest of the *Moments Musicaux*.

The first Duet *Sonata*, in B flat, Op. 30, was composed that year; the date "1824" is erroneous, and given because this early *Sonata* was associated with the second Duet *Sonata*, the more famous *Grand Duo*, in C major. Schindler gave the more acceptable date for the *Sonata* in B flat in his "Catalogue of Schubert's Works" of 1857. The B flat *Sonata* for pianoforte duet was published in 1823 by the Viennese firm of Sauer and Leidesdorf, and dedicated to Count Pálffy, owner and director of the Theater an der Wien. The work is in three movements, there is no scherzo, and its shortness should recommend it to players. Again one asks: why is this sonata neglected? It starts with a Mozartian theme, it is true, but Schubert soon forgets his assumed accent and speaks in his own voice. The first movement has a *codetta* and a development section of great interest and imagination. The work teems with Schubertian melody, and the touches of unusual harmony, the original modulations, the imitations of thematic figures between the players, especially in the finale, should place the work occasionally in concert programmes. Instead of perhaps one more orchestration of the *"Grand Duo" Sonata*, the bringing to light of this earlier one by two pianists would be a more rewarding effort.

The first of Schubert's many sets of *Marches Militaires* for pianoforte duet was composed at [this] time and published in 1824 as Op. 27; the music of the three marches, in b minor, C and D, is a little obvious, but entertaining, and in the "Trio" sections there is a quieter and more lyrical note. Like the overtures, the marches are all written to a pattern. But a fixed form is never a confining matter for Schubert, and his episodic departures from it usually produce music of great individuality. In later work in "March" style there is music as thoroughly Schubertian as anything in the chamber music of the period.

The last two pianoforte duets of the group are the *Overtures* in G minor and F major. The former work, composed in October 1819, was unknown to the nineteenth century. It came to light in 1896 in the posthumous papers of a friend of Ferdinand Schubert from whom he must have received the piece. The manuscript is a neatly written copy, and it has been suggested that the *Overture* was originally written for the orchestra. The pianoforte duet may therefore be an arrangement. It was published in the supplementary volume of the *Gesamtausgabe* (volume XXI). It is in the standard tripartite form: Adagio introduction, a main section in modified sonata-form, Allegretto, and an Allegro vivace coda. The Allegretto is a masterly piece of work having much in common with the Duet *Sonata in B flat*. It also shows a feature of Schubert's style in those years: a favourite harmonic clash between the diatonic seventh of a minor scale (F natural in the key of G minor) and the sharpened leading note (F sharp). Both *Sonata* and *Overture* derive tonal contrasts from the clash of F natural and F sharp—giving linkages between the keys D major/D minor/B flat major, and similar sets of keys. The second overture, in F major (with an Adagio introduction in F minor), was composed in November 1819 and published in 1825 as Op. 34. It is an extraordinary example of the inability of the individual to judge the merit of his own work that Schubert should have chosen to publish this markedly inferior composition rather than the previous *Overture in G minor*.[162] There is a legend, which originated with the untrustworthy Joseph Hüttenbrenner, that Schubert composed the *Overture in F* in his (Hüttenbrenner's) lodgings in the Bürgerspital in three hours! This information, he said, was actually written by Schubert on his manuscript. Needless to say Josef was not able to produce the manuscript as evidence of his anecdote: it was lost. He even added that Schubert wrote the words "and dinner missed in consequence." The reader may judge for himself whether this overture, occupying a dozen pages of print, could have been so composed....

[2. 1824]

To his friends and to his brother [Schubert] mentioned the compositions of the summer [1824]; the *Sonata in C major*, for pianoforte duet, known by the name which Diabelli bestowed on it, *Grand Duo*, when he published it as Op. 140 in 1838; the *Eight Variations on an Original Theme*, also for pianoforte duet, which was published soon after [Schubert] returned to Vienna, as Op. 35. The two duets were successfully played to the Esterházy family and their Hungarian friends, but Schubert wrote to [Moritz von] Schwind:

> As I do not wholly trust the Hungarians' taste, I leave it to you and
> the Viennese to decide.

A third pianoforte duet was written in September; it is the long, and very unequal *Divertissement à l'hongroise*. Only a few years ago a preliminary sketch for part of the *Divertissement* saw the light; it is for piano solo and consists of the Allegretto finale. Schubert called it "*Ungerische* [sic] *Melodie*". The manuscript bears in the composer's hand "Zseliz, September 1824", which enables us to place and date the composition with certainty. The duet was published in April 1826 by Artaria of Vienna, as Op. 54. It was widely known in the nineteenth century with results which are not too happy; in many cases, e.g. Wagner's, it was practically the only instrumental piece of Schubert's to be known, and gave a wrong impression of his stature. Schumann wrote in his diary on 9 October 1836 that Mendelssohn "stamped his feet" impatiently over the work.

Some *Marches* for pianoforte duet were published the following year as Op. 40. Two of them, in G minor and B minor, are charmingly lyrical: the "Trio" section of the first one is built on a melody so absolutely characteristic of its author in rhythm, harmony and contour, that it brings a smile to the face as if one were greeting an old friend. The fifth march, *funèbre* in style, in E flat minor, reminded a later friend of Schubert, Fritz von Hartmann, of his mother. He mentioned this in his diary and so conferred on this particular march a somewhat undeserved distinction.

Release from [Schubert's] not too congenial duties [at Zseliz] came in October. He travelled back to Vienna in the company of Baron Schönstein.... Schubert was delighted to be back in his old haunts, and he and Schwind resumed their former intimacy, becoming almost inseparable.... At the end of the year, on 22 December [1824], a new publisher's name appears, that of Thaddäus Weigl. In a *Musikalische Angebinde* (Musical Dedication), a collection of new waltzes, Weigl included as No. 29 a waltz of Schubert. It was a charming piece, in E flat major, composed for pianoforte duet in the previous July at Zseliz. Schubert arranged it in November for pianoforte solo especially for Weigl's collection, and so business relations between the composer and the publisher were initiated. In a year's time Schubert was selling full scale work to Weigl....

---

162 It is possible, however, that in 1825 he may no longer have had the manuscript of the G minor *Overture* to hand. Friends, it is evident, borrowed the work, and it may have been temporarily mislaid.

The Pianoforte Duets which [Schubert] composed in the summer of 1824 at Zseliz... form a very distinguished group. A set of six marches, the second and third of them the best he ever wrote, were published in May and September of 1825 as Opus 40 (Books I and II). The *Eight Variations on an Original Theme in A flat* is Schubert's masterpiece in variation-form. It has a majesty, a warmth and a poetry which infuse every bar. The Hungarian *Divertissement*, published as Op. 54 in 1826, was fairly well known in the nineteenth century and on the whole did not serve Schubert's reputation as an instrumental composer very well. Wagner's and Mendelssohn's derogatory judgements have been mentioned. They are not undeserved. Many of Schubert's faults are present in the duet: triviality (Wagner's complaint about the work), rhythmic monotony (Mendelssohn's complaint, due perhaps to the pseudo-Hungarian atmosphere), protracted repetition; but we find few of his virtues.

The group of duets is culminated by the *Sonata in C major*, published as the *Grand Duo*, Op. 140, in 1838, and dedicated by the publisher, Diabelli, to Clara Schumann. The term "Sonata" had ceased to be commercially profitable by 1838, and the appellation "Grand Duo" has apparently come to stay. It is a great example of the composer's epic style (observe the key), almost the supreme one, and each of its movements is so broadly planned and so generously filled with music, that the proportions of the work suggest a symphony rather than a sonata. The result is not surprising: writers ever since it was first published have wondered if it were a symphony in disguise. Schumann was the first one to propose the idea. He was of the opinion that Schubert had arranged a symphony for pianoforte duet until the manuscript came into his wife's possession, a gift from Diabelli, and he saw for himself Schubert's own title: *Sonata für Pianoforte zu vier Händen* ("Pianoforte Sonata for four hands"). But he could not give up the notion. "A man who composes so much as Schubert," he wrote, "is not too particular about the title he dashes down on his work, and it could be that he wrote SONATA at the head of his composition, whilst in his own mind he thought of it as a SYMPHONY."[163] He then went on to talk of the "symphonic" effects which are found in the duet, and the resemblances to Beethoven's symphonies: in particular the Andante of the *Second Symphony*, and the finale of the Seventh. His arguments ignore the facts: that Schubert was engaged in teaching two young piano pupils and providing them with material; that the manuscript of the work is beautifully written and represents Schubert's last word; that when he sketched a symphony in pianoforte score he did not hesitate to write at the top the word "Symphony"; that all Schubert's big compositons for the piano, from the *"Wanderer" Fantasia* at the beginning to the *Lebensstürme* Duet at the end, teem with "symphonic" effects, string *tremolandos,* horn and trumpet calls, drum rolls and woodwind "solos", all of which Schumann spoke of as if they were only to be found in the one work alone. Nearer our own day Sir Donald Tovey follows Schumann. In his *Essays in Musical Analysis*, Volume I, he writes on Joachim's orchestrated version of the duet, and says: "The GRAND DUO is unique among Schubert's four-handed works in the disconcerting nature of its orchestral style. Not even the FUNERAL MARCH FOR THE CZAR, Op. 55, is so full of the kind of orchestral things the pianoforte obviously cannot do, or so deficient in the things, pianistic or orchestral, that it can do with enjoyment." Tovey then proceeds to enlarge on another problem altogether, which had, during the nineteenth century, become entangled with the other: whether or not the *Grand Duo* was the lost "Gmunden-Gastein" Symphony. Even to entertain the idea that it might be so is to ignore, or to be ignorant of, irreconcilable dates, and other uncompromising facts. Joachim orchestrated the *Duo* in 1855; there are two other similar versions, by Anthony Collins (1939) and Karl Salomon (1946).

The most conclusive argument against the "symphony-in-disguise" theory of the *Duo* lies in the failure of any of these orchestral versions to convince. In its orchestral garb the work betrays, only too obviously, its pianistic origins. Liszt's orchestral version of the *"Wanderer" Fantasia,*

---

163 *Neue Zeitschrift für Musik*, Leipzig, June 1838.

without question conceived for the piano by Schubert, is more convincing. In so far as Schubert's organization of a sonata differs from his organization of a symphony, it is possible to see that the *Duo* belongs to the former type of work. And its first movement is a close relation of the two solo sonatas, in A minor and C major, which Schubert wrote in the following spring.

All three, for example, open with a pregnant, octave phrase coupled with a few soft chords marking the cadence. They each have a bold, fanfare-like episode of clanging chords, which assumes great importance as the movement proceeds. In the opening movement of all three sonatas there is another feature which gives an underlying unity, almost persuading us that Schubert was writing in them a three-fold expression of one, prevailing, creative mood. It is the way in which the second subject is derived from the first. The two subjects could be looked upon not as contrasting themes, but as two variants of the same theme. The three pairs of themes are briefly quoted here to illustrate the point:

Ex. 59.

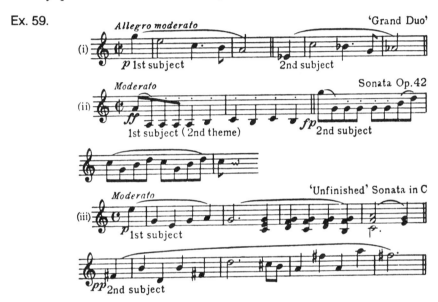

There was a similar evolution of the second subject in the first movement of the octet....

[3. 1828]

[The] summer months [of 1828] spent in Vienna were devoted to composition. Schubert, instead of recuperating from his work in the spring, drove himself harder. His desire to initiate publication in Germany, which could only be achieved by piano or chamber works, led him to write several pieces of this sort in the early summer. The great *Fantasia in F minor* was finished in April and played to Bauernfeld by Schubert and Lachner on 9 May. It has, in the highest degree, all those characteristic qualities of the composer which have endeared him to generations of music lovers, and the Scherzo section is one of his finest stretches of writing for the piano. Two other duets, one of May and one of June, although published separately and usually considered as independent compositions may have been designed as movements from a third "Sonata" for pianoforte duet, designed but not completed by the composer. The first is the *Allegro ma non troppo in A minor*, published by Diabelli in 1840 and given the catchpenny title *Lebensstürme* ("Life's Storms"). It is a strong, vigorous movement in sonata-form, and contains what is, in the opinion of many Schubertians, his loveliest melody. The melodic "tensions",... so remarkable a feature of the Schubert melody in the 1820s, lead, in this one, to some fascinating shifts from key to key. The second duet would have contributed, perhaps, the finale of the sonata. It is a *Rondo in A major*, published by Artaria as Op. 107 a month or so after the composer's death. Schubert had written it for the publisher. Again, the melodic charm of the work is irresistible; Schumann, who thought this *Rondo* one of Schubert's best compositions, has some remarkably interesting things to say of it (in a letter to Frederick Wieck, 6 November 1829). In the last episode of the rondo (at the change to C major) Schubert uses the sequence-structure to achieve some most admirable harmonic and tonal effects, so new and, for their day, so revolutionary, that we can understand some of the concluding sentences in Schumann's letter mentioned above:

> I remember playing that very Rondo at an evening party at Herr Probst's, but at the finish both players and listeners stared at one another, rather at a loss to know what to think, or to know what Schubert had meant by it all....

In considering the work of his last year it is difficult to avoid the belief that the composition of the songs of the *Winterreise* had a profound effect on his musical sensibilities and techniques. The new, *intellectual* quality in the development sections of his movements, although there were signs of it before the composition of the song-cycle, becomes very noticeable, in the *Lebensstürme* pianoforte duet, and in the pianoforte duet *Fantasia in F minor*, for example, as well as in the sonata-movements of the C major Symphony and the String Quintet. It derives from the styles and procedures in the *Winterreise* songs such as "*Die Wetterfahne*", "*Auf dem Flusse*" (this song particularly), "*Irrlicht*" and "*Der Wegweiser*". Another feature which was born in the *Winterreise* pervades the work of 1828: the tranquillity, the dream-like serenity of the "*Lindenbaum*". It is found in the Trio-section of the *Quintet*, in the slow movement of the *Sonata in B flat*, in the melodic interludes of the "*Lebensstürme*".

13. SCHUBERT AND THE DEVELOPING TRADITIONS OF PIANO FOUR-HAND MUSIC (EPILOGUE)

●DOUGLAS TOWNSEND, from Program Notes for Musical Heritage Society Recording MHS 3911/12/13 (works performed by Christian Ivaldi and Noel Lee, ca.1978)

Except for the madrigal there was possibly no other single form more dependent on non-musical stimuli than music for the piano, four-hands. Unlike the madrigal, which evolved from existing forms, music for piano duet was, at its inception, something new and untried, but its history reflects not only the rise and decline of a new type of music, but also the vagaries of a developing society; a society in which a new class—the middle class—was rising, with its own needs and desires. Like the madrigal, which suited the musical and social requirements of an era, music for the piano duet was in harmony with the requirements of a new society in a different era.

Previous to the eighteenth century, music was written [largely] for either the church or the court. Aside from the religious music it heard, the public rarely had the opportunity to hear music except at festivals and dances. Operas and concerts were for the benefit of the royal or aristocratic families who employed composers to write music for the entertainment of themselves and their friends.

From the early part of the eighteenth century the rising middle class began to exert more and more pressure on the bonds imposed on it by the vestiges of a feudal past. Their desire to learn and to experience some of the pleasures previously denied them became evident in the literature of the period as well as in the music. One-act comic operas, depicting everyday life, were sandwiched between the acts of longer and more serious operas dealing with the troubles in'some far-off land between royal families and the gods they looked up to. The heroic drama was gradually replaced by the comedy of manners or situation, and the middle class became increasingly more concert- and opera-conscious. Towards the middle of the eighteenth century the first public concerts were held in Germany, and a few years later, in the 1760s, public subscription concerts under Johann Christian Bach and Karl Friedrich Abel were introduced into England.

The desire of the middle class to attend concerts was accompanied by their desire to perform and sing for their own pleasure. If the royal families could have their court-composers, the middle classes would do the next best thing, which was to buy whatever music they could that suited their purposes, and to play it at home. It was because of their almost insatiable demand for more music that not only did music publishers pop up like flowers in spring, but also a tremendous amount of music for the home came to be written. Innumerable duets for violins, flutes, cello etc., were produced in addition to the traditional forms of chamber music.

The type of "*Hausmusik*" which virtually eclipsed all others in popularity with the middle-class amateurs was music for the piano, four hands. Here was a form of chamber music that required only two persons of moderate pianistic abilities,[164] and the symphonies of Haydn and Mozart came alive again when they were played on only one instrument. In addition to the numerous arrangements of orchestral works for four hands, many sonatas, sonatinas, suites, etc. were composed, as well as compositions for one piano, three hands and concertos for piano, four hands and orchestra. By 1800 piano duets had become as much of a social function among the middle classes and musical amateurs as string quartets, piano quartets and trios had among the professional musicians and dilettanti. ("Dilettanti" in this sense refers primarily to members of the royal or noble families who employed orchestras, composers, or chamber music groups to perform for their entertainment. Frequently members of such families were excellent artists, writers and instrumentalists.)

In the early part of the nineteenth century there were two notable occurrences which affected the development of music in general and of piano music in particular. One was the almost total disapppearance (except in isolated instances) of the court-composer and the emergence of the composer as a free agent. The composers, no longer responsible to royal courts, did not have to worry as their predecessors did about pleasing the royal palate. They now endeavored to live off their earning as teachers, performers, conductors, and whatever remuneration they received from the sales or performances of their music. The second important occurrence about this time was the improvement of the piano. Until then pianos were generally made along the lines laid down by Christofori and Silbermann. In the last years of the eighteenth century and the first quarter of the nineteenth, piano makers (among them Muzio Clementi) adopted the practice of adding additional notes to the keyboard, reinforcing the frames with steel, and the use of a new escape mechanism that enabled the pianist to play repeated notes in quick succession. All these, in addition to other changes, gave the newer pianos a more spectacular sound and created a need for a piano technique that was able to more fully exploit the possibilities of the improved instrument. The result was that during the second quarter of the nineteenth century a new pianistic technique was evolved which made greater use of the more brilliant upper, and richer, fuller lower registers.

The piano duets of this period, while greatly increasing the available literature, appeared to fall off in quality in almost inverse proportion to the quantity produced. Composers were so intent on satisfying the demands of the public for "showy" music that one might say they wrote first and thought afterwards. It is for this reason that there were produced, during the years from about 1825 to 1875, countless fantasies and potpourris on themes from the favorite operas, on folk tunes, and on themes from contemporary instrumental works. All these pieces were

---

164 Assuming, that is, that only music of moderate difficulty was chosen! (NA)

designed to show off the crystalline shimmer of the upper registers of the piano, while the lower register (played by the *secondo*), was generally relegated to playing uninteresting and inferior accompaniment figures. Not all the composers of the time wrote in this manner, of course, but for every first-rate work of Weber, Schubert, Schumann, Dvorak and Brahms there were dozens by Moscheles, Kalkbrenner, Czerny, and others. To some extent the last-named might be excused, since many of his duets are worthy of revival, but even he succumbed too many times to the demand for more flashy and superficial piano duets.

So great was the demand for piano duet music that a substantial proportion of eighteenth-century orchestral, chamber, and operatic music was arranged for four hands. While some of these compositions already had been been arranged as duets in the composer's own lifetime (needless to say, not by the composer, and without his permission), it was all gone over again in terms of the more brilliant piano of the middle and late nineteenth century. It came to be almost standard procedure for a composer to arrange his own works for piano duet, or entrust them to a friend or pupil, rather than have a publisher's hack do the work. Beethoven allowed his friend and pupil, Czerny, to do this work, even venturing suggestions on how certain passages might be improved, while Brahms and Tchaikovsky had many of their symphonies and suites arranged for piano four-hands by friends whom they trusted.

Not only were symphonies, chamber music, and operas arranged for four hands, but also works for piano solo passed over the "doctor's" table: Chopin *Nocturnes*, Bach *Two-Part Inventions* and organ works, sonatas by Haydn, Mozart and Beethoven were only some of the compositions to be operated on during these years.

With the advent of the phonograph, cinema, radio, and television, the useful days of the piano duet, so far as the general public was concerned, were over. Their function as a social force was replaced by the newer media of mass communication and entertainment. Four-hand music came to be in so little demand that publishers begged their composers *not* to write duets. Within a few years, indeed, publishers were complaining that they could not sell even the duets of Mozart, Schubert, and Schumann. More than one publisher was forced to drop these composers' duets from their catalogues not so long ago.

The explanation of public indifference towards these masterpieces, while based on individual reasons, comes down to the same thing: each era had its own form of private and public entertainment. The madrigal served a social and musical function in its time, as chamber music and *Hausmusik* did in a later era. The newer forms of entertainment made it easier to be amused by others, even if indirectly, than to entertain and amuse one's self. Remember that chamber music is essentially a social function in which two or more people get together to exchange ideas both musical and verbal. We can be certain that when Mozart's "*Haydn*" *Quartets* were first tried out, one summer's evening in 1784 at the Vienna apartment of the English composer Stephen Storace, there were refreshments and conversation as well as music. Similarly, in the last years of the nineteenth century, when a new Brahms symphony was played four-hands, or a new ballet of Tchaikovsky was tried out in parlors, such occasions were social no less than musical ones. The lay person, too, for whom so much of this music was actually written, would have friends over to perform his latest purchase of duets, trios, or other forms of *Hausmusik*.

In the past few years there has been a reawakening of interest in music for the piano, four hands. Some of the leading American composers have written first-rate compositions for this medium, and the piano-playing public seems to be rediscovering the original four-hand music of Schumann, Dvorak, Brahms, *et al.* Doubtless there are many possible explanations for this, none of which will be gone into here. Suffice it to say that a number of publishers are, once again, finding it to their advantage to print new collections of duets (varying from poor to excellent), and to reissue some of their previously withdrawn publications.

Piano teachers, too, are finding uses for duets which had previously eluded them: those of their young students who are not proficient enough to play alone at a student recital are assigned the pupil's part in one of the many student-teacher duets. Teachers have also noticed that, while a student may quickly lose interest in working on a composition himself, the thrill of working with a friend has not only been musically exciting, but also in many cases effective in welding friendships.

* * *

An especially interesting development in the history of the piano duet is the number and variety of compositions written for this medium by Schubert. In fact, Schubert wrote more music for piano duet than he did for piano solo, omitting the dances. The first three works are fantasies.... The finale of the first fantasy [D 1], composed in 1810, served as the basis for the overture to an operetta for children composed in 1831, by Schubert's brother Ferdinand.... At least one of [the Schubert] duets is known to nearly everybody. I am referring to the *Marche militaire* Opus 51 number 1, in D major, which has been arranged for piano solo, orchestra, band, and almost every conceivable combination of instruments.

In all Schubert wrote 17 marches for piano four-hands. Some of these were arranged for orchestra or piano solo by Liszt. Although these pieces are tuneful and delightful to play and listen to, their special charm lies in their exquisite trios, all of which possess that special quality one encounters so frequently in his *lieder*—a combination of folk and art music. The trio to the aforementioned *Marche militaire* is a fine example of this.

During the first quarter of the nineteenth century it was fashionable to end large-scale works (sonatas, concerti, etc.) with a polonaise, as for example Beethoven's *Triple Concerto*, Opus 56. Schubert wrote ten *Polonaises* for piano duet. Schumann was very fond of these works, and described them in his diary as "downright thunderstorms, with romantic rainbows." These pieces were the sources for his own youthful *Polonaises* for piano duet.

Schubert wrote four sets of variations, the first of which, Opus 10 (composed in 1818), was dedicated to Beethoven....

There is an interesting, if somewhat long-winded *Divertimento à l'hongroise* (1824), which Schubert wrote as the result of a stay with friends on the Esterházy estate in Hungary. It is one of the few times he ever actually employed folk-tunes in his music. Mendelssohn didn't particularly care for this work, but Liszt was very fond of it and arranged it for piano solo, and the middle movement (a march) he arranged for orchestra....

Schubert and his friends were particularly fond of his *Variations in A flat*, Opus 35, and they are frequently mentioned in the diaries and letters of the time. In August of 1824, Schubert wrote from Zseliz to his friend the painter Moritz von Schwind: "I have composed a grand sonata and a set of variations for four-hands, the latter of which are having a particularly great success here; but as I do not wholly trust the Hungarians' taste I leave it for you and the Viennese to decide." A year later, Schwind wrote to one of their mutual friends: "These new variations for four hands are something quite extraordinary. In eight pages they are quite independently and vitally developed, and yet each again seems to reveal the theme."...

The splendid *Fantasy in F minor*, Opus 103, is in four movements which follow one another without pause. The work is experimental in form, in that the last section is a varied repetition of the first. There are some glorious tunes in this piece, too, and several writers consider the melodies in this piece as some of the best Schubert wrote for an instrumental medium. The Scherzo section is a joy to play and listen to, while the closing fugue (on two subjects) is a truly memorable experience for the performers—and the listeners.... The *Grand Duo* in C [and, so many other works,] are all part of the wonderful legacy of piano duets Schubert has left us, the total consisting of some of the most unjustly neglected masterpieces in the entire literature of keyboard music.

BIBLIOGRAPHY

SELECTED BOOKS AND ARTICLES

Apel, Willi. *Harvard Dictionary of Music* (Cambridge MA: Harvard University Press, 1955).

Badura-Skoda, E. and Branscombe, P., eds. *Schubert Studies: Problems of Style and Chronology* (Cambridge: Cambridge University Press, 1982).

Bie, Oscar. *A History of the Pianoforte and Pianoforte Players*. Transl. E. E. Kellett and E. W. Naylor (New York: E. P. Dutton and Company, 1894).

Brown, M. J. E. *Essays on Schubert* (New York: St. Martin's Press, 1966).

_____(with Eric Sams). *The New Grove Schubert* (London: Macmillan, 1982).

_____. "New, Old and Rediscovered Schubert Manuscripts", *Music and Letters*, xxxvii (1957), 359.

_____. "Recent Schubert Discoveries", *Music and Letters*, xxxii (1951), 349.

_____. *Schubert: A Critical Biography* (London: Macmillan, 1961).

_____. "Schubert: Discoveries of the Last Decade", *The Musical Quarterly*, xlvii (1961), 293.

_____. "Schubert: Discoveries of the Last Decade", *The Musical Quarterly*, lvii (1971), 351.

_____. *Schubert's Variations* (London: Macmillan, 1954).

Cone, E. T. "Schubert's Beethoven", *The Musical Quarterly*, lvi (1970), 779.

Czerny, Charles. *Complete Theoretical and Practical Piano Forte School*. Transl. J. A. Hamilton (London: Messrs. R. Cocks & Co., 1839).

Dannreuther, Edward. *Musical Ornamentation* (London: Novello [n.d.]).

Dart, Thurston. *The Interpretation of Music* (London: Hutchinson, 1954).

Deutsch, O. E. "The Schubert Catalog: Corrections and Additions", *Music and Letters*, xxxiv, No. 1 (1953), 26.

_____(ed.). *Schubert: Memoirs by His Friends*. Trans. Rosamond Ley and John Nowell (London: Adam and Charles Black, 1958).

_____. *The Schubert Reader: A Life of Franz Schubert in Letters and Documents*. Trans. Eric Blom (New York: W. W. Norton and Company, 1947).

_____. *Schubert: A Thematic Catalogue of His Works* (New York: W. W. Norton and Company, 1951).

Dorian, Frederick. *The History of Music in Performance* (New York: W. W. Norton and Company, 1942).

Dürr, W., Feil, A., Landon, C. and others (ed.). *Franz Schubert: thematisches Verzeichnis seiner Werke in chronologischer Folge von Otto Erich Deutsch* (Kassel: Barenreiter-Verlag, 1978).

Eibner, F. "The Dotted-quaver-and-semiquaver Figure with Triplet Accompaniment in the Works of Schubert", *The Music Review*, xxiii (1962), 281.

Einstein, Alfred. *Schubert: A Musical Portrait* (London: Oxford University Press, 1951).

Ferguson, Donald. *Piano Music of Six Great Composers* (New York: Prentice-Hall, 1947).

Ferguson, Howard. *Style and Interpretation*, Vols. III, IV (New York: Oxford University Press, 1964).

Flower, Newman. *Franz Schubert, The Man and His Circle* (London: Cassell and Company, Ltd., 1949).

Frisch, Walter (ed.). *Schubert: Critical and Analytical Studies* (Lincoln NE: University of Nebraska Press, 1986).

Hanson, Alice. *Musical Life in Biedermeier Vienna* (Cambridge: Cambridge University Press, 1985).

Hellborn, Kreissle von. *The Life Franz Schubert*, 2 vols (London: Longmans, Green and Company, 1869).

Hoorickx, R. van. "About Some Early Schubert Manuscripts", *The Music Review*, xxx (1969), 118.

_____. "Franz Schubert (1797-1828): List of the Dances in Chronological Order", *Revue belge de musicologie*, xxv (1971), 68.

Note: for a more comprehensive listing see Schubert entry by Maurice J.E. Brown and Eric Sams in *The New Grove Dictionary of Music and Musicians*, ed. by Stanley Sadie (Grove's Dictionaries of Music, Inc., 1980, vol. 16), and Maurice J.E. Brown and Eric Sams, *The New Grove Schubert* (W.W. Norton and Company, 1983; orig. Macmillan Publishers Ltd., 1982).

_____. "Fugue and Counterpoint in Schubert's Piano Music", *The Piano Quarterly*, (Spring 1979), 48.

_____. "A Schubert Autograph at the Brussels Conservatoire", *Revue belge de musicologie*, xxii (1968), 109.

_____. "Schubert: Discoveries since 1970", *The Music Review*, Vol 45 (1986), 220.

_____. "Schubert's 'Pastoral' Mass", *Music and Letters*, xlii (1961), 53.

_____. "Some Unknown Schubert Manuscripts", *The Musical Times*, cxviii (1977), 1001.

_____. "Thematic Catalogue of Schubert's Works: New Additions, Corrections and Notes", *Revue belge de musicologie*, xxviii-xxx (1974-6), 136.

_____. "Two Essays on Schubert, I: Schubert's Variations, Op. 10, II: Ferdinand and Franz Schubert", *Revue belge de musicologie*, xxiv (1970), 81.

_____. "An Unknown Schubert Letter", *The Musical Times*, cxxii (1981), 291.

Hutchings, Arthur. *Schubert* (London: J. M. Dent and Sons, Ltd., 1947).

Marek, George. *Schubert* (New York: Viking Penguin Inc., 1985).

Newman, W. S. "Freedom of Tempo in Schubert's Instrumental Music", *The Musical Quarterly*, lxi (1975), 528.

Nowak, L. *"Das Autograph von Schuberts Rondo in D-dur, Op. 138"*, *Osterreichische Musikzeitschrift*, viii (1953), 325.

Osborne, Charles. *Schubert and His Vienna* (New York: Alfred A. Knopf, 1985).

Reed, John. *Schubert: The Final Years* (London: Faber and Faber, 1972).

_____. *Schubert: The Master Musician* (London: J. M. Dent, 1987).

Sams, Eric. "Schubert's Illness Re-examined", *The Musical Times*, cxxi (1980), 15.

_____. "Schubert's Piano Duets", *The Musical Times*, cxvii (1976), 120.

Schumann, Robert. *On Music and Musicians* (New York: Pantheon Books, 1946).

Stein, Erwin. *Form and Performance* (London: Oxford University Press, 1943).

Tovey, Donald. *Essays in Musical Analysis*, Vol. 1 (London: Oxford University Press, 1943).

Waissenberger, Robert. *Vienna in the Biedermeier Era* (New York: Rizzoli International Publications, 1986).

Wechsberg, Joseph. *Schubert: His Life, His Work, His Time* (New York: Rizzoli International Publications, 1977).

Weekley, Dallas and Arganbright, Nancy. "Schubert: Master of the Piano Duet", *The Piano Quarterly*, No.104 (Winter 1978-79), 41.

Whaples, M. K. "Style in Schubert's Piano Music from 1817 to 1818", *The Music Review*, xxxv (1974), 260.

Whitaker-Wilson, C. *Franz Schubert: Man and Composer* (London: W. Reeves, 1928).

Woodford, Peggy. *Schubert: His Life and Times* (Neptune City NJ: 1980).

MANUSCRIPTS

Allegro Moderato in C, D 968: Stadtbibliothek, Vienna.

Andante in A minor, D 968, Stadtbibliothek, Vienna.

Eight Variations on a French Song, Op. 10, D 624: Theme, Var. I, and part of Var. II, Nationalbibliothek, Vienna; remainder of Var. II, Var. III and part of Var. IV, Sibley Music Library, Univ. of Rochester, NY; twelve measures of Var. VII and seven measures of Var. VIII, Bibliotheque Nationale, Paris; remainder of Var. VIII, University Library, Leningrad.

Fantasy in G, D 1b (fragment), Männergesang-Verein, Vienna.

Fantasy on Gluck's Overture to "Iphigénie in Aulis", D 1d (fragment), Männergesang-Verein, Vienna.

Fantasy in G, D 1 (sketch only), pp. 9-24 Pierpont Morgan Library, New York.

Fantasy in G minor, D 9, Deutsche Staatsbibliothek, East Berlin.

Fantasy in C minor, D 48 (second version), Stadtbibliothek, Vienna.

Fantasy in F minor, Op. 103, D 940, Nationalbibliothek, Vienna.

Four Comic Ländler, D 354 (fragment), Stadtbibliothek, Vienna.

Fugue in E minor for Piano or Organ, Op. 152, D 952, Paris Conservatoire.

German Dances with Two Trios and Two Ländler, D 618, Stadtbibliothek, Vienna.

Kindermarsch, D 928, Gesellschaft der Musikfreunde, Vienna.

Rondo in D, Op. 138, D 608, Nationalbibliothek, Vienna.

Rondo in A, Op. 107, D 951, Deutsche Staatsbibliothek, East Berlin.
Variations on a Theme from Hérold's "Marie", Op. 82, No. 1, D 918, Staatsbibliothek, Marburg/Lahn, Germany.

FIRST EDITIONS

A. Pennauer, Vienna
  Grande Marche funèbre d'Alexandre I, Op. 55, D 859, Feb. 8, 1826.
  Grande Marche héroïque au Sacre de Nicholas I, Op. 66, D 885, Sept. 14, 1826.
Artaria and Company, Vienna
  Rondo in A, Op. 107, D 951, Dec. 11, 1828.
Breitkopf and Härtel
(Gesamtausgabe), Leipzig
  Fantasy in G, D 1, 1888.
  Fantasy in G minor, D 9, 1888.
  Fantasy in C minor, D 48, second version, 1888.
  Allegro Moderato in C, D 968, 1888.
  Andante in A minor, D 968, 1888.
  Overture in G minor, D 668, 1897.
  Overture to "Fierrabras", D 798, 1897.
Cappi and Company, Vienna
  Sixteen German Dances and Two Ecossaises, D 783a, Jan. 8, 1825.
  Overture in F, Op. 34, D 675, Feb. 28, 1825.
Cappi and Czerny, Vienna
  Six Polonaises, Op. 61, D 824, July 8, 1826.
Cappi and Diabelli, Vienna
  Eight Variations on a French Song, Op. 10, D 624, Apr. 19, 1822.
Diabelli and Company, Vienna
  Three Military Marches, Op. 51, D 733, Aug. 7, 1826.
  Four Polonaises, Op. 75, D 599, July 6, 1827.
  Fantasy in F minor, Op. 103, D 940, Mar. 16, 1829.
  Deux Marches caractéristiques, Op. 121, D 886, Feb. 1830.
  Rondo in D, Op. 138, D 608, May 1835.
  Sonata in C ("Grand Duo"), Op. 140, D 812, 1838.
  Duo in A minor ("Lebensstürme"), Op. 144, D 947, ca. 1840.
  Fugue in E minor for Piano or Organ, Op. 152, D 952, ca. 1844.
"Festschrift für Hugo Riemann", Leipzig
  German Dances with Two Trios and Two Ländler, D 618, 1909.
J. P. Gotthard, Vienna
  Four Ländler, D 814, 1869
  Kindermarsch, D 928, 1870.
  Fantasy in C minor, D 48, 1871 (First version)
  Overture "in Italian Style" in D, D 592, 1872.
  Overture "in Italian Style" in C, D 597, 1872.
Matthias Artaria and Company, Vienna
  Divertissement à la hongroise, Op. 54, D 818, 1826.
Sauer and Leidesdorf, Vienna
  Grand Sonata in B flat, Op. 30, D 617, Dec. 30, 1823.
  Trois Marches héroïques, Op. 27, D 602, Dec. 18, 1824.
  Variations on an Original Theme in A flat, Op. 35, D 813, Feb. 9, 1825.

Six Grand Marches and Trios, Op. 40, D 819, May 7 and Sept. 21, 1825 (in two books).
Overture to "Alfonso and Estrella", Op. 69, D 773, Feb. 20, 1826.
Schuberth and Company, Hamburg and Leipzig
Introduction and Variations on an Original Theme in B flat, Op. 82, No. 2, D 603, 1860.
Thaddäus Weigl, Vienna
Divertissement en forme d'une marche brillante et raisonnée, Op. 63, No. 1, D 823, June 17, 1826.
Andantino varié, Op. 84, No. 1, D 823, July 6, 1827.
Rondeau brillant, Op. 84, No. 2, D 823, July 6, 1827.
Tobias Haslinger, Vienna
Variations on a Theme from Hérold's "Marie", Op. 82, No. 1, D 908, Sept. 3, 1827.

AVAILABLE EDITIONS

Barenreiter: *Neue Schubert-Ausgabe, Werke für Klavier zu vier Händen*, Series VII, Vol. 4, *Märsche und Tänze.*
          Edited by Christa Landon. Kassel, 1972.
Trois Marches Héroïques, D 602, Op. 27
Trois Marches Militaires, D 733, Op. 51
Six Grandes Marches, D 819, Op. 40
Grande Marche Funèbre, D 859, Op. 55
Grande Marche Héroïque, D 885, Op. 66
Deux Marches caractéristiques, D 886, Op. post. 121
Marcia für Faust Pachler, D 928
Vier Polonaisen, D 599, Op. 75
Sechs Polonaisen, D 824, Op. 61
Deutscher mit zwei Trios, D 618
Zwei Ländler, D 618
Barenreiter: *Neue Schubert-Ausgabe, Werke für Klavier zu vier Händen*, Series VII, Vol. 2. Edited by Christa Landon. Kassel, 1978.
Sonate in C, D 812, Op. post. 140
Variations sur un thème original, D 813, Op. 35
Divertissement à l'hongroise, D 818, Op. 54
Divertissement sur des motifs origineaux français, D 823, Op. 63 and 84
Barenreiter: *Neue Schubert-Ausgabe, Werke für Klavier zu vier Händen*, Series VII, Vol. 5, *Ouvertüren.* Edited by Walburga Litschauer. Kassel, 1984.
Ouvertüre im "italienischen Stile" in D, D 592
Ouvertüre im "italienischen Stile" in C, D 597
Ouvertüre in g, D 668
Ouvertüre in F, D 675, Op. 34
Ouvertüre zu der Oper "Alfonso und Estrella", D 773, Op. 69
Ouvertüre zu der Oper "Fierabras", D 798
Dover: *Franz Schubert: Complete Works*, Vol. 4. Edited by Anton Door. New York, 1965. (A one-volume reprint of the Breitkopf and Härtel Critical Edition of 1884-1897, *Franz Schuberts Werke: Kritisch durchgesehene Gesamtausgabe*, Series 9.)
Three Marches (Marches héroïques), Op. 27
Six Marches, Op. 40
Three Military Marches, Op. 51
Funeral March on the Occasion of the Death of Emperor Alexander I of Russia, Op. 55
Heroic March on the Occasion of the Anointing of Emperor Nicholas I of Russia, Op. 66
Two Characteristic Marches, Op. 121

Children's March in G Major
Overture in F Major, Op. 34
Overture in C Major
Overture in D Major
Sonata in B-flat Major, Op. 30
Sonata in C Major, Op. 140 ("Grand Duo")
Rondo in A Major, Op. 107
Rondo in D Major, Op. 138
Variations in E Minor on a French Song, Op. 10
Variations in A-flat Major on an Original Theme, Op. 35
Variations in C Major on a Theme ("Was einst vor Jahren") from Hérold's Opera Marie, Op. 82, No. 1
Introduction and Variations in B-flat Major on an Original Theme, Op. 82, No. 2
Divertissement à la hongroise in G Minor, Op. 54
Divertissement (en forme d'une Marche brillante et raisonnée) in E Minor on French Motifs, Op. 63
Andantino varié in B Minor on French Motifs, Op. 84, No. 2
Lebensstürme (Storms of Life), Characteristic Allegro in A Minor, Op. 144
Fantasy in F Minor, Op. 103
Six Polonaises, Op. 61
Four Polonaises, Op. 75
Four Ländler
Fugue in E Minor, Op. 152
Allegro moderato in C Major and *Andante in A Minor*
Fantasy (written in 1810)
Fantasy (written in 1811)
Fantasy (written in 1813)
Henle: *Franz Schubert: Werke für Klavier zu vier Händen.* Edited by Willi Kahl. 3 vols. Munich, 1960.
   Volume I
      Fantasy, D 1
      Fantasy, D 9
      Fantasy, D 48
      Trois Marches héroïques, Op. 27, D 602
      Rondo, Op. posth. 138, D 608
      Four Polonaises, Op. 75, D 599
      Grand Sonata, Op. 30, D 617
      Deutscher with 2 Trios and 2 Ländler, D 618
      Variations on a French Air, Op. 10, D 624
      Overture, Op. 34, D 675
      Allegro moderato and Andante, D 968
      Introduction and Four Variations on an Original Theme, Op. posth. 82, No. 2, D 603
   Volume II
      Trois Marches militaires, Op. 51, D 733
      Sonata in C Major ("Grand Duo"), Op. posth. 140, D 812
      Four Ländler, D 814
      Variations sur un Thème Original, Op. 35, D 813
      Six Grande Marches and Trios, Op. 40, D 819
      Divertissement à la hongroise, Op. 54, D 818
      Grande Marche funèbre, Op. 55, D 859
      Divertissement über Französische Motive, Op. 63, No. 1, D 823
      Sechs Polonaisen, Op. 61, D 824

Volume III

Grande Marche héroïque, Op. 66, D 885

Deux Marches caractéristiques, Op. posth. 121, D 886

Variations on a Theme from Hérold's Opera "Marie", D 908

March ("Kindermarsch"), D 928

Fantasie, Op. 103, D 940

Duo ("Lebensstürme"), Op. posth. 144, D 947

Fuge, Op. posth. 152, D 952

Rondo, Op. 107, D 951

Kalmus: *Franz Schubert: Original compositions for piano four hands*. 5 vols. Miami, FL: Belwin/Columbia Pictures.

Volume I

Eight Variations on a French Song, Op. 10

Three Heroic Marches, Op. 27

Grand Sonata in B flat, Op. 30

Eight Variations on an Original Theme, Op. 35

Six Grand Marches and Trios, Op. 40

Volume II

Three Military Marches, Op. 51

Divertissement à la hongroise, Op. 54

Grande Marche funèbre d'Alexandre I, Op. 55

Six Polonaises, Op. 61

Divertissement en forme d'une marche brillante et raisonnée, Op. 63

Grande Marche héroïque au Sacre de Nicholas I, Op. 66

Volume III

Four Polonaises, Op. 75

Variations on a Theme from Hérold's "Marie", Op. 82, No. 1

Introduction and Variations on an Original Theme, Op. 82, No. 2

Andantino varié, Op. 84, No. 1

Rondeau brillant, Op. 84, No. 2

Fantasy in F minor, Op. 103

Volume IV

Rondo in A Major, Op. 107

Deux Marches caractéristiques, Op. 121

Rondo in D, Op. 138

Sonata in C ("Grand Duo"), Op. 140

Volume V

Lebensstürme (Storms of Life), Op. 144

Fugue in E minor, Op. 152

Overture in F, Op. 34

Grosse Sonate [same as *Fantasy in C minor*, D 48 but without fugue]

Four Ländler

Kindermarsch

Peters: *Schubert: Original Compositions for Piano Four Hands*. 4 vols. New York.

Volume I

Variations, Op. 10

Trois marches héroïques, Op. 27

Grande Sonate, Op. 30

Variations sur un thème original, Op. 35

Six grandes marches, Op. 40

Trois marches militaires, Op. 51

Divertissement à la Hongroise, Op. 54

Volume II

Grande Marche funèbre d'Alexandre I, Op. 55

Six Polonaises, Op. 61

Divertissement, Op. 63

Marche héroïque, Op. 66

Quatre Polonaises, Op. 75

Variations sur un thème de Hérold, Op. 82, No. 1

Variations (Original-Thema), Op. 82, No. 2

Andantino varié, Op. 84, No. 1

Rondeau brillant, Op. 84, No. 2

Volume III

Fantaisie, Op. 103

Grand Rondeau, Op. 107

Deux Marches caractéristiques, Op. 121

Rondeau, Op. 138

Grand Duo, Op. 140

Allegro (Lebensstürme), Op. 144

Fugue, Op. 152

Volume IV

Ouvertüre, Op. 34

Sonate [same as *Fantasy in C Minor,* D 48, but without fugue]

Vier Ländler

Kindermarsch

Schirmer: *Schubert: Selected Original Compositions for Piano, Four Hands in Two Volumes.* New York.

Volume I

Allegro moderato and *Andante*

Kindermarsch

Four Ländler

Marche Militaire, Op. 51, No. 1

Marche Héroïque, Op. 27, No. 1

Marche Héroïque, Op. 27, No. 3

Marche caractéristique, Op. 121, No. 1

Four Polonaises, Op. 75

Polonaise, Op. 61, No. 4

Rondeau, Op. 138

Grosse Sonate (1814)

Grande Sonate, Op. 30

Andantino Varié, Op. 84, No. 1

Volume II

Grand Rondeau, Op. 107

Allegro (Lebensstürme), Op. 144

Fantaisie, Op. 103

Divertissement à la Hongroise, Op. 54

Grand Duo, Op. 140

SUPPLEMENTARY COLLECTIONS

Dover: *Franz Schubert, Complete works*, vol. 18 (same as Breitkopf & Härtel *Critical Edition*, Series 21 of 1897). New York.
    Overture in G minor, D 668
    Overture to "Alfonso und Estrella", D 773
    Overture to "Fierrabras", D 798
Kjos: *Schubert's German Dances and Ecossaises*, Op. 33. Edited by Weekley and Arganbright, San Diego CA., 1983.

RECORDINGS

Allegro Moderato in C and *Andante in A minor*, D 968: see Rohmann & Schiff
Andantino varié, Op. 84/1, D 823/2: see Badura-Skoda & Demus, Gilels & Gilels, Hancock & Norwood, Ivaldi & Lee, Jones & DeRosa, Schnabel (K-U) & Schnabel (A), Weekley & Arganbright, Wentworth & Wentworth
Divertissement à la hongroise, Op. 54, D 818: see Badura-Skoda & Demus (3), Duo Crommelynck, Schnabel (K-U) & Schnabel (A), Vronsky & Babin
Divertissement en forme d'une Marche brillante et raisonnée, Opus 63/1, D 823/1: see Ivaldi & Lee
Duo [Allegro] in A minor ("Lebensstürme"), Op. 144, D 947: see Badura-Skoda & Demus (2), Brendel & Crochet, Ivaldi & Lee, Jones & DeRosa, Rohmann & Schiff, Schnabel (K-U) & Schnabel (A), Weekley & Arganbright
Fantasy in F minor, Op. 103, D 940: see Badura-Skoda & Demus (3), Brendel & Crochet (2), Corre & Exerjean, Duo Beer Shera, Fevrier & Tacchino, Gilels & Gilels, Haebler & Hoffman, Hambro & Zayde, Hancock & Norwood, Ivaldi & Lee, Jones & DeRosa, Kontarsky & Kontarsky, Menuhin & Ryce, Perahia & Lupu, Rohmann & Schiff, Salkind & Salkind, Schnabel (K-U) & Schnabel (H), Smith & Sellick, Weekley & Arganbright
German Dance [Deutscher (Deutscher Tanz) in G] with Two Trios and Two Ländler, D 618: see Duo Crommelynck
German Dances: see Hautzig & Valeses, Schnabel (K-U) & Schnabel (H)
    6 Ecossaien, after Op 18a, D 145 (two-hand German dances, played four hands): see Gilels & Gilels
Ländler (arr. Brahms): see Badura-Skoda & Demus
Four Ländler, D 814: see Ivaldi & Lee
Grande march héroïque, Op 66 (D 885): see Schlüter & Schlüter
Six Grandes marches et trios, Op 40, D 819
    2-6: see see Schlüter & Schlüter
    6: in E: see Badura-Skoda & Demus
Deux Marches caractéristiques, Op 121, D 886 (968b): see Badura-Skoda & Demus, Haebler & Hoffman, Rohmann & Schiff, Schlüter & Schlüter
    1: see Badura-Skoda & Demus
    2: see Badura-Skoda & Demus (2), Hancock & Norwood, Salkind & Salkind
Marches Héroïques, Op 27, D 602: see Schlüter & Schlüter
Three Marches militaires, Op. 51, D 733: see Klien & Klien
    1: see Badura-Skoda & Demus (3), Bauer & Gabrilowitsch, Fevrier & Tacchino
Overture in F minor/Major, Op 34, D 675: see Ivaldi & Lee
Four Polonaises, Op. 75, D 599: see Corre & Exerjean, Duo Crommelynck, Schnabel (K-U) & Schnabel (H)
Rondo in A, Op. 107, D 951: see Badura-Skoda & Demus (3), Duo Beer Shera, Fevrier & Tacchino, Gilels & Gilels, Rohmann & Schiff

Rondo in D ("Notre amitié est invariable"), D 608: see Badura-Skoda & Demus (2), Haebler & Hoffman, Jones & DeRosa, Schoettler & Dye

Rondeau brillant, Op 84/2, D 823/3: see Ivaldi & Lee

Grand Sonata in B Flat, Op 30, D 617: see Duo Beer Shera, Hancock & Norwood, Schnabel (K-U) & Schnabel (H) (2), Smith & Sellick

Sonata in C ("Grand Duo"), Op 140, D 812: see Badura-Skoda & Demus, Brendel & Crochet (2), Gold & Fizdale, Ivaldi & Lee, Kontarsky & Kontarsky, Schnabel (K-U) & Rowland, Weichert & Gicquel, Wentworth & Wentworth

Introduction and [4] Variations on an Original Theme in B Flat, Op 82/2, D 603 (D968a): see Badura-Skoda & Demus, Haebler & Hoffman, Schnabel (K-U) & Rowland, Weekley & Arganbright

[8] Variations on an Original Theme in A Flat, Op 35, D 813: see Badura-Skoda & Demus (3), Carlin & Carlin, Duo Beer Shera, Fevrier & Tacchino, Ivaldi & Lee, Weichert & Gicquel

¤ ¤ ¤

BADURA-SKODA, PAUL & DEMUS, JORGE
  ●*Schubert [Piano Four Hands]*
     Audax 766 (2 Stereo LPs, ca. 1980 [recorded 1978]; orig. distr. Discocorp, P.O. Box 771, Berkeley CA 94701)
  Divertissement à la hongroise, Op 54, D 818
  Fantasy in F minor, Op 103, D 940
  Ländler (arr. Brahms)
  Deux Marches caractéristiques (No. 2 in C), Op 121/2, D 886/2 (968b)
  Three Marches Militaires (No. 1 in D), Op 51/1, D 733/1
  Rondo in A, Op 107, D 951
  Rondo in D ("Notre amitié est invariable"), D 608
  [8] Variations on an Original Theme in A Flat, Op 35, D 813

  ●*Schubert [Piano Four Hands]*
     Deutsche Grammophon LPM 39107 (Monophonic LP; also ca.1966 as Stereo LP, SLPM-139107)
  Duo [Allegro] in A minor ("Lebensstürme"), Op 144, D 947
  Fantasy in F minor, Op 103, D 940
  Deux Marches caractéristiques (No. 2 in C), Op 121/2, D 886/2 (968b)
  Three Marches militaires (No. 1 in D), Op 51/1, D 733/1
  Rondo in A, Op 107, D 951

  ●*[Piano Four Hands]*
     Harmonia Mundi HM 30642 (Monophonic LP, ca. 1964; reissued ca.1968 as RCA Victrola VIC-1329 [mono] and VICS-1329 [reprocessed stereo])
  Divertissement à la hongroise, Op 54, D 818
  [8] Variations on an Original Theme in A Flat, Op 35, D 813

  ●*Schubert [Piano Four Hands]*
     Westminster 50-47 (Monophonic LP, ca. 1951; *also reissued ca.1957 as Westminster XWN 18344-45, *Schubert Piano Music, Four Hands, vol. 1-2*)
  *Fantasy in F minor, Op 103, D 940
  *Deux Marches caractéristiques (No. 1 in C), Op 121/1, D 886/1 (968b)
  *Rondo in A, Op 107, D 951
  *Rondo in D ("Notre amitié est invariable"), D 608

BADURA-SKODA, PAUL & DEMUS, JORGE [CONTINUED]
   ●*[Piano Four Hands]*
   Westminster 50-93 (Monophonic LP, ca.1952; *also reissued ca.1957 as Westminster XWN 18344-45,
         Schubert Piano Music, Four Hands, vol. 1-2)
*Sonata in C ("Grand Duo"), Op 140, D 812

   ●*Schubert [Piano Four Hands]*
   Westminster 51-47 (Monophonic LP, ca.1952; *also reissued ca.1957 as Westminster XWN 18344-45,
         Schubert Piano Music, Four Hands, vol. 1-2)
*Duo [Allegro] in A minor ("Lebensstürme"), Op 144, D 947
*Introduction and [4] Variations on an Original Theme in B Flat, Opus 82/2, D 603 (D968a)
*[8] Variations on an Original Theme in A Flat, Op 35, D 813

   ●*Schubert Piano Music, Four Hands, vol. 3*
   Westminster XWN-18790 (Monophonic LP, ca.1959)
Andantino varié, Op 84/1, D 823/2
Divertissement à la hongroise,, Op 54, D 818
Six Grand Marches and Trios (No. 6 in E), Op 40/6, D 819/6
Deux Marches caractéristiques, Op 121, D 886 (968b)
Three Marches militaires (No. 1 in D), Op 51/1, D 733/1

BAUER & GABRILOWITSCH
   ●*[Piano Four Hands]*
   Klavier 102 (LP)
Three Marches militaires (No. 1 in D), Op 51/1, D 733/1

BRENDEL, ALFRED & CROCHET, EVELYNE
   ●*[Piano Four Hands]*
   Murray Hill K-19565 (2 Cassettes)
Fantasy in F minor, Op 103, D 940

   ●*[Piano Four Hands]*
   Turnabout TV 34144DS (Mono LP; also as ca.1978-83 Stereo LP TVS-34516; see also Turnabout 34479;
         also cassette transfer KTVC 34144)
Duo [Allegro] in A minor ("Lebensstürme"), Op 144, D 947
Sonata in C ("Grand Duo"), Op 140, D 812

   ●*Schubert [Piano Four Hands]*
   Vox DL-1050 (Mono LP; also ca.1964 as Stereo LP STDL-501050)
Fantasy in F minor, Op 103, D 940
Sonata in C ("Grand Duo"), Op 140, D 812

CARLIN, SETH & CARLIN, MARYSE
   ●*Franz Schubert: Sonata in A Major, D 959 / Variations..., Op 35, D 813*
   Titanic TI-50, 43 Rice Street, Cambridge MA 02140 (Stereo LP, recorded 1980, issued 1983)
[8] Variations on an Original Theme in A Flat, Op 35, D 813 (17m)

CORRE, PHILIPPE & EXERJEAN, EDOUARD
   ●*Schubert [Piano Four Hands]*
   Pierre Verany PV-8309 (Stereo LP, ca.1984)
   Fantasy in F minor, Op 103, D 940
   Four Polonaises, Op 75, D 599

DUO BEER SHERA (SARA FUXON, BART BERMAN)
   ●*Schubert [Piano Four Hands]*
   Jerusalem ATD-8303 (Stereo LP, ca.1984)
   Fantasy in F minor, Op 103, D 940
   Rondo in A, Op 107, D 951
   Grand Sonata in B Flat, Op 30, D 617
   [8] Variations on an Original Theme in A Flat, Op 35, D 813

DUO CROMMELYNCK
   ●*[Piano Four Hands]*
   Pavane ADW-7027 (Stereo LP, ca.1980)
   Divertissement à la hongroise, Op 54, D 818
   German Dance [Deutscher (Deutscher Tanz) in G] with Two Trios and Two Ländler, D 618
   Four Polonaises, Op 75, D 599

FEVRIER & TACCHINO
   ●*Schubert [Piano Four Hands]*
   EMI Seraphim S-60317 (Stereo LP, ca.1979)
   Fantasy in F minor, Op 103, D 940
   Three Marches militaires (No. 1 in D), Op 51/1, D 733/1
   Rondo in A, Op 107, D 951
   [8] Variations on an Original Theme in A Flat, Op 35, D 813

GILELS, EMIL & GILELS, ELENA
   ●*Franz Schubert: Klaviermusik zu vier Händen*
   Deutsche Grammophon 2531 079 (Stereo LP, ca.1978)
   Andantino varié, Op 84/1, D 823/2 (10m)
   Fantasy in F minor, Op 103, D 940 (18m)
   6 Ecossaien, after Op 18a, D 145 (2m) [two-hand German dances, played four hands]
   Rondo in A, Op 107, D 951 (10m)

GOLD & FIZDALE
   ●*[Piano Four Hands]*
   Columbia ML 5717 (Monophonic LP; also ca.1962 as Stereo LP MS-6317)
   Sonata in C ("Grand Duo"), Op 140, D 812

HAEBLER & HOFFMAN
   ●*Schubert [Piano Four Hands]*
   Philips 802817 (also ca.1970 as Stereo LP SAL-3745)
   Fantasy in F minor, Op 103, D 940
   Deux Marches caractéristiques, Op 121, D 886 (968b)
   Rondo in D ("Notre amitié est invariable"), D 608
   Introduction and [4] Variations on an Original Theme in B Flat, Op 82/2, D 603 (D968a)

HAMBRO & ZAYDE
●*[Piano Four Hands]*
Command 11010 (Monophonic LP; also as Stereo LP 11010)
Fantasy in F minor, Op 103, D 940

HANCOCK & NORWOOD
●*Schubert [Piano Four Hands]*
Collectors Guild CG 641 (Monophonic LP, ca.1966)
Andantino varié, Op 84/1, D 823/2
Fantasy in F minor, Op 103, D 940
Deux Marches caractéristiques (No. 2 in C), Op 121/2, D 886/2 (968b)
Grand Sonata in B Flat, Op 30, D 617

HAUTZIG & VALESES
●*[Piano Four Hands]*
Turnabout CT-4006 (Cassette)
German Dances

IVALDI, CHRISTIAN & LEE, NOEL
●*Franz Schubert: Works for Piano, Four Hands* (vol 1)
Musical Heritage Society MHS 3911, 14 Park Road, Tinton Falls NJ 07724 (Stereo LP, ca. 1978; *also as
Arion ARN 268038 [2 CDs])
Andantino varié, Op 84/1, D 823/2 (9m)
**Fantasy in F minor, Op 103, D 940 (19m)*
Rondeau brillant, Op 84/2, D 823/3 (10m)

●*Franz Schubert: Works for Piano, Four Hands* (vol 2)
Musical Heritage Society MHS 3912, 14 Park Road, Tinton Falls NJ 07724 (Stereo LP, ca. 1978; *also as
Arion ARN 268038 [2 CDs])
**Divertissement en forme d'une Marche brillante et raisonnée, Opus 63/1, D 823/1 (10m)*
**Duo [Allegro] in A minor ("Lebensstürme"), Op 144, D 947 (12m)*
**Four Ländler, D 814 (3m)*
**[8] Variations on an Original Theme in A Flat, Opus 35, D 813 (19m)*

●*Franz Schubert: Works for Piano, Four Hands* (vol 3)
Musical Heritage Society MHS 3913, 14 Park Road, Tinton Falls NJ 07724 (Stereo LP, ca. 1978; *also as
Arion ARN 268038 [2 CDs])
**Overture in F minor/Major, Op 34, D 675 (8m)*
**Sonata in C ("Grand Duo"), Op 140, D 812 (Allegro moderato, 11m; Andante, 11m; Scherzo, 6m; Allegro
vivace, 9m)*

JONES & DeROSA
●*Schubert [Piano Four Hands]*
Musical Heritage Society MHS-1576, 14 Park Road, Tinton Falls NJ 07724 (Stereo LP)
Andantino varié, Op 84/1, D 823/2
Duo in A Minor ("Lebensstürme"), Op 144, D 947
Fantasy in F minor, Op 103, D 940
Rondo in D ("Notre amitié est invariable"), D 608

KLIEN, WALTER & KLIEN, B.
    ●*[Piano Four Hands]*
    Turnabout 4041 (Monophonic LP; also as Stereo LP 34041)
Three Marches militaires, Op 51, D 733

KONTARSKY, ALFONS & KONTARSKY, ALOYS
    ●*Schubert [Piano Four Hands]*
    Deutsche Grammophon 2531.050 (Stereo LP, ca.1980)
Fantasy in F minor, Op 103, D 940
Sonata in C ("Grand Duo"), Op 140, D 812

MENUHIN, YALTAH & RYCE, JOEL
    ●*[Piano Four Hands]*
    Everest 6112 (Monophonic LP; also as Stereo LP 3112)
Fantasy in F minor, Op 103, D 940

PERAHIA, MURRAY & LUPU, RADU
    ●*Mozart/Schubert [Piano Four Hands]*
    Columbia CBS IM-39511 (Digital Stereo LP; also as CD MK-39511 and as Cassette IMT-39511)
Fantasy in F minor, Op 103, D 940

ROHMANN & SCHIFF
    ●*Schubert [Piano Four Hands]*
    Hungaraton HCD-11941 (CD; *also as Stereo LP SLPX-11941, ca.1979)
Allegro Moderato in C and Andante in A minor, D 968
Duo [Allegro] in A minor ("Lebensstürme"), Op 144, D 947
Fantasy in F minor, Op 103, D 940
Deux Marches caractéristiques, Op 121, D 886 (968b)
Rondo in A, Op 107, D 951

SALKIND, M. & SALKIND, P.
    ●*Schubert [Piano Four Hands]*
    Friends 1027
Fantasy in F minor, Op 103, D 940
Deux Marches caractéristiques (No. 2 in C), Opus 121/2, D 886/2 (968b)

SCHLÜTER, KARL-HEINZ & SCHLÜTER, MICHAEL
    ●*4-Händige Klavierwerke Teil 1*
        Da Camera Magna SM 93145 (Stereo LP, ca.1980)
Six Grandes marches et trios (Nos. 2-4, 6), Op 40, D 819
Marches Héroïques (3), Op 27, D 602

    ●*4-Händige Klavierwerke Teil 2*
        Da Camera Magna SM 93146 (Stereo LP, ca.1981)
Grand march héroïque, Op 66, D 885
Six Grandes marches et trios (No. 5), Op 40, D 819
Deux Marches caractéristiques, Op 121, D 886

SCHNABEL, KARL-ULRICH & ROWLAND, JOHN (DUO SCHNABEL)
   ● *Schubert [Piano Four Hands]*
   Town Hall S-37 (Stereo LP, ca.1984)
   Introduction and [4] Variations on an Original Theme in B Flat, Op 82/2, D 603 (D968a)
   Sonata in C ("Grand Duo"), Op 140, D 812

SCHNABEL, KARL-ULRICH & SCHNABEL, ARTUR
   ● *[Piano Four Hands]*
   EMI Angel COLH 308 (Monophonic LP "Great Recordings of the Century" Series, recorded 1937; all
            three works reissued in HMV 3-LP mono set RLS 1435603; item * , also recorded 1937, ap-
            pears in the HMV set only)
   Andantino varié, Op 84/1, D 823/2
   Divertissement à la hongroise, Op 54, D 818
   [Duo] Allegro in A Minor ("Lebensstürme"), * Op 947*

SCHNABEL, KARL-ULRICH & SCHNABEL, H.
   ● *Schubert [Piano Four Hands]*
   SPA 49 (Monophonic LP)
   Four Polonaises, Op 75, D 599
   Grand Sonata in B Flat, Op 30, D 617

   ● *[Piano Music]*
   Town Hall S-8 (LP)
   German Dances (20)

   ● *[Piano Music]*
   Town Hall S-19 (2 LPs)
   Fantasy in F minor, Op 103, D 940
   Grand Sonata in B Flat, Op 30, D 617

SCHOETTLER & DYE
   ● *Schubert [Piano Four Hands]*
   Orion 79337 (LP)
   Rondo in D ("Notre amitié est invariable"), D 608

SMITH, C. & SELLECK, P.
   ● *Schubert [Piano Four Hands]*
   Nimbus NI-5178 (Monophonic LP; also CD version)
   Fantasy in F minor, Op 103, D 940
   Grand Sonata in B Flat, Op 30, D 617

VRONSKY & BABIN
   ● *[Piano Four Hands]*
   Columbia ML-2125 (Monophonic LP, ca.1950)
   Divertissement à la hongroise, Op 54, D 818

WEICHERT, G. & GICQUEL, A.
   ● *[Piano Four Hands]*
   Accord 200212 (CD)
   Sonata in C ("Grand Duo"), Op 140, D 812
   [8] Variations on an Original Theme in A Flat, Op 35, D 813

WEEKLEY, DALLAS & ARGANBRIGHT, NANCY
    ●*Weekley & Arganbright: The Art of the Piano Duet*
    London Archive LA 1533, 1532 Madison Street, La Crosse WI 54601 (Cassette; *also as LP GC 4204)
Andantino varié, Op 84/1, D 823/2 (9m)
Duo in A Minor ("Lebensstürme"), Op 144, D 947(12m)
Introduction and Variations on an Original Theme in B Flat, Op 82/2, D 603 (11m)

    ●*Weekley & Arganbright: Piano Duettists*
    Pro/Am Music Resources, Inc. MR 1535 (Cassette)
Fantasy in F minor, Op 103, D 940

WENTWORTH, JEAN & WENTWORTH, KENNETH
    ●*[Piano Four Hands]*
    Chandos ABRD-1093 (Digital Stereo LP, ca.1984)
Andantino varié, Op 84/1, D 823/2
Sonata in C ("Grand Duo"), Op 140, D 812

INDEX OF TITLES

and Lists of Works by Deutsch Catalog and Opus Numbers

Folio in **bold face type** = principal entry
Folio in *italicized type* = incipit or musical illustration

Allegros, etc.
Allegro in A minor: see *Duo in A minor*
Allegro Moderato in C and *Andante in A minor* (orig. publ. as *Sonatine*), D 968/ 6, **6**, *7*, 100, 101, 106
Andantino: see Variations
Andante: see Allegros, etc.
Dances, etc.
German Dance with Two Trios and Two Ländler [Deutscher in G, Deutscher Tanz mit 2 Trio], D 618/ **26**, 27, 102
Sixteen German Dances and Two Écossaises, Opus 33, D 783a/ **49**, *50*, *51*, 102
Four Ländler (in E^b, A^b, c, C), D 814/ **49**, *49*, 102
Divertissements
Divertissement à la hongroise (in g), Opus 54, D 818/ vii, **51**, *54*, *94*, *95*, *99*, 102, 117, 118, 123, 129
Divertissement en forme d'une Marche brillante et raisonnée, Opus 63, No. 1, D 823.1/ vii, *60*, **61**, *61*, 100, 102
Duos
Duo [Allegro] in A minor ("Lebensstürme"), Opus 144, D 947/ 69, **77**, *77*, *78*, *81*, 100, 101, 107, 118, 125, 126
"Grand Duo": see *Sonata in C*
Écossaises: see Dances, etc.
Fantasies
Fantasy in C minor (Grosse Sonata), D 48/ **7**, *8*, *9*, 15, 102, 106, 107
Fantasy in F minor, Opus 103, D 940/ vii, *8*, 20, 69, **71**, *71*, *73-76*, 79, 81, *86*, *88*, 90, 98, 103, 107-17, *109-15*, 118, 126, 129
Fantasy in G, D 1/ **3**, *4*, 102, 107, 129
Fantasy in G minor, D 9/ **5**, *5*, *9*, 102, 107
Fugue in E minor for Piano or Organ, Opus 152, D 952/ **79**, *79*, *80*, 100, 103, 107
Ländler: see Dances, etc.
Lebensstürme: see *Duo in A minor*
Marches
Marche brillante et raisonné: see Divertissements
Six Grand Marches [6 Grandes Marches] and Trios (in E^b, g, b, D, e^b, E), Opus 40, D 819/ **50**, *52*, *53*, *88*, *96*, 103, 123
Grande Marche funèbre d'Alexandre I (in c), Opus 55, D 859/ **64**, *65*, *95*, *96*, 103, 124
Grande Marche héroïque au sacre de Nicholas I (in a), Opus 66, D 885/ **64**, *65*, *66*, *96*, 103
Kindermarsch (in G), D 928/ 38, **68**, *97*, 104, 119
Deux Marches caractéristiques (in C, C), Opus 121, D 886 (968b)/ **65**, *66*, *67*, *87*, *96*, 104, 119, *119*
Three Marches héroïques (in b, C, D), Opus 27, D 602/ **22**, *22*, *96*, 103
Three Marches militaires (in D, G, E^b), Opus 51, D 733/ **38**, *38*, *39*, 65, *96*, 103, 119, 122, 129
"Notre amitié est invariable": see *Rondo in D*
Overtures
Overture "im italienischen Stile" in C, D 597/ vii, **15**, *15*, 17, 104
Overture "im italienischen Stile" in D, D 592/ **14**, *14*, 17, 104
Overture in F minor/Major, Opus 34, D 675/ **36**, *37*, *96*, 104, 122
Overture in G minor, D 668/ **36**, *36*, *96*, 104, 107, 122, 123
Overture to "Alfonso und Estrella", Opus 69, D 773/ **39**, *39*, 104
Overture to "Fierrabras", D 798/ **39**, *39*, 104

Polonaises

Four Polonaises (in d, B^b, E, F), Opus 75, D 599/ **21**, *21*, 29, 67, 96, 104, 121, *121*, 122, *122*, 129

Six Polonaises (in d, F, B^b, D, A, E), Opus 61, D 824/ **63**, *63*, *64*, 96, 104, 129

Rondos

Rondeau brillant sur des motifs orignaux français, Opus 84, No. 2, D 823.3/ vii, 60, **62**, 98, 100, 102

Rondo in A [aka Grand Rondeau] (Allegretto quasi Andantino), Opus 107, D 951/ 69, **81**, *81*, *85* 98, *99*, 104, 107, 126

Rondo in D ("Notre amitié est invariable"), Opus 138 (vers. b), D 608/ **18**, *18*, 98, 104, 119-21

Sonatas

Sonata fragment in F, 4

Grand Sonata in B Flat, Opus 30, D 617/ **25**, *26*, *85*, 100, 105, 106, 122

Grosse Sonata: see Fantasy in C minor, D 48

Sonata in C ("Grand Duo"), Opus 140, D 812/ vii, **44**, *45-47*, 86, 100, 101, 105-07, 117, 118, *118*, 122-25, *125*, 129

Sonatine: see Allegro Moderato in C and *Andante in A minor*, D 968

Variations

Andantino varié (in b), Opus 84, No. 1, D 823.2/ vii, 24, 60, **61**, 62, 97, *98*, 100, 102

Introduction and [4] Variations on an Original Theme in B Flat, Op 82 No. 2, D 603 (D968a)/ **23**, *23-25*, 48, *86*, 105

Eight Variations on a French Song in E minor, Opus 10, D 624/ vii, **28**, *28*, 48, 91, *91*, 105, 121

[8] Variations on a Theme from Hérold's "Marie" (in C), Opus 82, No. 1, D 908/ 23, **67**, *67*, 87, 98, 106

[8] Variations on an Original Theme in A Flat, Opus 35, D 813/ **48**, *48*, 97, *97*, 105, 107, 123, 124, 129

OTHER SCHUBERT WORKS MENTIONED IN TEXT:

Adrast (overture)/ 36

Choral

"*Don Gayseros*" (partsong)/ 94

Mass (German) in F, D 872/ 60

Die Schlacht (cantata)/ 22

Fantasy in C for violin & piano, Opus 159/ 94, 110

Incidental music

Rosamunde/ 35, 39, 42

Die Zauberharfe/ 32, 33, 39

Octet in F, Opus 166/ 42, 44, 125

Operas & Operettas

Alfonso und Estrella/ 35, 39

Claudine von Villa Bella/ 18

Fierrabras/ 35, 39, 90

Der Graf von Gleichen (sketch)/ 35

Der Spiegelritter/ 6

Die Verschworenen/ 44

Die Zwillingsbrüder/ 7, 31, 32

Piano solo

Impromptus

Opus 90.1/ 90, *91*

Opus 142, D 935/ 42, 60, 117

Moments musicaux, Opus 94, D 780/ 60, 117, 122

Sonata in B, Opus 147/ 24, *24*

"*Wanderer*" *Fantasy*/ 8, 79, 98, 110, 117, 124

Quartets for strings

No. 13 in A minor, Opus 29/ 42, 94, 108

No. 14 in D minor (*Der Tod und das Mädchen*)/ 42

No. 15 in G, Opus 161/ 113

Quintets for strings
  in C, Opus 163/ 126
  in C minor *(Overture)*, D 8/ 5
Songs *(Lieder)*
  "Am Erlafsee"/ 17
  "An die Musik"/ 12
  "Auf dem Flusse"/ 126
  "Augenlied"/ 13
  "Die Dioskuren"/ 13
  "Der Erlkönig"/ 12, 33, 34
  "Erstarrung"/ 89, 90
  "Die Forelle"/ 12, 17, 99
  "Ganymed"/ 13
  "Hagars Klage"/ 5, 6
  "Der Hirt auf dem Felsen"/ 69
  "Im Frühling"/ 99
  "Irrlicht"/ 126
  "Die junge Nonne"/ 59
  "Leichenfantasie"/ 7
  "Lob der Tränen"/ 120
  "Memnon"/ 13
  Die schöne Müllerin (cycle)/ 42, 59, 90
  "Der Tod und das Mädchen"/ 12
  "Wasserfluth"/ 89, 90
  "Der Wegweiser"/ 126
  "Der Wetterfahne"/ 126
  Winterreise (cycle)/ 60, 90, 108, 126
Symphonies
  No. 8 in B minor ("Unfinished")/ 79, 96, 108
  No. 9 in C ("The Great")/ 69, 108, 118, 126
Trios for piano & strings
  in B flat, Opus 99/ 118
  in E flat, Opus 100/ 60, 70

PIANO DUETS BY DEUTSCH CATALOG NUMBER

D 1   *Fantasy in G*
D 9   *Fantasy in G minor*
D 48   *Fantasy in C minor*
D 592 *Overture "im italienischen Stile" in D*
D 597 *Overture "im italienischen Stile" in C*
D 599 *Four Polonaises, Opus 75*
D 602 *Three Heroic Marches, Opus 27*
D 603 *Introduction and Variations on an Original Theme in B Flat, Opus 82/2 [later D 968a]*
D 608 *Rondo in D ("Notre amitié est invariable"), Opus 138*
D 617 *Grand Sonata in B Flat, Opus 30*
D 618 *German Dance with Two Trios and Two Ländler*
D 624 *Eight Variations on a French Song in E minor, Opus 10*
D 668 *Overture in G minor*
D 675 *Overture in F, Opus 34*
D 733 *Three Marches Militaires, Opus 51*

D 773   *Overture to "Alfonso und Estrella", Opus 69*
D 783a   *Sixteen German Dances and Two Écossaises, Opus 33*
D 798   *Overture to "Fierrabras"*
D 812   *Sonata in C ("Grand Duo"), Opus 140*
D 813   *Variations on an Original Theme in A Flat, Opus 35*
D 814   *Four Ländler*
D 818   *Divertissement à la hongroise, Opus 54*
D 819   *Six Grand Marches and Trios, Opus 40*
D 823   *Divertissement en forme d'une marche brillante et raisonnée, Opus 63/1; Andantino varié, Opus 84/1;*
             Rondeau brillant, Opus 84/2
D 824   *Six Polonaises, Opus 61*
D 859   *Grande Marche funèbre d'Alexandre I, Opus 55*
D 885   *Grande Marche héroïque au sacre de Nicholas I, Opus 66*
D 886   *Deux Marches caractéristiques, Opus 121 [later 968b]*
D 908   *Variations on a Theme from Hérold's "Marie", Opus 82/1*
D 928   *Kindermarsch*
D 940   *Fantasy in F minor, Opus 103*
D 947   *Duo in A minor ("Lebensstürme"), Op 144*
D 951   *Rondo in A, Opus 107*
D 952   *Fugue in E minor for Piano or Organ, Opus 152*
D 968   *Allegro Moderato in C* and *Andante in A minor* (orig. publ. as *Sonatine*)
D 968a: see D 603 — D 968b: see D 886

PIANO DUETS BY OPUS NUMBER

Op 10   *Eight Variations on a French Song in E minor, D 624*
Op 27   *Three Heroic Marches,D 602*
Op 30   *Grand Sonata in B Flat, D 617*
Op 33   *Sixteen German Dances and Two Écossaises, D 783a*
Op 34   *Overture in F, D 675*
Op 35   *Variations on an Original Theme in A Flat, D 813*
Op 40   *Six Grand Marches and Trios, D 819*
Op 51   *Three Marches Militaires, D 733*
Op 54   *Divertissement à la hongroise, 818*
Op 55   *Grande Marche funèbre d'Alexandre I, D 859*
Op 61   *Six Polonaises, D 824*
Op 63/1 *Divertissement en forme d'une Marche brillante et raisonnée, D 823*
Op 66   *Grande Marche héroïque au sacre de Nicholas I, D 885*
Op 69   *Overture to "Alfonso und Estrella", D 773*
Op 75   *Four Polonaises, D 599*
Op 82/1 *Variations on a Theme from Hérold's "Marie", D 908*
Op 82/2 *Introduction and Variations on an Original Theme in B Flat, D 603 (D968a)*
Op 84/1 *Andantino varié, D 823*
Op 84/2 *Rondeau brillant, D 823*
Op 103 *Fantasy in F minor, D 940*
Op 107 *Rondo in A, D 951*
Op 121 *Deux Marches caractéristiques, D 886 (968b)*
Op 138 *Rondo in D, D 608*
Op 140 *Sonata in C ("Grand Duo"), D 812*
Op 144 *Duo in A minor ("Lebensstürme"), D 947*
Op 152 *Fugue in E minor for Piano or Organ, D 952*

Other Music Titles Available from Pro/Am Music Resources, Inc.

GUITAR

THE AMP BOOK: A Guitarist's Introductory Guide to Tube Amplifiers *by Donald Brosnac.*

ANIMAL MAGNETISM FOR MUSICIANS: Making a Bass Guitar and Pickup from Scratch *by Erno Zwaan.*

ANTONIO DE TORRES: Guitar Maker—His Life and Work *by José L. Romanillos. Fwd. by Julian Bream.*

THE ART OF PRACTICING *by Alice Artzt.*

CLASSIC GUITAR CONSTRUCTION *by Irving Sloane.*

THE FENDER GUITAR *by Ken Achard.*

THE FLAMENCO GUITAR, REISSUE *by David George.*

THE GIBSON GUITAR *by Ian C. Bishop.* 2 vols.

GUITAR HISTORY: Volume 1—Guitars Made by the Fender Company *by Donald Brosnac.*

GUITAR HISTORY: Volume 2—Gibson SGs *by John Bulli.*

GUITAR HISTORY: Volume 3—Gibson Catalogs of the Sixties *edited by Richard Hetrick.*

GUITAR REPAIR: A Manual of Repair for Guitars and Fretted Instruments *by Irving Sloane.*

THE HISTORY AND DEVELOPMENT OF THE AMERICAN GUITAR *by Ken Achard.*

AN INTRODUCTION TO SCIENTIFIC GUITAR DESIGN *by Donald Brosnac.*

LEFT HANDED GUITAR *by Nicholas Clarke.*

LIVES AND LEGENDS OF FLAMENCO, 2ND EDITION *by D. E. Pohren.*

MANUAL OF GUITAR TECHNOLOGY: The History and Technology of Plucked String Instruments *by Franz Jahnel. English vers. by Dr. J.C. Harvey.*

THE SOUND OF ROCK: A History of Marshall Valve Guitar Amplifiers *by Mike Doyle.*

THE STEEL STRING GUITAR: Construction and Repair, UPDATED EDITION *by David Russell Young.*

STEEL STRING GUITAR CONSTRUCTION *by Irving Sloane.*

A WAY OF LIFE, REISSUE *by D. E. Pohren.*

PIANO / HARPSICHORD

THE ANATOMY OF A NEW YORK DEBUT RECITAL *by Carol Montparker.*

EUROPEAN PIANO ATLAS *by H. K. Herzog.*

GLOSSARY OF HARPSICHORD TERMS *by Susanne Costa.*

KENTNER: A Symposium *edited by Harold Taylor. Fwd. by Yehudi Menuhin.*

LIPATTI *by Dragos Tanasescu & Grigore Bargauanu.*

THE PIANIST'S TALENT *by Harold Taylor. Fwd. by John Ogdon.*

THE PIANO AND HOW TO CARE FOR IT *by Otto Funke.*

THE PIANO HAMMER *by Walter Pfeifer.*

PIANO NOMENCLATURE, 2ND EDITION *by Nikolaus Schimmel & H. K. Herzog.*

RAVEL ACCORDING TO RAVEL *by Vlado Perlemuter & Hélène Jourdan-Morhange.*

TECHNIQUE OF PIANO PLAYING, 5TH EDITION *by József Gát.*

THE TUNING OF MY HARPSICHORD *by Herbert Anton Kellner.*

See also:

ALKAN (2 volumes) *(Smith).*

LISZT AND HIS COUNTRY, 1869-1873 *(Legány).*

PERCY GRAINGER: The Man Behind the Music *(Dorum).*

PERCY GRAINGER: The Pictorial Biography *(Simon)..*

RONALD STEVENSON: A Musical Biography *(MacDonald).*

SORABJI: A Critical Celebration *(Rapoport).*

A SOURCE GUIDE TO THE MUSIC OF PERCY GRAINGER *(Lewis).*

Other Music Titles Available from Pro/Am Music Resources, Inc.

BIOGRAPHIES & COMPOSER STUDIES

ALKAN, REISSUE *by Ronald Smith.* Vol. 1: The Enigma. Vol. 2: The Music.
BÉLA BARTÓK: An Analysis of His Music *by Ernő Lendvai. Intr. by Alan Bush.*
BÉLA BARTÓK: His Life in Pictures and Documents *ed. by Ferenc Bónis.*
BERNARD STEVENS AND HIS MUSIC: A Symposium *compiled and edited by Bertha Stevens.*
JANÁCEK: Leaves from His Life *by Leos Janácek. Edited & transl. by Vilem & Margaret Tausky.*
JOHN FOULDS AND HIS MUSIC: An Introduction *by Malcolm MacDonald.*
LIPATTI *(Tanasescu & Bargauanu): see* PIANO, above.
LISZT AND HIS COUNTRY, 1869-1873 *by Deszo Legány.*
MASCAGNI: An Autobiography Compiled, Edited and Translated from Original Sources
    by David Stivender.
MAX REGER *by Gerhard Wuensch.*
MICHAEL TIPPETT, O.M.: A Celebration *edited by Geraint Lewis. Fwd. by Peter Maxwell Davies.*
THE MUSIC OF SZYMANOWSKI *by Jim Samson.*
MY LIFE WITH BOHUSLAV MARTINU *by Charlotte Martinu.*
PERCY GRAINGER: The Man Behind the Music *by Eileen Dorum.*
PERCY GRAINGER: The Pictorial Biography *by Robert Simon. Fwd. by Frederick Fennell.*
RAVEL ACCORDING TO RAVEL *(Perlemuter & Jourdan-Morhange): see* PIANO, above.
RONALD STEVENSON: A Musical Biography *by Malcolm MacDonald.*
SORABJI: A Critical Celebration *edited by Paul Rapoport.*
A SOURCE GUIDE TO THE MUSIC OF PERCY GRAINGER *edited by Thomas P. Lewis.*
VERDI AND WAGNER *by Ernö Lendvai.*
THE WORKS OF ALAN HOVHANESS: A Catalog, Opus 1–Opus 360 *by Richard Howard.*
ZOLTAN KODALY: His Life in Pictures and Documents *by László Eosze.*

GENERAL SUBJECTS

AMERICAN MINIMAL MUSIC, REISSUE *by Wim Mertens. Transl. by J. Hautekiet.*
A CONCISE HISTORY OF HUNGARIAN MUSIC, 2ND ENL. ED. *by Bence Szabolozi.*
THE FOLK MUSIC REVIVAL IN SCOTLAND, REISSUE *by Ailie Munro.*
GOGOLIAN INTERLUDES: Gogol's Story "Christmas Eve" as the Subject of the Operas by
    Tchaikovsky and Rimsky-Korsakov *by Philip Taylor.*
THE JOY OF ORNAMENTATION: Being Giovanni Luca Conforto's *Treatise on Ornamentation* (Rome,
1593) *with a Preface by Sir Yehudi Menuhin and an Introduction by Denis Stevens.*
THE MUSIC OF INDIA *by Reginald Massey & Jamila Massey.*
THE MUSICAL INSTRUMENT COLLECTOR, REVISED EDITION *by J. Robert Willcutt & Kenneth R. Ball.*
MUSICOLOGY IN PRACTICE: Collected Essays by Denis Stevens *edited by Thomas P. Lewis.*
    Vol. 1: 1948-1970. Vol. 2: 1971-1988.
THE PRO/AM BOOK OF MUSIC AND MYTHOLOGY *compiled, edited & with commentaries by*
    Thomas P. Lewis.
THE PRO/AM GUIDE TO U.S. BOOKS ABOUT MUSIC: Annotated Guide to Current & Backlist
    Titles *edited by Thomas P. Lewis.* 2 vols.
SOMETHING ABOUT THE MUSIC 1: Interviews with 17 American Experimental Composers
    by Geoff Smith & Nicola Walker.
SOMETHING ABOUT THE MUSIC 2 *edited by Thomas P. Lewis.*
TENSIONS IN THE PERFORMANCE OF MUSIC: A Symposium, REVISED & EXTENDED EDITION
    edited by Carola Grindea. Fwd. by Yehudi Menuhin.

WEEKLEY AND ARGANBRIGHT, husband and wife, began their Schubert research in 1960. Shortly thereafter they moved to Vienna in order to experience in a personal way Schubert's beautiful city, and especially to further their studies with the Schubertian authority Dr. Otto Erich Deutsch (1883-1967) and other prominent scholars in the field.

As concert piano-duettists, Weekley and Arganbright have met with outstanding success in the United States and abroad, and have been called "America's foremost one-piano, four-hand team." A critic for the London *Times* wrote: "Weekley and Arganbright ably and winningly demonstrated that the piano duet is a successful medium for the widest range of musical expression. Though limiting their repertoire to original works for four hands at one piano, their program affords both variety and substance..." Through their concert tours, recordings, more than twenty publications (Neil A. Kjos Music Publishers), workshops, and annual Four-Hand Festivals they have dedicated themselves to popularizing the four-hand medium. Weekley and Arganbright are faculty members at the University of Wisconsin — La Crosse. Dallas Weekley holds a doctorate from the Indiana University School of Music.